WILLIAM & CATHERINE

To Katie,
Always x

WILLIAM & CATHERINE

The Intimate Inside Story

RUSSELL MYERS

EBURY SPOTLIGHT

EBURY SPOTLIGHT

UK | USA | Canada | Ireland | Australia
India | New Zealand | South Africa

Ebury Spotlight is part of the Penguin Random House group of companies whose addresses can be found at global.penguinrandomhouse.com

Penguin Random House UK
One Embassy Gardens, 8 Viaduct Gardens, London SW11 7BW

penguin.co.uk

First published by Ebury Spotlight in 2026

1

Copyright © Russell Myers 2026
The moral right of the author has been asserted.

Penguin Random House values and supports copyright. Copyright fuels creativity, encourages diverse voices, promotes freedom of expression and supports a vibrant culture. Thank you for purchasing an authorised edition of this book and for respecting intellectual property laws by not reproducing, scanning or distributing any part of it by any means without permission. You are supporting authors and enabling Penguin Random House to continue to publish books for everyone. No part of this book may be used or reproduced in any manner for the purpose of training artificial intelligence technologies or systems. In accordance with Article 4(3) of the DSM Directive 2019/790, Penguin Random House expressly reserves this work from the text and data mining exception.

Typeset by seagulls.net

Printed and bound in Great Britain by Clays Ltd, Elcograf S.p.A.

The authorised representative in the EEA is Penguin Random House Ireland, Morrison Chambers, 32 Nassau Street, Dublin D02 YH68.

A CIP catalogue record for this book is available from the British Library

Hardback ISBN 9781529985016
Trade Paperback ISBN 9781529985023

Penguin Random House is committed to a sustainable future for our business, our readers and our planet. This book is made from Forest Stewardship Council® certified paper.

CONTENTS

Introduction   1

Chapter One: The Boy Who Would Be King   5
Chapter Two: Kate from Berkshire   25
Chapter Three: The Start of Something New   42
Chapter Four: Behind the Fairy Tale   58
Chapter Five: A Parting of Ways   78
Chapter Six: A Royal Engagement   94
Chapter Seven: The Windsors and the Wedding   112
Chapter Eight: Mapping Out   129
Chapter Nine: The Next Generation   145
Chapter Ten: Drifting Apart   163
Chapter Eleven: All Change   185
Chapter Twelve: All Alone   206
Chapter Thirteen: Creating a Modern Monarchy   225
Chapter Fourteen: The Cambridge Way   241
Chapter Fifteen: The World Mourns   258
Chapter Sixteen: In Sickness and in Strength   275
Chapter Seventeen: Healing   295
Chapter Eighteen: A New Era   313

Acknowledgements   327
Image Credits   330

INTRODUCTION

The emergence of the Prince and Princess of Wales as two of the most prominent and popular figures of the British royal family comes at a crucial time in the monarchy's history. William and Catherine embody both the weight of centuries-old tradition and the momentum for modern change. Together, they represent both continuity and the opportunity for the renewal of a one-thousand-year-old institution.

But who are the people behind the titles and what will their legacy be in such a rapidly changing world?

The royal family is in a state of flux not seen for nearly a century. The abdication in 1936 of King Edward VII changed the course of history and laid the foundations for Britain's longest-serving monarch, Queen Elizabeth II, and her family to write their own story. A tenure spanning seven decades may have brought with it a certain level of cohesion and stability, but recent years have seen such infighting and scandal at the heart of the monarchy that questions have been raised as to what purpose the institution really serves.

In producing a comprehensive portrait of the Prince and Princess of Wales, I have sought to reveal the most intimate insight ever documented of their lives as individuals, as well as their time together. Like many, I have been aware of the royal family for as long as I can remember. I was born in the same year as William and Catherine, and we have grown up in a world marked by the rapidly evolving values and pace of the twenty-first century.

I have been a journalist for two decades, and for the last eight, as a royal correspondent, I have been fortunate enough to be given a front-row seat to witness these dramatic changes. In that time I have spoken to members of the royal family, prime ministers, private secretaries, courtiers and friends of both the couple and their extended network. What I have since discovered in documenting the lives of two of the most famous people in the world, a sentiment that is almost universally shared by those that know them best, is that the Prince and Princess of Wales have formed a formidable partnership based on love, mutual respect and understanding. Their desire to create a monarchy in their image, that is fit for the modern age and that aligns with their desire to prepare their children for life amid unparalleled public scrutiny, is balanced with their dedication to public service, personal conviction and global visibility. However, in their two decades together, they have been forced to tackle challenges within their relationship, contend with pressure from those closest to them and periods of self-doubt as they have striven to forge their own path.

Despite this, both William and Catherine steadfastly believe that their lives, while anchored in service, must be responsive to the needs and concerns of the people the monarchy seeks to represent. History and duty will of course always be central to the roles they carry out, but amid uncertainty at home and throughout the Commonwealth on the future of the monarchy, questions remain over whether they can learn from the mistakes of the past and convince the public that humanity is at the heart of their mission.

The deaths of Prince Philip and Queen Elizabeth II brought a seismic shift, representing the loss of a generation for whom reverence was almost guaranteed. With King Charles III as the

INTRODUCTION

head of a slimmed-down monarchy, something that has brought its own pressures, the family has had to further contend with the departures of the Duke and Duchess of Sussex and the exile in disgrace of the former Duke of York. William and Catherine's personal experiences of these moments are revealed here in great detail, as are their reflections on decisive periods in their lives, in particular their tour of the Caribbean in 2022 and the subsequent health battles faced by the King and the Princess of Wales. All of this has contributed to a renewed outlook on their future and the ways in which they intend to face the challenges of preparing for their roles as king and queen.

While he has spoken of wanting to create 'change for good', William's long-standing commitment to mental health advocacy, environmental conservation and supporting vulnerable communities reveals a consistent focus on causes that transcend national boundaries. In turn, Catherine's thoughtful approach to duty, and her dedication to initiatives centred on early childhood development, family well-being, and mental health have been emboldened by a reverence for life informed by her personal experiences of an existence beyond the institution they both serve.

I am in huge debt to the numerous sources who have been beside William and Catherine for key moments in their lives, and who have so generously given their time and understanding to convey knowledge of many situations unknown to the public before now.

This biography traces the couple's paths from childhood, and the experiences that shaped their lives before they entered the national and global stage. It is a portrait not only of two individuals, but of a partnership at the heart of an institution that is continually striving to define its relevance in a changing world.

I

THE BOY WHO WOULD BE KING

From the moment Prince William entered the world on 21 June 1982, his life has been governed by the weight of immense privilege and tremendous expectation. As the firstborn son of Prince Charles and Princess Diana, his destiny as a future king would be shaped by the traditions of a thousand-year-old institution and guided by those responsible for navigating his upbringing. The weight of such certainty from early childhood, and the pressure he experienced from knowing that one day he would be expected to rule, inevitably influenced his sense of duty, identity and personal development. The era into which he arrived would also offer the sorts of obstacles that none of his ancestors would have had to face. Not only his life but the lives of those around him would become intensely scrutinised in an often polarised world; and questions would be asked about who the royal family really served and even whether it was suitable in a modern society. Yet, perhaps even more defining than his royal role was the environment of his early years. Born into a world marked by both deep affection and painful conflict, William was forced to grow up in the full glare of his parents' very public struggles within their marriage. The young prince has navigated love and turmoil in equal measure, experiences that would profoundly shape the man and the leader he has become today.

CHAPTER ONE

As heir to the throne, Prince Charles had grown up under a similarly intense spotlight. His life, perhaps much like that of his two sons, has been distinguished by numerous sliding-door moments, not least in his courtship of, and eventual marriage to, Diana. His adolescence was typified by isolation and his own reluctance to accept his public role. A somewhat awkward and reluctant bachelor, the Prince of Wales would go on to have several high-profile relationships with a string of aristocratic girlfriends, as pressure from his family and the outside world led to mounting questions concerning his capacity to find a suitable royal bride and his suitability to rule.

By his mid-twenties, the much-maligned prince would be characterised by the burden of his bachelorhood. A three-year relationship with Lucia Santa Cruz, the daughter of the Chilean ambassador to London, ended in 1970 although with the benefit, in his eyes, of an introduction to Camilla Shand. Jonathan Dimbleby, in *The Prince of Wales: A Biography*, noted how Charles would pursue Camilla relentlessly with 'elaborately worded love notes' and late-night telephone chats. By the end of 1972, Charles considered proposing marriage to Camilla, but was hesitant about taking the next step. The result was heartbreak the following year. While serving overseas with the Royal Navy, Camilla, who had serious reservations about becoming involved with Charles, and little intention of joining the goldfish bowl of the royal family, would announce her engagement to glamorous army officer Andrew Parker Bowles.

Charles's inability to hold down a partner would create the almost inevitable situation in which the decision was taken out of his hands. In the 1970s, Lady Diana Spencer was a shy teenager from an aristocratic family; she was also struggling for direction. The Spencers were long-time friends of the royal family. Diana's father, Earl Spencer, had served as an equerry to both King George VI and Queen Elizabeth II, marking her as a potentially suitable option to marry the future king in the eyes of Queen Elizbeth II and the Duke of Edinburgh. The pair met for the first time in 1977, when Diana was 16 years old. Two and a half years later they would begin a courtship characterised by Charles's fleeting affection as he struggled to come to terms with his feeling of rejection and what he saw as an obligation for him to marry. At just 19, Diana was considered in royal circles to be the perfect candidate for Charles. Young enough to be moulded into what was expected and naive about the world she was about to enter. Pressure was applied to the prince from all directions. His father, Prince Philip, had urged him to stop playing the field and settle down, leading to a knee-jerk reaction from Charles, who believed he was about to be forced to marry. As the press got wind of the relationship, Diana was caught in a whirlwind of interest, the subject of acres of coverage in the national media and harassed by paparazzi as she struggled to go about her daily life. On 24 February 1981, after meeting just 13 times, having spent barely any time together and certainly not having discussed a combined future, Charles and Diana were engaged.

Their wedding five months later, on 29 July 1981 at St Paul's Cathedral, was a wedding for the ages. A beautiful young bride marrying a prince and future king, cementing the end to his own forlorn pursuit of happiness. The Queen and Prince Philip had given the relationship their blessing, believing their son 'would grow to love Diana' and begin to dedicate himself to the role he was born to do. The British public had been willing participants in the construct of the 'fairy tale' relationship. 'Here is the stuff of which fairy tales are made – the prince and princess on their wedding day,' said the Archbishop of Canterbury during the service. And Diana was soon dubbed the 'People's Princess'.

CHAPTER ONE

However, soon after the marriage of these two poorly suited people who barely knew each other, cracks in the relationship started to appear. Diana was already beginning to suffer as she battled with life as part of the family known since the time of King George VI as 'The Firm'. Taken from everything she had known and placed in private apartments in the overwhelming environment of Buckingham Palace, Diana soon became tormented by her very existence. With incredibly little life experience, Diana was still troubled by having grown up in an unhappy household; her parents had separated when she was six. Diana's mother, Frances Ruth Roche, was deemed unfit to care for her and her three siblings after engaging in an affair and losing custody in extremely acrimonious court proceedings, where her own mother had given evidence suggesting she was incapable. At just seven years old and completely unaware of the court battle, Diana was left in the sole custody of her father, leading to significant feelings of abandonment and a hidden and immensely damaging eating disorder that would hurt her mental and physical health. In tapes made in answer to written questions from Andrew Morton, who wrote the best-selling book *Diana: Her True Story*, the princess spoke of her unhappy childhood. She recalled how she was forced to watch her mother cry after her father, John Spencer, slapped her mother, Frances, across the face, and how she was told by the family – including her mother, brother and even Charles – that she was stupid.

Having been thrust into the spotlight as Charles's handpicked bride, and barely 20 when she walked down the aisle, Diana's feelings of abandonment would once again surface in the infancy of her marriage as Charles struggled to create the safety she so craved. In Andrew Morton's book, Diana would later admit how, pregnant with her first child and with her mental state spiralling out of control, she threw herself down the stairs at the royals' Sandringham estate in Norfolk. She had lost all sense of reality, and also any fear of the consequences of such actions. The couple should have been basking in the glow of their wedding, which had brought joy to the country, but behind the curtain of their public life their marriage was already beginning to crumble. The royal family were ill equipped to deal with Diana's escalating emotional crisis, especially after her bulimia took hold as soon as they left for their honeymoon on board the royal yacht *Britannia*. Penny Junor's book, *The Duchess: The Untold Story*, gives an account of how blazing rows were followed by Diana destroying Charles's personal artwork and the painting materials he had packed for the trip. The honeymoon would be further marred by furious arguments following Diana's discovery of a pair of cufflinks Camilla had sent to Charles before they boarded the boat. Two intertwined Cs, the iconic symbol of the Chanel brand, which also carried a deeper meaning, threw Diana into a jealous rage that could not be calmed by the poor excuses offered by Charles. The trip ended as it had started, with tension and unhappiness. What had started as a means to be seen to be moving on with his life had soon resulted in Charles having to focus his efforts on trying to save his marriage from complete destruction.

Charles and Diana resolved to at least attempt to meet in the middle to rescue the relationship. There was, of course, no way of backing out, and soon the pressure would be on both of them to secure the royal bloodline. Diana consoled herself with the thought that having children would provide a focus to distract her from the troubles in the relationship. But neither she nor Charles would dare to seek mediation from family members, who would no doubt have little sympathy for their experience.

In June 1982, less than a year after they were married, their first son, Prince William, was born. Diana's pregnancy provided

CHAPTER ONE

little in the way of enjoyment or respite from the intolerable situation that had manifested. Besieged by sickness, she would also have to contest with opposition to her decision to have her child in hospital, doing away with centuries of tradition – royal babies were typically born within the confines of Buckingham Palace. The Queen and Queen Mother were aghast and quietly appealed to Diana – through aides that the princess would later describe disparagingly as 'the men in grey suits' – to rethink her course of action. Diana's choice of a hospital birth whipped the media into a frenzy. For days on end, dozens of reporters and photographers camped outside the Lindo Wing of St Mary's Hospital in Paddington. Finally, Diana decided she could not bear the pressure any longer and elected to be induced early. She later revealed that it was the impact of the media's attention, not medical advice or intervention, that stripped her of her desired delivery, saying, 'William had to be induced because I couldn't handle the press pressure any longer, it was becoming unbearable. It was as if everyone was monitoring every day for me.'

Under the direction of the Queen's own surgeon, gynaecologist George Pinker, who had looked after the princess throughout her pregnancy, Diana safely delivered William Arthur Philip Louis, weighing 7lb 1oz (2.65 kg), at 9.03pm on 21 June 1982. It later emerged that Diana had chosen to employ birthing methods espoused by the renowned childbirth educator, anthropologist and feminist icon Sheila Kitzinger. Diana's decision was considered by those in royal circles to be a sign of modern rebellion, but Kitzinger praised the princess, saying in her 2015 memoirs:

> The late Diana, Princess of Wales, may have been much criticised by some, but her contribution to reclaiming birth for women actually kick-started radical changes in

hospitals ... When she was pregnant with Prince William, I was asked to advise the private Lindo wing of St Mary's in Paddington, London. It was the first active royal birth – a complete contrast to the Queen's reflection that, with modern anaesthesia, birth had become 'a sleep and a forgetting'.

For Charles, whose own father had opted to play squash with his private secretary instead of attending the birth of his son, instructing an aide to deliver him the news when it occurred, the occasion had been overwhelming. Diana was delighted that he had decided to break that antiquated tradition by being by her side for the birth of their son. The prince was overcome with emotion. 'When you look at the early days of their relationship, it was incredibly testing for both of them. But he was absolutely riding high on the emotion of bringing his son into the world. That was undoubtedly the happiest he had ever been in his life at that moment,' a friend said. Excitedly, Charles told friends he was 'utterly elated', remarking on 'an astonishing experience and one that has meant more to me than I could ever have imagined'.

In his biography of Charles, Jonathan Dimbleby quotes a letter Charles wrote in 1982 to his closest friend and confidant Hugh van Cutsem and his wife Emilie: 'I got back here just before midnight – utterly elated but quite shattered. I can't tell you how excited and proud I am. He really does look surprisingly appetising and has sausage fingers just like mine.' Charles had certainly graduated from the sensitive, shy and introspective character who had once struggled to display his emotions. His exuberance at sharing in William's birth was further demonstrated in a letter to his beloved godmother Patricia Knatchbull, the Countess of Burma and the daughter of Charles's beloved great-uncle Earl Mountbatten, announcing, 'I am so thankful I was beside Diana's

CHAPTER ONE

bedside the whole time because by the end of the day I really felt as though I'd shared deeply the process of birth and as a result was rewarded by seeing a small creature which belonged to us even though he seemed to belong to everyone else as well!'*

At the age of just 21 Diana had, in the words of the Queen Mother, 'fulfilled her duty'. A child, she believed, would provide her the opportunity to focus on something other than her loneliness and the state of her marriage. Diana, who was ready to bask in the glow of motherhood, would later tell journalist Andrew Morton that the period following William's birth, up until the arrival of their second son, Harry, in 1984, was the happiest the couple had together. But no sooner had the couple celebrated in their shared joy of their new baby than the reality of their situation was laid bare. Not long after the delivery, an elated Charles, flanked by his personal protection officer, made his way outside the hospital to speak to the press pack. Buzzing with emotion, he told them he was 'relieved and delighted' at the safe arrival of his son, adding that the boy was 'in marvellous form'. Faced with quickfire questions from the media, Charles revealed the baby boy had a thatch of 'fair hair, rather than blondish', before he was promptly whisked away by officers from Scotland Yard. The heir, and indeed the country, was on a high. But the young princess, who was left shattered by the long and arduous labour, at once became filled with dread at the thought of having to face those same reporters, camera lenses and members of the public outside the hospital doors.

Within a few hours, Diana's fears were realised: the world was waiting for the first pictures of the future king. Having barely slept, somewhat delirious from exhaustion, and still in excruciating pain from a 16-hour labour, Diana mustered the energy to dutifully pose for a few minutes before being driven

---

* *The Prince of Wales: A Biography*, Jonathan Dimbleby, page 480.

away to the couple's Kensington Palace home. In what was, perhaps, a sign of the troubles that would besiege their relationship, as Charles went about his business and continued to spread news of his joy, Diana immediately shut herself away with her baby. Central to Charles and Diana's reconciliation had been the prince opening up to his wife about the nature of his upbringing and the torment that had marked his childhood. Even if he didn't know how, he was determined to bring his children into a world where they would not suffer the same absence of love and affection that he had endured growing up.

Almost at once Buckingham Palace courtiers began making plans for William's christening, arranged to coincide with the Queen Mother's 82nd birthday. Diana would later say that she was not consulted about the occasion, with her role limited to turning up to the 'ghastly' photoshoot. 'She was just expected to get on with it,' a former palace aide suggests. 'It was part and parcel of the process, and while she didn't quite understand why she had to perform as such, there certainly wasn't much discussion over how she was coping or how she was feeling as she was left to her own devices.' Now, six weeks after giving birth, sitting in the ornate Music Room at Buckingham Palace and already suffering silently from the early stages of post-partum depression, the princess knew the latest public ritual she was being forced to perform was a sign of things to come. Like Charles, Diana, whose own childhood had been scarred by loneliness and abandonment, was determined that history would not repeat itself.

Despite their apparent happiness, the couple's tour to Australia and New Zealand in March 1983 would expose the jealousy and self-loathing at the heart of their relationship. The visit, which had been postponed due to Diana's pregnancy, was hurriedly put together to take advantage of the princess's worldwide appeal as the young and glamorous face of a modern

CHAPTER ONE

monarchy. Diana would cause further dismay from palace aides when she insisted on taking nine-month-old William on the trip. According to courtiers around at the time, the Queen appealed to Charles to 'talk some sense' into his wife, although the prince decided to adhere to Diana's demands, to 'keep the peace'.

In the lead-up to the tour, the palace had been rocked by the press interest in Diana's mental state, exemplified by a sensational story by James Whitaker of the *Daily Mirror* regarding the princess's worsening eating disorder, under the headline 'Concerns for Di's health'. The front-page article had enraged the palace and set courtiers on a quest to enquire where such information had been garnered from. In an interview years later, Whitaker, the paper's royal editor – known as the 'doyen' of royal reporters for the number of royal scoops he secured during his 40-year career – revealed his sourcing had been the stuff of Buckingham Palace's nightmares. Recalling the 'absolute furore' over his story, he later claimed the story had been told to him directly by a Spencer family member.

Diana would go on to describe the six-week trip to Australasia as 'utterly traumatic', while Charles's jealousy over his wife's popularity exposed his juvenile desire to always be the centre of attention. Despite their tentative closeness, Charles had been angered by Diana's refusal to toe the party line and leave William behind, just as he had been left behind when his own mother went on royal tours. In Diana's eyes, this wasn't consistent with his description of his unhappy childhood, and was at odds with his ambition to create a different future for his children. Diana, for one, was not prepared to put the 'rules' of the Crown ahead of her own family's happiness. As she told one friend before the tour, she was a 'mother first and show pony second'.

Following the tour, which back home and across the countries they'd visited had been marked as a resounding success, the couple became ever more distant. They split their time between Kensington Palace and Charles's Highgrove estate in Gloucestershire, though were rarely under the same roof at the same time. While William would spend the week in London, living at Kensington Palace with Diana, his weekends would be spent in Gloucestershire. His parents kept out of each other's way by only staying at Highgrove on alternate weekends. Despite Diana describing her relationship with Charles as 'nonexistent', the pressure to have another child, a 'spare' as she would later remark, was all too present and she fell pregnant by the end of 1983. According to those close to Diana, while the relationship did have its happy moments, the problem was that Charles's desire to be a present father, to be different from his own parents, did not materialise in his actions. Diana's second pregnancy would once again be dogged by sickness, forcing her to cancel engagements, which further infuriated her husband. Sources describe how Diana's mental health deteriorated, while she clung to the hope that the introduction of a second child would repair her marriage.

Diana had kept the sex of their baby secret from her husband in an attempt to surprise him at the birth. Charles had made no secret of wanting more children, nor of his preference for a daughter. Again he was present for the duration of the nine-hour labour. But the heir to the throne's initial reaction to the arrival of their second son would cut Diana to the core. When the baby was delivered, weighing 6lb 14oz, at 4.20pm on 15 September 1984, Charles somewhat foolishly forgot himself, crying out 'Oh God, it's a boy', then commenting with unsubtle surprise on the fact his son had a mane of red hair. The outburst was another devastating blow to their already fractured relationship. The media and the public celebrated the arrival of the new baby, named Henry Charles Albert David, but in the tapes that Andrew Morton later used in his book, Diana would say of that

CHAPTER ONE

moment: 'something inside me closed off. Our marriage, the whole thing went down the drain.'

A year later William was enrolled in Jane Mynors' nursery school in west London. Before she married into the royal family, Diana had been a nursery assistant at the Young England Kindergarten school in Pimlico, south London – a school that taught using the Montessori method, an approach to classroom learning that emphasises pupils' independence and choice. She wanted her son to be enrolled in a nursery that followed similar principles. Charles had been the first heir to attend school rather than be solely educated by a private tutor, but had not joined the education system until he was nearly eight. Diana's choice was yet another break from tradition and further evidence of her desire to give her children a more rounded upbringing outside the confines of the institution they had been born into.

However, the young prince couldn't escape the influence of the institution entirely. Dozens of photographers and reporters gathered outside to witness William, decked out in new bright red strapped shoes, matching red shorts with white ankle socks, and a red and white checked shirt and a red, blue, white and green striped jumper, arriving promptly at 9.30am on his first day. Those journalists present to witness the occasion filled column inches by somewhat playfully noting the young royal's eagerness to get into the classroom, and no doubt away from them, by scurrying down the school steps on his own. More snarky commentators observed that the other parents dropping their children off were not afforded a curtsy from the teachers.

Those same members of the media would capture William walking out of the school later that afternoon, his hair slightly ruffled, a creased jumper under his arm, and clutching both a drinks bottle and a handmade finger puppet. Photocalls like this were a carefully managed operation, with palace press officials and Scotland Yard police officers on hand to curate the historic occasion. It would come to signify a new order between the royals and the press. While the royal family understood that there was interest in William and Harry's lives, and accepted that occasions such as this would be chronicled, they also wanted the young princes to be left alone to continue their education away from the spotlight.

William moved to Wetherby School in Notting Hill in 1987. Wearing the school's distinctive double-breasted red blazer and matching cap and red tie, the prince, by now used to the typical royal photocall, duly obliged the waiting press with a smile and a wave at the school door on his first day. William quickly adapted to the structured environment, taking a keen interest in reading and writing from a young age. Known for being courteous and sensitive as well as showing a proficiency for his early academic studies, he delighted in accompanying his younger brother to the same ritual two years later, guiding Harry through the process while helpfully instructing him how to greet his teacher and wave to the gathered media. Until he had started school, William was not given an indication of what his future would look like. Charles and Diana had both been cautious, agreeing that he should be allowed to explore as much as possible and live without burdens weighing on him.

But in the intervening years, Diana and Charles had once again been at loggerheads. Diana's mental health had deteriorated after Charles engaged in an affair, from 1986 onwards, with Camilla Parker Bowles. Charles and Diana's marriage had crumbled to the point that they only communicated when they needed to discuss their children's location and welfare. Aside from their deep marital issues, this time there was a distinct difference of opinion over the direction of their children's education. The princess, with her background in the early-years development of children,

CHAPTER ONE

which William's future wife would also be drawn to, was adamant in her desire to give her boys a more 'normal' upbringing. She took both boys on trips to theme parks, the cinema and even the fast food restaurant chain McDonald's. While the British press lapped it up, Charles was horrified. He questioned her motives to a former aide, asking, 'does she do it just to spite me?' He also believed Diana's displays of normality served to drive a wedge between him and the general public. But her natural unwillingness to bend to conformity meant she wanted to give her children real life experiences that they might not have received if they'd stayed bound by royal protocol. Visits to hospitals and homeless shelters followed, some in private and others with a small, handpicked press pack. Diana's actions only caused more difficulty in her relationship with Charles, who responded by refusing to involve himself in his children's education, and making references to his wife's 'hysterical' nature. 'He was at a point where he didn't see the relationship progressing or even surviving,' said one former aide. 'So he threw in the towel and allowed Diana to go about her business. If it was going to be a battle of popularity with the public he was astute enough to know he wasn't going to win by taking the boys to fast food restaurants, so he maintained his relationship with them in private.'

By the late 1980s, such was the fevered and continued press speculation as to whether Charles and Diana's relationship would last, Charles could no longer hide the failure of his marriage from his parents. Instead of accepting equal blame, he raged at being forced into a marriage with a 19-year-old he had barely met, and in whom he had lost interest. By 1986, he was also fully engaged in his extra-marital affair with Camilla, refusing to stop seeing her even when questioned by his own father. It fell upon Queen Elizabeth, keen to keep things inhouse, to try and shore up the pretence of family union.

As a result of Diana's growing influence over her children and, at the time, Charles's lack of it, the Queen set about subtly constructing her own authority over the future king. Together with Charles, she delicately introduced William to the concept of his destiny, while also making clear that the family was supposed to be dedicated to its people and not to serving one's own purposes. However, while this rather unique education could perhaps be classed as favouritism, and none of the other grandchildren received this attention, both the Queen and the Queen Mother were intent on instilling in William the tools that would be essential for his future as a monarch.

The Queen Mother, in particular, doted on William, sending him small gifts and letters of encouragement throughout the years, and early on became the biggest enforcer of William's concept of his destiny. During family occasions, the Queen Mother would insist William be seated beside her, further reinforcing his position as heir and sowing the seeds of the unspoken difference between him and Harry. William's craving for normality throughout his life can perhaps be drawn back to these very moments. While he has certainly grown into his position and place in the world, his understanding of his destiny was marked by internal conflict over choices that he perceived as being taken away from him before he had the chance to explore a future of his own.

Diana smothered the boys with affection, equipping them with her sense of humour, her appetite for fun, and her appreciation for the privilege she enjoyed – the qualities that she became renowned for throughout the world. Diana believed this sense of normalness, no matter how small the gestures, would equip these boys for what lay ahead when they became central figures within the institution. The brothers already shared a deep bond, with William forging the protective instincts he would display for decades. As an understanding of the slow death of their parents'

CHAPTER ONE

relationship crept up on them, William made sure he was always accessible to Harry. Former BBC royal correspondent Jennie Bond told how Diana wanted the boys to be brought up in a way no royal princes had been in the past. 'She set up what she called "work days and play days",' Jennie said,

> On work days she totally accepted that they should wear suits and ties and behave like royalty. But on play days she wanted them to be as normal as possible – wearing jeans and baseball caps, eating burgers and enjoying go-karting. She wanted them to see what life was like outside the ivory tower of the palace, which is why she took them to meet the homeless and to hospitals to comfort the sick and dying. She also wanted them to be able to express their emotions freely. She told me: "I shower my boys with cuddles and love, because I didn't have any as a child."

For a brief period the boys would be separated when William enrolled in Ludgrove School in Berkshire, a boarding preparatory school for boys aged 8 to 13. Harry followed him three years later. The boys' time at Ludgrove coincided with Charles and Diana's worsening marital problems, which were widely covered in both the print and broadcast media at the time. Diana's mental state was crudely splashed over the newspapers as the media exposed cracks in their relationship, but Charles and Diana's households were equally responsible for briefing against one another. Ludgrove's headmaster, Gerald Barber, banned newspapers in the library and ordered all pupils' television viewing to be restricted and monitored to save William and Harry the embarrassment of being confronted by daily headlines about their parents' marital woes. 'Ludgrove was extremely good at protecting him and later Harry,' a palace source said. 'It took them out of troubled waters.'

A year after starting at Ludgrove, William would summon that same maturity to protect his younger brother from the realisation that, after years of speculation, their parents' marriage was all but over. The boys were spending weekends with just one parent at a time, either at Highgrove (as Charles and Diana shared the property) or with visits to Diana's sisters' homes in the country. Despite the acrimoniousness of the breakdown, both Charles and Diana attempted to shield their children from the furious rows that were tearing them apart, often with little success. The following spring, Andrew Morton would publish *Diana: Her True Story*, his blistering tell-all of the collapse of the Waleses' marriage, Charles's relationship with Parker Bowles, and Diana's own mental health struggles. It set the royals on a collision course. In December 1992, a month after a disastrous royal tour to South Korea, where the couple barely acknowledged each other, leading to the British media labelling them 'The Glums', British prime minister John Major announced that the couple had formally separated. The announcement unleashed a tsunami of bitterness, dubbed 'The War of the Waleses' by the tabloid press. In the summer of 1994, Charles gave a bombshell television interview to Jonathan Dimbleby on ITV, in which he devastatingly admitted infidelity, leading Diana to collude with BBC *Panorama* journalist Martin Bashir to deliver her own broadside, where she famously decreed that 'there were three of us in the marriage, so it was a bit crowded.' A year later, the couple's fairy tale was over and they were granted a divorce. In 2021, Diana's torment would be laid bare in an investigation into Bashir's methods of gaining access to the princess. Lord Dyson, the retired judge who led the inquiry, found Bashir 'deceitful', concluding that he seriously breached BBC rules by mocking up fake bank statements to gain access to the princess. Bashir also showed the fake documents to Diana's brother, Earl Spencer, to gain his trust so that he would

CHAPTER ONE

then introduce Bashir to Diana. This was how the journalist was able to persuade Diana to agree to give the interview, which led to what was then considered to be the scoop of the century.

Throughout this time of intense turbulence, in 1995, William, aged 13, became the first senior family member to be sent to Eton College in Windsor. A stark difference from Gordonstoun, the Scottish school both his grandfather Prince Philip and his father – who described the harsh educational environment as 'Colditz with kilts' – were sent to. Again, this was under Diana's direction, driven by her belief that Eton's more relaxed environment would better suit her son. William was already a dashing and confident young man, given the right company. Those close to him, however, suggest he had been scarred by his parents' battles and relished the opportunity to leave for school.

Eton gave teenage William his first taste of freedom. Away from his family and the feverish press attention on Charles and Diana's split, which he was increasingly conscious of, he developed close bonds with a group of young men his age, such as Guy Pelly and Tom Inskip. They became part of a protective inner ring, maintaining a distance from those outside their tight circle that would remain constant into adulthood. Those same friends would prove invaluable when, on 31 August 1997, William and Harry's world changed irreversibly. The brothers, then just 15 and 12, were staying at Balmoral Castle with Charles and the Queen when the news came of their 36-year-old mother's tragic death, along with her lover Dodi Fayed, following a high-speed car crash in a Parisian tunnel. William later described feeling 'completely numb' with shock when his father delivered the news to him. The true effect of his grief would not be felt for many years.

By the turn of the millennium, both William and Harry had learned to lean on each other as their father adapted to life as a single parent. While Charles's personal conduct would draw criticism and commentary, those close to him relay a sadness that 'he never really got the credit he deserved'. One friend said:

> There were all sorts of stories about how he abandoned the boys, which was absolute nonsense. Of course he was finding his feet, as anyone in that situation would be, but there was a closeness with his sons that never really cut through. I think in their adulthood both William and Harry really came to have a newfound respect for the way their father did step up in an extraordinary situation.

On a holiday in the summer of 1998, William developed his deep, enduring love of Africa. It would provide the solace he had been craving as he struggled to come to terms with life without his mother. It was also the first time he met the beautiful Jecca Craig, daughter of the British businessman Ian Craig and his wife Jane. The trip provided two pivotal moments in his life: first, Jecca would become a lifelong friend; and second, the time William spent on the Craigs' 55,000-acre game farm led years later to his becoming heavily involved with the Tusk Trust, a charity that partners with leading and emerging conservationists across Africa. Activities like rhino spotting or joining anti-poaching patrols offered an experience, craved by William, that was a world away from school and the palace.

In 2000, with his A-levels completed, William expressed a desire to take a year out before starting university. Whereas Charles had previously encouraged the following of traditions, he was now highly supportive, believing it would be a chance for William to spread his wings away from home. William enrolled in a programme with the charity Raleigh International, setting off to join a project to build accommodation and teach English in southern Chile. 'He mucked in like the rest of us,' a fellow

CHAPTER ONE

volunteer recalled. 'If anything, he was the first to make tea when we were freezing.' Mixing with other young people from different backgrounds provided William with his first real taste of life beyond the palace walls and his well-heeled aristocratic set. After Chile, William spent more time in Africa, the continent that would go on to become one of the pillars of his future working life. Members of the royal household at the time said he returned from Kenya 'full of life' and yet 'no doubt questioning what his life could have been like' outside the confines of his future responsibilities. 'He was bright enough to realise what life could be like for a senior member of the family, although took little interest in what his father or family members were specifically up to,' said one former palace aide. 'But his craving for normality, whatever that was for someone of his position, probably did make him stop to think "What if?" around that time.'

In the year 2000, William's first serious relationship blossomed when he began dating Rose Farquhar, an aspiring singer who would later appear on the reality show *The Voice* in 2016. She was also the youngest daughter of Captain Ian Farquhar, a close friend of Charles and former equerry to the Queen Mother. Friends recall their relationship as 'sweet', rather than a love affair. 'It was a break from the constant expectation that weighed heavily on him,' recalled one associate. 'He was a young man having fun, without worrying about saying or doing the wrong thing with people looking at him all the time.' The pair belonged to the same close-knit friendship group, one that appreciated the sensitivities of William's life. Though their romance was brief, lasting little more than a summer, this period cemented something William had long understood: anyone he loved – or married – would need to navigate the rarefied, scrutinised sphere of the 'royal set'. It was into this world that Catherine Middleton, years later, would step with remarkable poise.

2

KATE FROM BERKSHIRE

When Carole and Michael Middleton walked out of the Royal Berkshire hospital in the winter of 1982 to begin the drive back to their modest three-bedroom semi-detached home, their only thought was of the enveloping joy of welcoming their firstborn child into the world. Thoughts of princesses, castles and dashing young princes would be reserved for lighting up the bedtime stories of their darling daughter Catherine, born on a cold grey day on 9 January.

Life for the Middletons in the quaint village of Bradfield Southend within the Royal County, named as such due to its significant connections to the British monarchy and nearby Windsor Castle, hardly epitomised what life was like for millions in 1980s Britain. Great societal upheaval and cultural change was being orchestrated by Prime Minister Margaret Thatcher's government, resulting in rising unemployment, inequality and social disruption in places like London, which was just an hour away from Carole and Michael's home. Despite coming from very different backgrounds, the couple had pursued the typical quiet rural life of Britain's middle class, away from the turbulence and division experienced around the country.

Carole Goldsmith was born on 31 January 1955 into a distinctly working-class family, with roots connecting them to generations of steely coal miners from County Durham. Her father, Ronald, was a hard-working and mild-mannered decorator, while her

CHAPTER TWO

mother, Dorothy, joyfully known as 'The Duchess' in local circles because she always looked so impeccable, worked as a part-time sales assistant in a jewellery shop. When Carole was a child, she lived in local authority housing with her family in Ealing, before moving to a small home in Southall, west London. She and her brother, Gary, who was born a decade later than her in 1965, studied at the local high school and lived a happy life, with the self-employed Ron and Dorothy doing the best they could in often difficult circumstances. There were various bouts of financial hardship. Carole was inspired by her parents' work ethic, instilled in her from a young age. She had grown up watching both her parents work hard to make ends meet and ensure that, even though money was not abundant, the children grew up in a safe and loving home.

In contrast, Michael, born in Leeds, Yorkshire, on 23 June 1949, came from a wealthy family with ties to the British aristocracy. His father, Peter, served in the Royal Air Force during the Second World War and later worked as a commercial pilot. His mother, Valerie Glassborow, was the daughter of a bank manager and served as a Voluntary Aid Detachment nurse with the British Red Cross during the Second World War. She also famously worked at the Government Code and Cypher School at Bletchley Park, an agency that played a crucial role in helping Britain to win the war. Michael's paternal grandmother, Olive Middleton, was an Edwardian society beauty and daughter of wealthy Yorkshire wool merchant Francis Martineau Lupton, a prominent lawyer, justice of the peace, and member of Parliament for the Liberal Party. According to the city's archives, the family represented 'landed gentry, political and business dynasty'. During the Victorian era the family boasted connections to industrialists, solicitors and civic leaders, as well as prominent merchants and ministers. Their endeavours as woollen cloth merchants and manufacturers flourished during the Industrial Revolution, and they traded throughout northern Europe, the Americas and Australia. Such were their connections to the British aristocracy, they would on several occasions host Princess Mary, the Queen's aunt, while another relative before the First World War was a friend of Queen Victoria's son Prince Arthur and also of the future George V.

On 6 January 1914, Olive married respected solicitor Richard Noel Middleton, who would go on to broker the transfer in 1958 of the family textiles business William Lupton & Co, to AW Hainsworth in Pudsey, West Yorkshire, closing a chapter of more than 160 years in business. The rich heritage of both firms, renowned for manufacturing British woollen cloth and high-performing technical textiles, led, in 2004, to AW Hainsworth being granted a Royal Warrant under Queen Elizabeth II in recognition for services to the Crown. In contrast to this mixed legal and aristocratic background, Michael had always dreamed of becoming a pilot. He was educated at the independent boarding school Clifton College in Bristol – following in the footsteps of his father and grandfather – and then attended the University of Surrey, graduating with a BSc in 1973. After university he trained as a pilot with British European Airways (BEA). But after six months he switched to a ground crew role, as a dispatcher with British Airways. It was here that he would meet his future wife.

With money scarce at home, Carole decided to leave school at the age of 16, after landing a job as a secretary at the financial services company Prudential, in Holborn, central London. Having seen her parents deal with the ups and downs of both being self-employed, she was determined to rise up the ranks of a big corporation, believing she could expand on the entrepreneurial spirit her parents had attempted to foster at home. But within two months she recognised her complete aversion to spending her time in a nondescript office filled with rows of chain-smoking colleagues sitting in silence at their desks. When her father returned home from work early one evening, Carole summoned the courage to tell him of her plan to return to education – she had dreams of becoming a teacher. She would go on to achieve four A-levels in art, economics, English literature and geography. But, despite their pride in their daughter's achievements, Ron and Dorothy could not afford to send Carole to college, and so at the age of 18 she was forced to return to work.

With newfound confidence in her abilities and bolstered education, Carole set about plotting a career in retail and was accepted for a trainee scheme at upmarket high street store John Lewis. The job would prove just the tonic for ambitious Carole, particularly her stint in the china and glass department at John Lewis's sister store Peter Jones, in west London's fashionable Sloane Square. Two years after starting at Peter Jones, in April 1975, Carole replied to an advert in the local newspaper to become a secretary for British Airways airline, which had been formed just a year earlier as part of a deal established by the British government to manage two nationalised corporations, British Overseas Airways Corporation and British European Airways, and two regional airlines, Cambrian Airways and Northeast Airlines. The new venture was another opportunity to expand her horizons, and at the age of 21 she was accepted to work as ground crew, before moving to join British Airway's international flight steward team in 1976.

After they had become acquainted during staff training sessions at the airline's London Heathrow base, Carole told friends of her fondness for her colleague Michael, who she described as handsome but rather shy. Eventually, though, Michael, having also confessed his feelings for Carole, was urged by two of her friends to ask her out for a date at a local pub. From then on, their relationship developed at pace, with Carole arranging to see him whenever she had leave from her demanding travelling schedule. Within 18 months the couple had moved into a rented flat together in Slough, near Heathrow, before getting engaged.

When the couple married on 21 June 1980, at St James's Parish Church in Dorney, Buckinghamshire, their union signified much more than the love that had blossomed from their early shy exchanges in the staff canteen. Michael's quiet confidence and upper-middle-class polish, mixed with Carole's determined ambition and pragmatism, would prove to be the force that would undoubtedly shape their future children's characters.

A little over 18 months later they were blessed with the arrival of their first child, Catherine Elizabeth Middleton, born on 9 January 1982. A second daughter, Philippa, affectionately known as Pippa, followed on 6 September 1983. As they settled into the contentment of family life, in May 1984 Michael was suddenly offered a posting to Amman, the capital of Jordan, as an aero manager for an international air station. There was a lucrative package, and the possibility of a unique cultural experience for their young family. With Carole on maternity leave, they agreed it was too good an opportunity to turn down. Michael signed a two-year contract with the option of an extension, flying out ahead of Carole and the children to set up their accommodation and their new life abroad.

In the early 1980s, Amman had a growing population of just under 700,000 and was in the midst of an early boom, making Jordan an attractive place to explore both economically and culturally. The Middletons had moved to a city straddling modernity and a traditional Islamic society. International organisations had been lured there by offers of tax breaks from a government keen to grow its economy, modernise and develop its technology sectors, alongside opening up as a tourist destination for the West. The family rented a two-storey villa, close to a park and overlooking a landscape of ochre hills and bustling streets alive with the scent of freshly baked bread and cardamom coffee. Keen to maximise his career possibilities, Michael threw himself into work while Carole focused on settling into life within the expat community. They were both excited by the journey that lay ahead. For Carole, life in Jordan was a lesson in resourcefulness. Home comforts that young children in the 1980s might be accustomed to, such as certain breads and fruits, were not available, but the family soon adapted to the new culture, trying local delicacies such as hummus, falafel and tabbouleh.

But Carole relished the challenge, forming a tight-knit circle with other expatriate families. Michael worked long hours during the week, but reserved weekends for family adventures. Whether it was playing tennis or walking round the manicured gardens of the British Embassy Club or making visits to local souks, he, Carole, Catherine and Pippa were always together. The weather and security of the area allowed Michael and Carole to provide a safe environment for the children to grow up in and explore a different culture, something that Michael and Carole believed would be invaluable for Catherine and Pippa's personal development. Trips to ancient ruins and picnics in the desert under skies so wide they seemed to swallow the horizon were a highlight for the family during their time in the country. In an interview with the UAE's *National* newspaper in 2011, Hanna Hashweh, a BA agent in Amman, remembered the family well, describing Michael as 'straightforward and honest' and 'a man of integrity' and Catherine as 'a very beautiful little girl'.

At the age of two and a half, Catherine started at the £1,000-a-year Assahera nursery, a significant fee for the area at the time. The experience would offer young Catherine the opportunity to mix with children from a variety of backgrounds and cultures.

The class timetable, which ran from 8.30am to 12.30pm, Sunday to Thursday, gave Carole the time to organise activities such as playdates with other expat families, or trips to the local markets to try produce such as fruits, vegetables and citrus crops from the Jordan Valley. In the mornings, the class, who hailed from more than a dozen countries, would gather in a circle to sing typical nursery rhymes such as 'Incy Wincy Spider', often reciting them in both English and Arabic. Nursery teachers said both Catherine – known as Kate at the time – and Pippa, who enrolled 18 months later, thrived in their environment and delighted in seeing their father on the occasions when he would appear to collect them. In the *National* newspaper article from 2011, Sahera al Nabulsi, the founder of the now-closed nursery, said: 'Kate's father used to pick her up sometimes in his work uniform and the kids used to get very excited and run to see him. But most of the time the mother picked her up. She was always on time.'

While the Middleton family were from a Christian background and Catherine herself was baptised into the Church of England as an infant, her ancestry was rather more eclectic. Her paternal great-grandparents were married in a Unitarian church and her extended family tree included relatives ejected from the Puritan clergy in the 17th century. In Jordan, Catherine was introduced to the diversity of faith through learning alongside fellow international children in the traditionally Islamic country. Teachers would recite verses from the Quran to improve the children's Arabic and read stories about the Prophet Muhammad's companions, such as his father-in-law Umar ibn al-Khattab. According to Sahera, 'The idea was to reinforce concepts such as respect and love. Foreign children also learnt Arabic words when we grouped the children together. The teacher used to ask in Arabic, "Who is wearing red today?" so that the children would recognise the colours [in Arabic].'

CHAPTER TWO

The carefully structured day would include all the children sitting down with each other every morning at 9.30am to enjoy a breakfast of hummus, cheese and labneh, a soft Middle Eastern cheese made from strained yogurt. In the afternoons they would read, put on plays, play in the sandpit and care for the rabbits and ducks kept on site. As part of the nursery's global appreciation for other cultural traditions, the children would celebrate many cultural holidays – including Christmas, where Sahera even dressed up as Santa Claus – and the Islamic holy festival of Eid, where a traditional Jordanian band was invited to entertain the children. The cultural experience was extended to trips outside the classroom; twice a month the children would enjoy excursions to nearby places of historical interest. A favourite at the time was the Haya Cultural Center, inaugurated by King Hussein and Queen Alia Al Hussein.

Life in Jordan was welcoming and comfortable for the Middletons. They had the help of a nanny and there were regular social events at the British Embassy. But Carole yearned to return to England: 'I wasn't convinced I wanted to be an expat mum and Mike's job there was coming to an end,' she said in the *Daily Telegraph* in 2018, her first interview with the media. So, in September 1986, just over two years after the start of the Jordanian adventure, the family decided to move back to the UK. Days before the family packed up their belongings and flew home, Carole discovered she was pregnant.

As soon as they had unpacked the boxes and rearranged their house, which had been rented during their absence, Michael started back at British Airways, at its Heathrow base. Carole, however, following an extended maternity leave and faced with constant pressure to make the transition as smooth as possible for the children, struggled with the reintegration into home life. In Jordan, the children had made friends, enjoyed the country club and the ability to play outside at all hours. Now they missed the life they had become accustomed to. In addition to this, during their final months in Jordan, the desire to pursue a career on her own had resurfaced in Carole, and she began researching the possibility of setting up her own business. The pivot away from simply returning to the airline would not only provide her with the freedom of striking out on her own, but also more time to spend with her children.

For a child who had lived between two different countries and been immersed in two entirely different cultures, Catherine settled well at St Andrew's School in the tiny hamlet of Buckhold, Berkshire. Teachers remember her as a polite and well-mannered child, who was hard working and conscientious. The family life was stable, idyllic even. But Carole, who had come from a hard-working background, wanted more than being a stay-at-home mum. In the months leading up to giving birth to James William on 15 April 1987, she put into action her idea for a one-stop place where you could get everything you needed for a children's party. One example of her tenacity involved driving 100 miles to Birmingham with all Catherine, Pippa and baby James in tow, to visit a trade fair where she made contact with several suppliers and came away with her first purchase of paper plates and cups for sending out to party organisers. With dogged determination, she stuck up a self-designed flyer at Catherine's local playgroup in Bucklebury and began stuffing bags for orders from her kitchen table. From there the business Party Pieces was born.

At the end of the summer of 1987, with orders trickling in, Carole used what little capital she had to advertise in a mail order children's book club she had subscribed to. By early 1988, the business was pulling in orders from all over the country, leading her to free up the kitchen table and start renting a small unit in the nearby market town of Hungerford. After years of feeling that she hadn't reached her potential, or possibly never would, Carole felt like she was finally going to make her mark. Throughout the next year, Carole's days were long and her nights were spent sitting at the kitchen table with Michael after putting the children to bed, mulling over the next financial decision. Realising they had a scalable business, in 1989 Michael decided to quit his job to help Carole full time. As Party Pieces steadily grew, the business morphed into a completely family affair, with all three children – who by now were together at the same school – joining in the endeavour, modelling some of the products for order catalogues.

By the time she was eight, Catherine was already excelling in sport, achieving honours for the school in both athletics and swimming as well as taking an interest in the arts. Aged 11, she shone in the role of Eliza Doolittle in the school's production of *My Fair Lady*, and later, aged 13, starred in the Victorian melodrama *Maria Marten, or The Murder in the Red Barn*. Classmates remember her quiet determination, perhaps fostered by her entrepreneurial family environment. Many years later, after having her own children, Catherine would pay tribute to her parents' drive to succeed and foster a grounded environment in which she could thrive. Speaking in February 2020 to the actress and presenter Giovanna Fletcher on her *Happy Mum, Happy Baby* podcast, Catherine would recall: 'I had a very happy childhood. It was great fun and I'm very lucky I come from a very strong family. My parents were hugely dedicated. I really appreciate now as a parent how much they sacrificed for us. They came to every sports match, they'd be the ones on the sideline shouting and we'd always have our family holidays together.'

As Carole and Michael increased their time at the family business, Catherine and Pippa would often have to be dropped off at school before 8am and stay at school until 6pm. Encouraged by their parents, they would finish their homework before taking part in various extra-curricular activities such as netball, athletics and tennis. On occasion, while the girls were representing the school at hockey, swimming, or netball, James, who was now five, would be picked up by a family friend and be brought to Carole and Michael's office while they finished up for the day.

By the early 1990s, Party Pieces was in full swing and growing exponentially. But despite their busy schedules, Carole and Michael remained steadfast in their commitment that weekends were to be enjoyed as a family, with Carole also working around the summer holidays. At a young age and with their growing personal involvement in the business – Pippa even wrote for the company blog in the early days of the internet – the children started to ask for help in setting up their own enterprises. In 1995, aged just 13 and 11, Catherine and Pippa approached their teachers at St Andrew's about helping at the school summer fete, asking their friends' parents to donate items they then auctioned off with raffle tickets, raising hundreds for Cancer Research and a local animal shelter. The small primary school had provided the shy Catherine in particular with the comfort of being able to grow in a small and safe environment before she embarked on her next chapter.

In the September of that year, Catherine started at the independent Downe House girls' school in Newbury, just a ten-minute drive away. Carole and Michael had discussed the potential for Catherine to board full time but, together with their daughter, decided Downe House was near enough for her to attend as a day pupil and stay close to the family. After the initial excitement of new beginnings, though, Catherine's time there quickly turned into an unhappy one. While she has never publicly described her ordeal, she found it difficult to settle and make friends during her first term. Shocked by how quickly

CHAPTER TWO

her daughter had become withdrawn – she wasn't showing the same enthusiasm for sports or her schoolwork as previously – Carole contacted the school on a number of occasions before Christmas, appealing to the headmistress to identify the cause of this change in attitude. In January, before the start of the second term, Carole and Michael both visited the school to demand why their fun and caring daughter had become so desperately unhappy and withdrawn at home. They threatened to pull her out of the school if improvements were not made. Katie Nicholl, in her book *Kate: The Future Queen*, recounts how the teachers believed that Catherine was being teased, something they saw as part and parcel of a competitive environment in which girls were growing up and establishing a pecking order. However, pupils who studied alongside her at the time have revealed that while many of the young girls at Downe House were subject to typically teenage taunts about their appearance or conscientious attitude to school work, Catherine's experience was sadly marred by groups of young girls who had already formed a bond, having attended the school from age 11 (Catherine did not join until she was 13). Catherine's initial exuberance at joining one of the top schools in the country was quickly extinguished by feelings of being an outsider. 'Looking back on it, it definitely was bullying,' a fellow pupil remarked. 'She was very quiet and bookish, and girls had already made their friendship groups, so it was harder for her to settle in. She also played different sports to what was popular at the time, like tennis and track over lacrosse, which only made things worse for her.' Catherine's feelings of inadequacy were exacerbated when she failed to impress during a try-out for the lacrosse team. It was a doomed attempt at assimilation, mostly because she had never played the sport before.

By Easter, Carole and Michael had made enquiries about transferring Catherine to the prestigious independent

Marlborough College in Wiltshire. The co-educational school, which currently charges annual fees of £40,000, was founded in 1843 for the purpose of educating the sons of clergymen. It boasted an exemplary reputation and esteemed alumni such as artist William Morris, the poets John Betjeman and Siegfried Sassoon, and Lord Janvrin, Private Secretary to Queen Elizabeth II between 1998 and 2007. On their first visit the Middletons fell in love with the environment, believing Catherine would thrive with the promise of extra care and attention in the cosy all-girls Elmhurst boarding house. An added benefit was she already knew a handful of the pupils, who had attended St Andrew's with her. Catherine started the term after the Easter break. A March 2023 article in the *Daily Mail*, 'Inside Kate's Marlborough College days', featured an interview with Catherine's dorm mate Gemma Williamson. 'She had very little confidence,' recalled Williamson, who described Catherine as 'thin and pale' when she joined. But she was seen as a kind, dependable and considerate friend, certainly a person who steered clear of any teenage drama. Over time, after battling eczema caused by the stress from her brief time at Downe House, her quiet determination grew and she settled in with a group of girls who would remain lifelong friends. Excelling in academics and sports, including becoming captain of the hockey team and co-captain of the rowing and tennis teams, she forged strong friendships with contemporaries who joined her in her favourite pastimes: listening to music, watching the American sitcom *Friends* and reading. In 1997 Pippa followed her sister to Marlborough; untainted by Catherine's unfortunate previous experiences, she was seen by contemporaries as the more naturally confident of the Middleton pair.

Still, by the age of 16, Catherine had blossomed, settling into her studies, achieving 11 GCSEs and growing in confidence. She was freed from the train-track braces that she had been forced to wear for over a year, leading her friends to describe her as a 'real beauty'.

In February 1998, with her confidence growing following a hockey tour where she excelled for the school, she began her first foray into a relationship. Just before the summer term she had experienced her first kiss with Woody St John Webster, the elder brother of one of her close friends, Alice. A year later, Catherine entered a year-long romance with fellow Marlborough boy Harry Blakelock, who was captain of the rugby team and not short of admirers. According to a 2020 article in the *Mail on Sunday*, the relationship blew hot and cold, and with Harry in the year above Catherine it fizzled out after he left school. She was, for a short time at least, left 'heartbroken'. When Harry finished his studies and announced he was taking a gap year to travel round the world, Catherine told friends she believed they would get back together, even travelling to Florence at the same time as him, but a rekindling never materialised. After her brief emotional setback, Catherine entered her final year and concentrated on her studies, with her heart set on being accepted to study history of art at Edinburgh University, drawn by its strong academic reputation and vibrant cultural life, and the fact that two of her friends had elected to study in the Scottish capital.

On track to get the required results to go to her chosen university – she had already confirmed her course choice and been accepted at Edinburgh – she surprised her parents with a shock announcement. Arguing she needed space to grow beyond the confines of boarding school and the well-heeled Marlborough set, Catherine presented a plan to Carole and Michael ahead of starting university. After attaining three A-levels, with As in maths and art and a B in English – the results she needed for Edinburgh – Catherine set off to spend three months in Florence, studying Italian and history of art at the British Institute of Florence. In Tuscany, Catherine shared an apartment with four other girls and enjoyed the freedom to roam round the city, away from the pressures of exams. When she wasn't busy photographing the cathedral and local architecture, Catherine made time for a visit from Carole and Michael, taking them round the piazzas and coffee shops in her local neighbourhood near the pretty central square of Piazza degli Strozzi. After returning home at the end of the summer, she succeeded in convincing her parents to let her take a year out, presenting the possibility of enrolling on a course in Chile with the charity Raleigh International. This was testament to the respect Carole and Michael had for their daughter, as well as their confidence that she would make the right decision, but also a victory that revealed an independent streak. She had clearly matured considerably from that shy schoolgirl who arrived at Marlborough just four years earlier.

Back in Berkshire, Catherine helped out with the family business; in return Carole and Michael paid her a small allowance that she put towards her travels. And then, in January 2001, Catherine set off for ten weeks in Chile, where she joined up with the Raleigh International programme. Here she camped in rugged terrain, helped local communities, took part in a three-week marine survey – travelling in a rigid inflatable boat and helping British and Chilean scientists to analyse marine life – and helped fit the windows and roof cladding during the construction of a new fire station. Catherine set off for Chile with a newfound confidence and soon made friends on the excursion. She also returned with another new idea to present to her parents: instead of going to Edinburgh, she wanted to study at the University of St Andrews.

The timing of Catherine's announcement to her parents would, years later, result in accusations that she changed her mind about Edinburgh because she wanted to follow the dashing young Prince William to St Andrews, where in August 2000 he had announced he would be studying. But the truth is that during the trip she had met a fellow student, an 18-year-old girl from Somerset who was set to go to the University of St Andrews, in Fife on the east coast of Scotland, to study engineering. The two hit it off so well that Catherine decided to explore the option of changing her course while she was still away.

At first, Carole and Michael were dead set against the idea, with Carole in particular worried about her daughter losing academic momentum, but after listening to Catherine explain that she believed she would be suited to the quieter surroundings of St Andrews rather than the city life that Edinburgh would provide, they agreed to her decision.

By coincidence, Prince William also had plans to travel to Chile for his own ten-week expedition. The prince had recently completed a trip to Belize with the British Army Training Support Unit Belize (BATSUB) for jungle training, as well as taking part in a research project on Rodrigues, a smaller island off the coast of Mauritius, where he conducted research on coral reefs for a 10,000-word university dissertation. In his first ever public interview, attended by the royal rota of journalists including the national broadcasters and newspaper reporters, William, with his father by his side, posed for pictures in the walled garden of his father's Highgrove estate. He announced his A-level results, his intention to study at St Andrews, and said he was looking forward to the experience with Raleigh International because he 'wanted to do something constructive'. The interview gave him a glimpse of the life he would be expected to immerse himself in, working with the press he had grown to distrust after the tragic death of his mother. 'I mean, I could do other work but I thought this was the way to try to help people out and meet a whole range of different people from different countries.' At just 18, he was showing signs of the leadership that he would one day rely on.

In Chile, Malcolm Sutherland, 41, was in charge of leading both William and Catherine's groups and spoke in a 2012 interview with the *Evening Standard* of that 'absolutely crazy' time. Sutherland noted that, 'With the expedition that William was on, there was a clear understanding of who he was, while Kate was like you and I. She was like everyone else; she didn't have a profile. She was by herself, like most people. She was definitely one of the fitter and stronger members of her group, which assisted her for sure. At times it was physically demanding. She was pretty easy going.' Rachel Humphreys, the group leader on the programme, recalled Catherine being 'always very in control of herself and impeccably behaved'. These experiences undoubtedly shaped her worldview and deepened her appreciation for life beyond the privilege she had enjoyed through her school years.

In the summer of 2001, just before heading to university, Catherine worked as a deckhand for two months on a BT Global Challenge yacht in Southampton. Here she met the handsome Ian Henry, who was about to study at Oxford. The two 19-year-olds were said to have enjoyed a fleeting summer romance, although Ian would later coyly suggest they were simply 'very good friends'. A 2019 article in the *Mail on Sunday* revealed that fellow crew mates dubbed her 'Fit Kate', a further sign of her emergence from her awkward teenage years. While the relationship did not progress to anything more substantial, the couple remained friends for many years. As the sun set on the summer months, Catherine returned to Berkshire, emboldened by the experiences and fun she had carved out for herself, ready to embark on another adventure, which would change her life for ever.

3

THE START OF SOMETHING NEW

From the moment it was announced that Prince William would embark on a history of art degree at St Andrews, the university had been inundated with applications: they were up a staggering 44 per cent on the previous year's figures. Just days before he was due to begin studying there, the 'Prince William effect' was linked by the national press with filling St Andrews with the brightest undergraduates it had ever received.

The teenage prince's decision to embark on the next stage of his education in Scotland had raised eyebrows in certain quarters. The future king was expected by senior courtiers, as well as the majority of his family, to follow in his father's footsteps by enrolling at Trinity College, Cambridge. Charles, as the first heir to go to university, had established the route and, finally freed from the hellish Gordonstoun, had 'enormously' enjoyed the experience. William's uncle Prince Edward and his great-grandfather King George VI (King George VI was not born the heir, but became the monarch after his brother, Edward VII, abdicated in December 1936) had also attended Cambridge.

But the four-year history of art course at St Andrews, considered one of the best in the UK, appealed to the prince, who was keen to postpone a life of royal engagements for as long as possible. William had the backing of the Queen and his father, who were both in agreement that he should be allowed to experience as much life as possible, without the burden of the responsibility that would come with his future public role. And for Charles, who had also shown capacity to adapt to his circumstances when unhappy at Cambridge by switching from archaeology and anthropology to history in his second year, there was nothing but pride at his eldest son's achievements and decision to strike out on his own. He told the media how elated he had been on hearing William's grades.

In the days leading up to the start of term, much of the world's attention was fixed on what kind of student life the future King of England would lead. In his address at Highgrove, William said he hoped for a continuation of his experience at Eton, where he was able to forge new and loyal friendships away from the media glare. His gap year had seen him visit six countries and included everything from sleeping under the stars in the Chilean outback to working as a farm hand on a Cornish estate. Rising before dawn to milk cows, William had shown he was not averse to quite literally getting his hands dirty, mucking out the livestock while earning £3.20 an hour, the minimum wage for workers under 21 in the UK at the time. Although not glamorous by any means and considerably harder than he had imagined, it was a slice of the normality William craved. On the farm, he was William and, despite his initial reservations, no one treated him any differently than the other farm hands working their shifts.

While he was hugely looking forward to beginning his course, meeting other students from a variety of backgrounds and enjoying long walks along the windswept Scottish coast, William had enjoyed his time on the farm and the time away from his family and the press. He readily admitted he wished he could have prolonged the experience of his gap year, as well as his short-lived romance with Rose Farquhar and no doubt the anonymity that came with being abroad. Just as they had honoured the agreement to leave William alone during his school years, the press had somewhat surprisingly kept their distance during his gap year. William had certainly been nervous as he approached his 18th birthday and prepared to leave school, fearing that the attitude of an industry that was inevitably deeply interested and invested in his future would change radically.

Catherine had begun life at St Andrews by scoping out the hockey and tennis societies. She also joined an organised wine-tasting evening at Ma Bells, a basement bar in the nearby St Andrews Golf Hotel. The local town, with its three main streets and distinct lack of bars, was a far cry from the bustling city universities, such as her previous choice of Edinburgh, but as she found her feet in the first few weeks, Catherine enjoyed the quiet, serene surroundings.

The press had been ready to set off for the east coast of Scotland in time for William's freshers' week, hoping to catch the prince downing pints of beer, or better still, locking lips with a fellow student; just like thousands of other first years across the country letting loose before starting their university careers. But much like his father, William decided to arrive a week after the start of term, knowing that his presence ran the risk of causing a media frenzy. 'Plus,' he said of the decision in an interview, 'I thought I would probably end up in a gutter completely wrecked, and the people I had met that week wouldn't end up being my friends anyway. It also meant I could have another week's holiday.' A somewhat cute response to a pointed question, perhaps, although the Prince of Wales's most senior aides were all concerned about the potential pitfalls that lay ahead. During his school days, the press had largely respected the wishes of the palace and, owing to his age, stayed clear of publishing stories about his lifestyle. But now he was an adult, in new surroundings, with people he did not know, there was a feeling of intense nervousness at the palace. There were real concerns that the press would now see him as fair game.

The university had similar anxieties. Aware that it was responsible for both educating the future king and also looking after his welfare for the next four years, St Andrews had, in William's absence, organised a seminar from Guy Black, director of the Press Complaints Commission, to focus students' minds on 'media attention'. The university's principal, Dr Brian Lang, also delivered a lecture with a stark warning to undergraduates about respecting each other's privacy. The advice from both sessions was of course directed to all students, but the reason for their introduction was clear. Fleet Street editors and members of the royal rota, the cohort of reporters and photographers whose job it was to cover the royal family, as well as agency staff who regularly supplied the national press, had also been individually contacted by the palace to convey that any intrusion into the prince's life would not be tolerated.

Back at St Andrews, on 23 September 2001, around 2,000 students and locals gathered to greet the prince, some holding banners aloft while a small crowd chanted anti-war slogans, which could be heard faintly among the screams of young women hoping to catch a fleeting glimpse of the young royal. In an attempt to travel incognito through the cobbled streets of the small town, Charles got behind the wheel of a nondescript green Vauxhall Omega saloon car, which was usually seen around the royals' Balmoral estate, maneuvering it into the quadrangle outside William's halls of residence, St Salvator's. William emerged from the vehicle dressed in baggy jeans, trainers and a sweater, and was greeted by Brian Lang. After a brief exchange, he hesitantly joined his father for a walk along the road to greet the crowds before taking some questions from the waiting reporters – as a gesture of co-operation with the

Scottish media, St James's Palace had arranged just one interview with the press ahead of William's first day.

While William was no doubt concerned about being so far away from his family home and the protections that afforded, he was excited by the move to Scotland, telling the press that he loved the scenery, and that studying at the university would offer him the opportunity to move north of the border in search of a new experience.

The prestigious Edinburgh University had, at one stage, been mooted as a potential location for the future king to study, but William had decided it was 'too busy' for his liking; he believed that St Andrews had a real community feel to it. He was excited also to live near the sea, which he'd never done before.

The palace had stipulated that this would be his first and last interview while at university, and so the press that gathered on that windswept day across the road from the Royal and Ancient Golf Club of St Andrews decided to pose some rather pointed questions in an attempt to get a top line to their story. Their relaying of newspaper reports from that week of over-eager female students having already ordered wedding dresses in anticipation of his arrival did little to faze him: 'I suppose they're saying that tongue-in-cheek,' he said, 'but people who try to take advantage of me and get a piece of me – I spot it quickly and soon go off them.'

When another newsman asked whether the prince would be able to make friends with people from a variety of backgrounds, even if they held anti-monarchist views, his response gave a telling insight into the mind of the man who would one day become king:

> Someone can hold a view about something without it
> making a difference to who they are. Everyone has opinions

and they are entitled to them. I still get on with them, even if I don't agree with what they believe. It's not as if I choose my friends on the basis of where they are from or what they are. It's about their character and whether we get on. I just hope I can meet people I get on with. I don't care about their backgrounds.

Prince Charles might have thrown himself into Cambridge's amateur dramatics clubs but he wasn't exactly the most social of beings. By contrast, William was a young man for the age. Good-looking, straight-talking and intent on being left alone so that he could enjoy himself. Princess Diana's determination to show her children a version of life that would have never otherwise been presented to them had clearly resulted in many of the traditional barriers being broken down.

William insisted that he wanted to be treated like an ordinary student. Naturally, he was aware that the experience would be somewhat different to the immense privilege he'd encountered at Eton; he now found himself in an environment where six in ten of the university's 6,500 students hailed from state schools. To help achieve the sense of normality he craved, he decided to forgo his proper title of 'His Royal Highness', wishing to be known simply as William Wales. In his book *William at 40*, Robert Jobson revealed how, midway through his first term, in another attempt to create further distance from his actual identity, William took on the sobriquet 'Steve'. 'It was the most normal one he could think of at the time and it just stuck,' said a former aide. This inclination for anonymity did little to calm the interest across Fleet Street, with reporters already filing numerous stories on topics ranging from William's future career options to his rumoured love interests.

Despite the palace drawing its battle lines early, William had already been linked to a long list of young society beauties

CHAPTER THREE

including Davina Duckworth-Chad, Isabella Anstruther-Gough-Calthorpe and Emma Parker Bowles, Camilla Parker Bowles's niece, connections that had been routinely denied. While William had been in several short-lived relationships before arriving at university, he was single at the time. The palace and the prince were in little doubt that details of a future relationship would emerge at some point, and both parties wanted to have control over any potential story. In an attempt to pre-empt the media frenzy that would no doubt explode once it was confirmed that William had a love interest, senior palace aides met with the editors of all the major British newspapers to reaffirm their request that the prince should be given as much space as possible. It was acknowledged by the editors that while William was no longer a child at school and the situation had clearly changed, none of them would publicly break ranks owing to the tense relationship between the press and Buckingham Palace following Princess Diana's passing. The palace aides left their meetings feeling optimistic about the sentiments expressed, if not entirely confident that their concerns had been fully understood.

Just a few weeks into William's first year in the small, historic seaside town on Scotland's east coast, fate took an unexpected turn when he crossed paths with Catherine Elizabeth Middleton, a poised and down-to-earth young woman from Berkshire.

Fresh from her gap-year experiences, Catherine was equally keen to prove to herself, and her parents, that her bold decision to change universities was correct. Following the advice of friends who had previously attended St Andrews, Catherine signed up for the same accommodation as William. St Salvator's Hall, affectionately known as 'Sallies', was known as the 'posh hall'. Despite the basic decor and furnishings of the student rooms, the imposing gothic-style building was certainly impressive, with sea views to the rear and a large front lawn that served as a meeting ground for students from across the campus. Inside, each student had their own bedroom with a basin, with a basic bedside table, two lamps, a bulletin board and, if they were lucky, a bookcase. William had actually requested a room without an en suite, fearing criticism if he was seen to be rejecting the full student experience of queuing for the showers with everyone else. During the interview William and Catherine gave to ITV News anchor Tom Bradby in November 2010, after they were engaged, Catherine also clarified that her room did not, as some sections of the media had reported, have pictures of the young prince on her bedroom wall. Instead she had posters of a male model wearing Levi's jeans.

Costing £2,000 a year in rent, St Salvator's was certainly at the upper end of the student budget at the time. Fortunately for William, who only had the culinary skills to make a humble cheese toastie, the halls were also fully catered.

Contrary to some reports, Catherine had never met William before university despite occasionally moving in the same social circles. Their first introduction at Sallies was informal and friendly, as part of a small group of students in the early weeks of term. There was no instant thunderbolt of romance. But before long, William became one of several faces Catherine recognised around campus, whether in the dining hall, during hallway conversations, or walking to lectures down the cobbled streets of the town. Their early conversations were brief, even tentative, discussing timetables and coursework for their history of art classes. William, despite his towering public profile, was shy at first, conscious of how his presence might affect others. Catherine was calm and approachable, but never overawed by William; something that immediately put William at ease. Friends recalled that she 'didn't play up to him or try to impress' anyone, emboldened by the independence her gap-year experiences had brought her. William, however, did make the first move. Despite the terrible weather in the first autumn term, William invited Catherine to join him on a run around the campus and down to the beach, along a route his personal bodyguard had mapped out for him. Within a few days they were seen together trudging the perimeter in the howling wind and rain, prompting rumours that they were now an item.

Far from chasing William, Catherine, with typical modesty, later admitted that she was overcome with embarrassment the first time she saw him and felt awkward about how to act. 'I went bright red and scuttled off,' she confessed to Tom Bradby. From their first interactions, a sincere yet purely platonic relationship blossomed. Catherine spent much of her time with two school friends from Marlborough College, Emilia Jardine-Paterson and Alicia Fox-Pitt, forming close relationships that have stood the test of time. William also relied on trusted friendships from his schooldays, such as the loyal Fergus Boyd, who he knew from Eton. William and Fergus became close with Catherine and also Olivia Bleasdale, known as Livvy. Away from the public eye, they formed a protective circle around the prince.

Within weeks of the start of term, Catherine – who quickly gained a reputation for her good looks, being voted the 'prettiest girl at Sallies' by some of the young men in residence – had caught the eye of charming final-year law student Rupert Finch. Rupert was popular and well liked, but their romance was short-lived. William had also started an intimate relationship with English-language and creative-writing student, Carly Massy-Birch. According to Carly, they had met 'through the general St Andrews melee'. She continued by saying that, 'it's such a small place that it was impossible not to bump into William, and after a while there was nothing weird about seeing him around.' The two had shared interests. Like William, Carly had a love for the countryside, having been brought up in Devon in the south-west of England. And Carly believed that they'd have got on well whether anything romantic happened or not. Carly was renowned for throwing dinner parties at her townhouse, which was just a stone's throw from the university, and had welcomed the prince into her sociable yet exclusive friendship group, despite being in the year above.

For William, who had shied away from drinking in the town's bars and pubs, as well as other organised student events, it was the perfect introduction to university life. In an interview with royal journalist Katie Nicholl, published in *Vanity Fair* in December 2010, Carly explained what drew the couple together. 'I'm a real country bumpkin. I think that was why we had a connection.' They would spend hours discussing plays and literature and sharing their love of the countryside. On other evenings they would enjoy pints of cider at the cosy Old Castle Tavern on North Street and play board games or enjoy dinner parties with their friends. 'There wasn't really a club at St Andrews, so we tended to go to pubs and bars, and there was always a good dinner party going on,' Carly told *Vanity Fair*.

But according to friends, William decided to cool the relationship, as he still harboured an affection for another striking society beauty, who he'd met in the summer of 2001 – Arabella Musgrave, the 18-year-old daughter of Cirencester polo club manager Major Nicholas Musgrave. Arabella was a close friend of Guy Pelly and Hugh van Cutsem and part of the so-called 'Glosse Posse', the name given to William and Harry's inner circle, who often frequented parties in the basement of Highgrove, Prince Charles's home in Gloucestershire. Their relationship had taken off in the summer before William left for university, ending by mutual agreement in the weeks ahead of his first term. However, William still desired Arabella, leaving St Andrews at weekends to return to Highgrove in the knowledge that she would be waiting for him.

CHAPTER THREE

By Christmas 2001, William was somewhat conflicted about university life. He missed his friends, his brother Harry and the freedom of his gap year. Robert Lacey's book, *Battle of Brothers*, quotes Charles's former press secretary, Colleen Harris, who recalled how William 'was really nervous when he arrived' at university, adding that 'all the press were there – cameras from all over the world – and it suddenly hit him. He was very unsteady for a while after that.' William told his father he wanted to leave St Andrews and enrol at the University of Edinburgh instead. Rather than admonish his son, Charles listened and, noticing his son was on the verge of quitting, took William's concerns on board.

A former courtier with knowledge of the exchanges said it was clear during the festive period that William recognised that he and his father were developing a new closeness. This would be a turning point in a relationship that had undergone several tough moments since Princess Diana's tragic death in August 1997. Both William and Harry had accused Charles of struggling to adequately address and support their immense grief. But over several days of the Christmas holidays, Charles conveyed his own, similar, experiences at Gordonstoun and Cambridge, and implored his son to persevere with his studies. Charles argued that the experience of university would be enriching, as well as advantageous to William's well-being. The courtier said:

> The Prince of Wales was concerned that William was ready to throw in the towel at such an early stage and had perhaps the most honest and candid discussions with him that he had ever had. He explained to him that there was a whole world to be experienced, but perhaps he would live to regret turning his back on the experiences that lay right in front of him if he left university so soon.

During further discussions with William, Charles warned him of the potential fallout were he to formally quit his studies in Scotland. And, although anxious about creating further pressure on his son, Charles reminded William that such a decision would impact his reputation and also that of the monarchy at large. William later reflected that, 'I think the rumour that I was unhappy got slightly out of control. I don't think I was homesick. I was more daunted.' Praising his father's intervention, he added, 'We chatted a lot and in the end we both realised – I definitely realised – that I had to come back.'

William's relationship with Catherine was also growing. After spending time together in the common room, and then on weekly runs along the beach, William had come to appreciate her sincere and calm approach to life. Catherine was far more interested in playing sports or listening to music, two of William's passions, than going out to pubs or attending the odd dinner party. Their burgeoning friendship remained platonic at this stage, but, as William considered whether he wanted to stay on at St Andrews, he began to wonder whether perhaps it could be more. As well his father, William had shared his dilemma with his friends, who had picked up on the prince's creeping self-doubt. But, in a sign of their increasing closeness, Catherine would be the one to convince him to stay, laying out the new term's advantages and reminding him that, in the months that followed, students would get to choose who they'd live with when they moved into private accommodation. William hadn't particularly enjoyed the halls environment, believing it to be too restrictive. He hated the lack of his own space. 'As soon as he stepped out of his room, he recognised and noticed people stopping midway through a conversation to look in his direction. It was quite an uncomfortable experience so he was desperate to have a place of his own, where he would have more of an opportunity to relax,' said a source.

CHAPTER THREE

The dynamic between William and Catherine began to shift in March 2002, at a student charity fashion show. It would be the catalyst for a relationship characterised by the quiet anonymity that William craved – certainly less full-on than his affair with the exuberant and outgoing Carly Massy-Birch, who William described to friends as intense. On 27 March 2002, William paid £200 to sit in the front row of a fashion show at the local Fairmont Hotel, organised by a group of international students to raise money for charity in the aftermath of 9/11. The 'Don't Walk' concept reflected its mission: rather than walking past problems in society, people should use creative expression, including fashion, to raise awareness and make a positive impact on the world. What William did not know was that Catherine had agreed to pose in a daring black lace dress worn over a black bandeau bra and bikini briefs. The sheer dress in question was actually a skirt, until Catherine decided to alter its presentation, placing it just below her tousled curls as she strode confidently along the stage. It was enough to catch William's eye, who remarked to Fergus Boyd seated next to him, 'Wow, Kate's hot.'

Just ten days later, a Sunday newspaper reported that William, Catherine, Olivia Bleasdale and Fergus would move into a shared flat in their second year. William and Fergus had come up with the idea. Having already decided to live together, they believed that Catherine and Olivia would make the perfect housemates. 'They were already spending a lot of time together as a foursome and enjoyed each other's company. An added bonus was that the girls were fantastic cooks, whereas William and Fergus could barely boil an egg,' joked a source. A week later, on 15 April 2002, reports followed that William had elected to change his university course, switching his major from history of art to geography. Though St James's Palace denied the story, William had in fact discussed his plan with his father at Christmas. And, having been through the same process, Charles was supportive. Courtiers were duly informed and negotiated for William to change course.

William's second year in September 2002 began with the excitement of moving into 13A Hope Street, a £400,000 maisonette in the centre of St Andrews. He and his housemates each paid £100 a week for their new digs. They walked to and from lectures together and threw their own cosy dinner parties, similar to those they experienced in their first year. As the term progressed, William became more settled, with a routine that revolved around home cooking, playing water polo and listening to music on his stereo. Years later, in 2022, when presenting DJ Simon Mayo with his MBE at Buckingham Palace, William would reveal that his favourite tracks of the time included 'Insomnia', the 1995 club track by British electronic band Faithless, as well as 'Groovejet (If This Ain't Love)', a 2000 chart-topper by the Italian DJ Spiller and Sophie Ellis-Bextor. Catherine had slowly been introducing him to cooking basic meals like spaghetti bolognese, and eventually he managed to muster, with a fair bit of assistance, a steak and ale pie, certainly a step up from cheese toasties. He had been made captain of the university water polo team and, alongside Fergus, would dedicate two hours to training every Thursday, playing matches on either Friday nights or Saturday afternoons.

But while William and Catherine's chemistry may have been clear to their friends, who had noticed them spending an increasing amount of time together – such as going out for lunch together at the Northpoint Café, and being spotted enjoying a post-lecture drink alone in Ma Bells – it seems it was not yet apparent to the couple themselves. From those early days of joining each other on morning runs around the town, to taking afternoon dips in the freezing North Sea or relaxing in the Sallies common room together, rumours of their connection had always swirled around the university.

CHAPTER THREE

The couple would not share their first kiss until March 2003, when they slipped away for an evening drink together at Ma Bells. A source who knows the couple suggests it was William who made the first move, in a 'spur of the moment' reaction to how the night had gone. However, the couple were both unsure about what would, or should, happen next. William was wary of entering into a romance, considering how his previous dating history had panned out, even though, sources suggest, something about this connection felt different to the prince. So William and Catherine decided not to tell anybody about the kiss. While it had acted as proof of their mutual feelings for one another, they were housemates and hadn't as yet discussed the possibility of a relationship. Just two months later, however, their secret would be out. At a dinner party attended by around 20 people in May 2003, towards the end of the summer term, William was left furious when his former flame Carly Massy-Birch audaciously confronted the couple with the rumours that they were seeing each other. They were all playing the drinking game 'Never have I ever', where players take turns revealing something they have never done, beginning each statement with 'Never have I ever ...' The game involves one person mentioning something they have never experienced but knows or suspects another person in the group has. In front of a squirming William, who was sitting beside Catherine, Carly announced, 'Never have I ever dated two people in this room.' Shocked by the reactions of those at the table, William shot Carly a thunderous look before quietly voicing his astonishment that she had revealed his secret. Catherine saw this immediately as a lesson in who both she and William could trust. The tense exchange hit William hard, forcing him to evaluate the direction of his friendship group and his willingness to expose himself so publicly by opening up such a part of his life.

In the same month, as rumours of his daughter's closeness to the future king spread beyond St Andrews, Michael Middleton addressed reporters outside the family home. 'I spoke to her a few days ago and can categorically confirm they are no more than just good friends. They are together all the time because they are the best of pals. But there's nothing more to it than that.' Much to the waiting press pack's delight, Michael also revealed that he and his wife Carole had been speculating about the future, adding, 'We're very amused at the thought of being in-laws to Prince William, but I don't think it is going to happen.'

While Catherine had not been so bold as to tell her parents she had in fact shared a kiss with William, it was clear that whatever path the couple chose, they would not be able to keep news of their relationship from the wider public for long.

4

BEHIND THE FAIRY TALE

Adhering to the unwritten agreement that allowed Prince William the space and time to enjoy his university career had become an issue for Fleet Street. With his 21st birthday in June 2003 fast approaching, editors wanted an exclusive on the young prince's life in Scotland or, better still, to confirm the rumours that the heir to the throne had finally engaged in a hot love affair. Newspapers had caught wind of William and Catherine being in a relationship, but as yet they had not been pictured together.

But when, in March 2003, a Sunday newspaper appeared to reveal that their bond had progressed beyond cups of tea in the common room, the pressure was mounting. Palace communications chiefs refused to confirm or deny any of the speculation, which had by the beginning of 2003 extended beyond the British media, choosing not to respond to the regular calls filling the palace press lines. One former courtier recalled: 'None of us were foolish enough to think the news of the prince's relationship would stay out of the public domain forever, but in a very short space of time, the floodgates were well and truly open.' As requests for clarification from the palace from all over the world began to flood in, William was asked by his father's most senior aides whether he would like to engage with the press. Unsurprisingly, he did not. In fact, although the press interest was not yet classed by the palace as intrusive, stories linking him to other young women, including fellow geography student Bryony Daniels, who was merely his friend, had begun to appear. William vowed to challenge the media if they persisted in interfering with his affairs.

The media's interest in William and Catherine showed no sign of abating when, in June 2003, just weeks after Michael Middleton's well-meaning statement to the press, the Middletons threw a grand bash to celebrate Catherine's 21st birthday. After celebrating her birthday in January, Catherine had been busy helping Carole with preparations for the official party, which was intended to take advantage of the summer weather. A marquee was erected in the grounds of the family home, with 250 guests attending a champagne reception and sit-down dinner for the 1920s-themed event. Catherine looked stunning in a long, shimmering, sleeveless black and silver cocktail dress, complete with headdress, perfectly pulling off the theme of the evening. Among the throng of old school friends and university associates, in slipped Prince William. He was slightly late, blaming traffic for his delay. Catherine was delighted to see him. She complimented him on his dapper suit and tie and then the pair chatted alone before being seated for dinner. Aware that William's attendance would no doubt result in scrutiny from the guests, many of whom he did not know, Catherine decided it would be best if she and the prince sat apart, although he made an impression on her friends who he chatted to animatedly throughout the meal as well as the speeches by Carole and Michael. As the party kicked off after supper, William quietly pulled Catherine aside to say goodbye before making his exit. As they were still establishing their relationship during these first tentative months, and keen to prevent gossip, the couple had agreed to take things slowly.

Catherine would not have to wait long to see William again. Two weeks later she arrived as a guest to his 21st birthday celebrations at Windsor Castle. The 'Out of Africa'-themed evening, inspired by the prince's time in Africa during his gap year, brought senior royals, including Queen Elizabeth II and Prince Charles, together with members of the Spencer family for the first time since Princess Diana's funeral in 1997. Relations between the Spencers and the royals remained tense after Diana's brother, Earl Spencer, had delivered a eulogy that was critical of the royal family, but the evening was all about celebrating William's coming of age. Catherine arrived at the security gates at the 11th-century castle with a group of St Andrews students William had also invited, none of whom knew that she and William had recently become more than good friends. While Catherine was certainly not thinking too far ahead, she could be forgiven for wondering whether one day she would be attending events alongside William as part of the royal family.

The couple had begun to discuss how and when they would manage to see each other during the summer holidays. William had a trip to France planned with his male friends, while Catherine was planning to go to Ibiza with her sister. It would be the first time they had spent time apart since that first secret kiss, and they both wondered whether the break would bring them closer together or force them to drift apart.

The castle's ancient rooms were transformed into spectacular scenes from the African bush, including, in pride of place, a life-sized papier-mâché elephant. African band Shakarimba were flown in specially from Botswana, where William had heard them perform while on holiday with Prince Harry and their former nanny Tiggy Legge-Bourke in 1999. More than 300 guests arrived in an array of outfits, including a lion suit topped with a gold crown, a full Foreign Legion uniform, a Biggles-esque pilot, a banana, and a top-hatted witch doctor. Charles Spencer donned a light-coloured safari-type suit, followed by the comedian Rowan Atkinson and his wife in linen and colonial-style attire. As the party started, other guests were spotted, including the late socialite Tara Palmer Tomkinson, dressed as a lion and mixing with William's friends from university, and Tarzan and another banana. The presence of the Prince of Wales's partner Camilla Parker Bowles was a notable inclusion on William's birthday and the clearest indication yet that the prince had given her relationship with his father his blessing.

On the eve of the party, William gave an interview to the Press Association, to be pooled with the UK media, where he railed against intrusion into his life and the impact it had on his inability to have a significant relationship, while denying he was romantically involved with anyone. And, in a further sign of his growing unease with the speculation about his relationship with Catherine, the prince also lamented the fact that he felt he was unable to protect his female friends from the kind of scrutiny he had become used to over the years. 'I'm used to it because it happens quite a lot now. But it's very difficult for them, and I don't like that at all,' he said.

Although delighted to see her, it is telling that William took a cautious approach to seeing Catherine throughout the evening, partly so he could enjoy the evening with friends but also to stop the aristocratic set from gossiping. It has been suggested, for instance in Katie Nicholl's *The Making of a Royal Romance*, that Catherine was put out by the lack of affection William showed, and the fact he had seated Jecca Craig next to him on the top table. Friends of the couple, however, say that these reports are 'wide of the mark', and that with the relationship in its infancy, Catherine realised she couldn't be seen to be 'hanging off' William, especially given guests included many senior members of the royal family.

Among those female friends at the party were a host of rumoured former flames, including the polo-playing Natalie

Hicks-Löbbecke and party girl Davina Duckworth-Chad, who had joined William for a summer cruise in 1999 with Charles and Camilla. In that Press Association interview, William claimed he was happy to ask a woman out, but wary of causing them difficulties. 'Only the mad girls chase me, I think,' he said, jokingly, adding: 'No, I've never been aware of anyone chasing me, but if they were, could they please leave their telephone number?'

William went on to explain how he had developed a fear of opening himself up to a relationship due to the pressure exerted by both the press and the public. 'I don't have a steady girlfriend,' he claimed. 'If I fancy a girl and I really like her and she fancies me back, which is rare, I ask her out. But at the same time I don't want to put them in an awkward situation because a lot of people don't quite understand what comes with knowing me, for one, and secondly, if they were my girlfriend there is the excitement it would probably cause.'

William also disclosed that he had been considering how the life of duty that he had been born into would affect his choices in the years to come. He reflected that his priority was to get through university, but that he thought about his future frequently (sometimes with anxiety). What he was certain of was that his future would involve helping people with dedication and loyalty. This was a key time in William's development, not only as an adult enjoying the freedom of his university years, but also as somebody who was considering what a life after St Andrews might look like.

While the prince was prepared to disclose his vision as a future senior figure within the institution, he had remained silent about Catherine. William's responses could have been a source of angst for Catherine, but the couple were by this point engaged in an exclusive relationship, and she had come to appreciate his desire to operate under the radar. William appealed again to the media to allow him privacy at university, saying, 'I don't think either side wants to return to the free-for-all of the old days. The media can be tricky at times, but so can most people. It's something that I want to handle with the most maturity I can. So it is difficult, but it's not impossible.'

On publication of this interview, Catherine was questioned by friends as to what she thought of this apparent public snub. 'I remember she was relaxed about it,' said one friend close to the couple. 'She didn't see it as an issue and certainly didn't present that she was remotely bothered about it.' What was clear to their inner circle was that the couple wanted to live in the moment and enjoy their time together without worrying about the outside world. 'Their relationship was hardly typical at the time, with all the external pressures, whether that was gossiping students or the wider media issue. But behind closed doors it was as normal as you could expect,' said the friend.

William and Catherine kept in touch over the summer although they did not manage to meet in person. At the beginning of the summer term, 13A Hope Street's residents had decided to go their separate ways. Fergus would stay in the flat, while Olivia was moving across town with another group of girlfriends, leaving William to suggest to Catherine that they move in together with Oliver Baker, a mutual friend. At first, Catherine was apprehensive. As part of a foursome, she and William had enjoyed the opportunity to get to know each other without the pressure of labelling the relationship during its early days. Now, having been secretly seeing each other for several months, she had to decide whether to take the next step.

William had already been offered alternative accommodation, which would provide greater privacy. The four-bedroom sandstone cottage Balgove House, set within Strathtyrum, a 400-acre private country estate, was owned by Henry Cheape,

CHAPTER FOUR

a distant cousin of the prince and friend of the royal family. William suggested they take a road trip to see the house, which was an hour away from St Andrews and came complete with outbuildings that would allow his personal protection officers to remain on site. Catherine fell in love with the area and believed it would provide a sanctuary in which their relationship could deepen, away from the growing media curiosity. In turn, William had made no secret of his fondness for Catherine, both to his close friends and to his father, who had proposed Balgove House as a possible home.

On 14 September 2003, the couple moved their belongings into the 18th-century farmhouse. They would be protected by round-the-clock security, with panic alarms linked directly to the local police station. Armed officers could arrive within three minutes. Aside from the CCTV cameras that surrounded the property, and its bomb-proof doors and windows installed by the royalty protection squad, William and Catherine felt at home. They enjoyed solitary romantic walks along the windswept coastline and invited friends over for picnics on the estate. Their new life together was a world away from the goldfish bowl of the university town. In moving there, William felt at ease for the first time. Now that they were staying out of town, their time was mostly spent having groups of friends over for dinner parties and weekend stays.

Shortly after the 2003 Christmas break, Prince Charles enlisted the services of a new press secretary, Patrick 'Paddy' Harverson. Described by a former colleague as 'intimidatingly bald and with a trim, gingery beard, and easy to mistake for a nightclub bouncer', the six-foot-tall former journalist could equally have been mistaken for one of the royal household's legion of protection officers, with a stern reputation to match. Paddy had begun his professional career in journalism and spent

12 years working at the *Financial Times* in roles as diverse as economics reporter, Wall Street correspondent (based in New York) and sports correspondent. In 2000, he took the well-trodden path of public relations to become the first director of communications at Manchester United Football Club. Four years later, Paddy's leaving party in an upmarket jazz bar in the city featured a video message from the club's legendary manager Sir Alex Ferguson. 'Good luck. You're going to the only place madder than Manchester United,' the Scottish behemoth said, to rapturous laughter from those gathered.

On joining the royal household in February 2004, one of Paddy's first appointments was to travel to Scotland for an introductory meeting with Prince William. Arrangements were made for the pair to meet at a local Italian restaurant, a haunt of William's throughout his first year that was familiar and comfortable. Paddy arrived earlier than the agreed 7pm reservation, in case the prince (whose tardiness had been joked about by his own father) arrived late. At 7pm, though, William pushed open the door to the intimate candlelit restaurant and made his way over to Paddy's table. 'Paddy, lovely to meet you. This is Kate,' the prince said, pulling a seat out for his surprise guest. According to a palace source, Paddy was caught unaware when met with the prince's love interest, but remarked to a colleague on his return that 'it must be serious' if William was ready to introduce Catherine to someone he had never met. During the hour and a half meeting, the two men bonded immediately over their interest in football, as Prince Charles's 'new man' laid out his experience of dealing with a rabid international press and of representing some of the highest-profile individuals on the planet. In the meeting, Catherine kept to small talk, not being a football fan, let alone a high-ranking executive from the royal household. 'The report back was that she was very polite and pleasant,' said a former courtier. 'It was obviously a major deal that William was introducing her to Paddy, which certainly focused our attention that firstly, we had to be ready when the press started speculating on the details of their relationship which would certainly present its own issues.'

In that initial meeting, William relayed his explicit wish to be left alone to concentrate on his studies, as well as repeating his desire to live as 'normal' a life as possible. The prince also confirmed that not only was he in a relationship with Catherine, but that he wished for the full weight of the palace machine to get behind him and the young woman he cared so deeply for. William had seen the way media intrusion damaged his parents' marriage and was determined to protect that part of his life. Catherine had confided to her parents before the Christmas break that she was seeing Prince William and had expectations the relationship could progress. Family friends suggest Carole was incredibly excited and, while she was well aware of the need to maintain the couple's secret, she had to be urged by Catherine to calm down, such was her nervousness of anything leaking to the press given William's distrust of the media. Naturally, they were sworn to secrecy but, when Catherine later told them that William had brought her to meet one of the Prince of Wales's senior aides, they realised that the relationship was becoming serious.

One former courtier said, 'It was a huge moment for William and for the team. Essentially, we were instructed to act for an individual who was not part of the family, but both sides could see the clear pitfalls of not being prepared for what was clearly on the horizon. From that moment on, the palace was acting in an unofficial manner for Kate.' Though Clarence House would continue to deny its involvement in Catherine's affairs for years.

With Clarence House's backing, William and Catherine started taking tentative steps towards a more public relationship.

The prince had invited his girlfriend to stay at Highgrove on several occasions, and they had also enjoyed a weekend together at the Queen's Sandringham estate. The stays were organised by William for when his father and grandmother were not in residence, allowing the couple the freedom to enjoy themselves without Catherine worrying about meeting his family. 'He was very concerned she would be completely overawed by the whole thing,' said a former courtier. 'Kate had wealthy friends who had nice piles in the country, but it's a different story when you're dating a prince whose granny is the Queen. He was still very much in the mode of "Let's take it slow and see what happens," while being pretty nervous that the press was going to find out what was going on and ruin it for them.'

But before long, William's request for protection for both himself and Catherine was to prove prophetic. On 1 April 2004, the *Sun* ran a front-page splash story under the headline 'Finally. Wills gets a girl'. Dressed in complementary red and black ski gear, the beaming William and Catherine had been photographed skiing at the luxury Klosters resort in Switzerland. Over the next four pages, billed as a 'world exclusive: the royal romance', the prince was pictured again with Catherine, skiing and riding lifts together. The paper identified her as 'his first serious girlfriend'. Suddenly, William and Catherine's relationship, which they had worked so hard to safeguard against idle gossip and intrusion, had moved from an open secret at St Andrews to a Fleet Street exclusive.

The couple had flown out with the Prince of Wales, Prince Harry and a group of friends including Harry Legge-Bourke, the younger brother of William's nanny 'Tiggy', the brothers' exuberant pal Guy Pelly, and William van Cutsem (son of Charles's Norfolk-based friend Hugh) and his girlfriend Katie James. The headlines interrupted plans for what was intended to be a close-knit family holiday. The palace was also furious, accusing the *Sun* of breaking an agreement to leave William in peace: four days beforehand he had posed alongside his father during an official photocall when they both joked with photographers about their skiing abilities. Clarence House relayed William's immense disappointment about the apparent breach of the agreement, adding that the palace was considering banning the newspaper from further engagements.

The publication of the images, taken by the well-known celebrity photographer Jason Fraser instead of one of the *Sun*'s own staff photographers, looked as if it would be a turning point in the royals' relationship with the media. The agreement between the press and Buckingham Palace that was supposed to protect the royal princes while they studied was already under strain because news organisations believed they were being deliberately shut out. The newspaper industry accused the palace of reneging on its side of the entente, which involved giving regular official access to both princes at key milestones during their schooling. Sir Michael Peat, the Prince of Wales's private secretary, had attempted to ease unrest among tabloid newspapers by promising to provide information about the student prince at least once a term. In a letter to Les Hinton, the chairman of the Editors' Code of Practice Committee, sent in September 2004, Sir Michael even made the candid admission that the palace had failed to give the press sufficient access to William during his time at university. While many outside the media industry would regard this behaviour as wholly unpalatable, the royal household acknowledged that there was mileage in keeping the peace. By giving up some ground to the newspapers, they hoped to allow William to maintain a degree of privacy.

Although there was no picture of the pair in a romantic embrace, the rest of the world was now in no doubt that

Prince William and his attractive housemate were more than just friends. The palace communications team reacted furiously, admonishing the *Sun* and warning other newspapers off using the photographs. Yet the goalposts had clearly moved. Reporters from rival publications were immediately dispatched to track the young prince and his partner down, hungry for the next scoop.

Having grown up under the media glare his entire life, William was clearly aware of what lay on the horizon. For Catherine, however, it was entirely new territory. William had done his best to inform her about how the media operated, but now she was the subject of their pursuit things felt incredibly different. 'She was spooked by the attention,' a former courtier said. 'No matter how much you're told about what can happen, you literally can't have any idea about it until you're on the other side, and now she was very much on the other side.'

Refusing to bow to the palace's pressure, the *Sun*'s then editor Rebekah Brooks ordered the release of a statement insisting the story about Prince William and his 'girlfriend' was '100 per cent true, therefore there is a strong public interest in publishing these delightful photographs'. The statement added, 'One of William's girlfriends could become Queen one day. Her subjects will be entitled to know all about her.' The palace threatened to shut out the paper's veteran royal photographer, Arthur Edwards, who had been with the *Sun* since 1977 and was known by all the royals, from royal events. In response, Brooks said she would launch an 'Our Arthur Is Innocent' campaign. Battle lines had been drawn.

Hundreds of column inches followed and William and Catherine found themselves at the centre of a media storm. While the palace would not officially confirm the relationship, its reaction to the *Sun*'s pictures effectively did so. One former Fleet Street editor said: 'The world had been waiting for the news that William had a proper love interest and once it was all but confirmed by him or the palace, it marked a turning point for sure. The public were desperate to know if the future king had found his queen and what that would mean for the future of the monarchy in an ever-changing world.'

William, along with palace officials, had long feared that the unofficial pact with the British media to safeguard the privacy of the young princes would break down at the first sign of a girlfriend. William was now ready to take matters into his own hands. Seven weeks after the publication of the photographs, the evening before a prearranged press call with his father, which would take place on a visit to Duchy Home Farm in Gloucestershire, William stunned the royal press pack by striding into the nearby Hare and Hounds Hotel, where they were enjoying a drink after dinner.

William ordered at the bar after offering to get in a round of drinks, welcoming those who had made the journey up from London. After engaging in some small talk, William addressed the royal photographers to convey his feelings on the Klosters episode. Former *Daily Mirror* chief photographer Kent Gavin, who won Royal Photographer of the Year an unprecedented seven times throughout his four-decade career, said:

> William lowered his voice very purposely and said: 'That business on the slopes, totally uncalled for, don't you think?' We knew he wasn't asking the question, it was more of a dressing down, which was pretty extraordinary.
>
> He then said he was making himself very clear, that there was absolutely no way we are going back to the old days. I remember him saying, 'There is absolutely nothing I would not do to protect my family or those close to me from those times, so we are not going back.' We were all pretty dumbfounded, but understood where he was coming from.

Having finished his pint of cider, William then said his goodbyes and exited the bar, leaving the newsmen astonished at the frankness of the conversation. It was no secret that the prince remained deeply scarred by the circumstances of his mother's death, particularly the actions of paparazzi photographers on motorbikes in the moments before her tragic demise. One thing was clear, though: William was now ready to act independently of the palace communications team. In turn, the palace did not think William's intervention was particularly wise. 'When you start breaking that wall, it's only going to cause problems,' a former courtier said. 'But he was upset, he was angry and there wasn't much you could argue with. He already felt he had given up a lot of his life to the press and was going to have to in future, so it was his way of laying a marker down.'

Close friends of the prince described how a 'sudden change' came over him following the Klosters trip. In the following weeks, the couple were involved in several tense exchanges that completely caught Catherine off guard.

> William could be quite volatile at times, mainly in his reactions over having to deal with his father's aides or having to take part in interviews. But during that time before the summer holidays there was a sudden change in his attitude. He was thinking about going to Sandhurst, joining the army, maybe some travelling and what that would lead to. It certainly gave his head a wobble, wondering how much time he would have to dedicate to that and what that would mean for other things in his life, such as a serious relationship.

With such significant plans on the horizon, it wasn't clear that Catherine would remain a priority for William after university. He was still just 22, and friends suggested he was afraid both of

CHAPTER FOUR

losing his sense of independence so young, and of the mounting media speculation about a possible engagement.

While Catherine did not doubt the burden of responsibility William felt as a senior member of the monarchy, she was left in shock at his sudden change of direction. 'William suggested he needed to clear his head and come up with a plan, he was a bit all over the place and just left Kate hanging,' the friend said. With Catherine somewhat stunned, William suggested that, over the summer of 2004, they take a break from the two-year relationship.

And so, as the summer term ended, William made plans to join Guy Pelly on a sailing holiday in Greece, while Catherine retreated to her family home in Berkshire. Reports in the press emerged that William and his pals were on a booze-fuelled trip, catered for by an all-female crew. Although Catherine had vowed not to read anything in the press regarding William, concerned friends made her aware of at least two stories that summer.

Contact between William and Catherine was sparse. William was away, having organised a number of trips abroad following on from the holiday in Greece, including a holiday to Tennessee. He travelled to America with a group of friends, many of whom studied at Edinburgh University. The group included the glamorous American heiress, Anna Sloan. Anna had tragically lost her legendary horseracing father, George, in 2001, after his shotgun discharged while he was climbing a fence on the family's sprawling 320-acre estate in Nashville. Anna and William bonded over the devastating loss of a parent and had kept in touch following his trip to Tennessee. After Catherine was told about William's travel arrangements, as well as further rumours that he was pursuing Isabella Anstruther-Gough-Calthorpe, she broke the silence William had engineered to confront him about what she'd heard. William did not respond until almost a week later. He was having fun, even if he wasn't pursuing anyone else, and he was torn about whether he wanted to continue his relationship with Catherine. On the one hand he missed her, and on the other the attention from the media had left him so incensed that he had started telling friends that he didn't believe he would ever be left alone to have a normal relationship.

By October, the couple were heading back to St Andrews, where they would resume living together. Understandably there was nervousness on both sides and issues that undoubtedly needed addressing. Would things be different? Could they move on from their summer blip? Catherine was emboldened after confiding in her parents over the summer and told William she would not tolerate their relationship's stop-start pattern. Soon after starting the new term, the couple had a heart-to-heart while walking around the estate near their home. William broke down and apologised, suggesting he was struggling to deal with the claustrophobic nature of the questions from his father and other family members about what he planned to do after finishing university. The Queen and Prince of Wales had allowed him to avoid royal duties while he was concentrating on his studies, but soon that time would end. William was under pressure to deliver a coherent plan for his future, and as yet he had none. 'He was a bit all over the place,' a friend said. 'There was a certain pressure from above, but he was becoming consumed with it. It was more to do with him not having an idea of what he wanted to do after university, so the pressure was self-induced, actually.' William told Catherine he wanted to make a serious go of the relationship and in a peacemaking gesture he invited her to his father's 56th birthday celebrations at Highgrove. Unbeknown to Catherine, it was Charles who had insisted on William having an honest conversation with her. Friends of the Prince of Wales have always maintained that, despite his ups and downs with both his sons, and that while he

CHAPTER FOUR

may have struggled to adequately show his love at times, he has been capable of delivering astute advice when required. Charles explained to William that if he did indeed love Catherine, then his actions suggested the opposite, and he risked throwing a valuable relationship away.

The couple reunited quietly and without fanfare. With the lessons of the previous six months behind them, their final terms at St Andrews were marked by consolidation and stability. While not necessarily bound by the pressure of having to achieve a strong degree to establish career prospects, William applied himself to his studies, keen to outdo the 2:2 his father had achieved at Cambridge.

At home, more changes were afoot for Prince William. Before William returned to Scotland at the end of January, after a Christmas spent together with his family at Sandringham, Charles asked both his sons to join him on a walk around the grounds of Highgrove, where he told them of his intention to propose to Camilla. While William, then 22, and Harry, 20, were happy their father had found happiness again, they were in no mood to give their father's desire to marry Camilla their blessing. In his memoir, *Spare*, Harry recounted how, after the boys had begged their father not to marry again, they were faced with the reality that he was going to, whatever they thought. 'Despite Willy and me urging him not to, Pa was going ahead. We pumped his hand, wished him well. No hard feelings. We recognised that he was finally going to be with the woman he loved, the woman he'd always loved.'

As well as telling his sons, Charles had used the Christmas break to discuss the matter with his mother and with Sir Michael Peat, his private secretary, before the palace communications team was informed. Nevertheless, Clarence House was caught on the hop when, on 10 February 2005 the *Evening Standard* published a world exclusive, announcing 'Charles to Wed Camilla in the Spring'. The journalist behind the article, Robert Jobson, who was awarded the London Press Club Scoop of the Year for the story, also revealed that Queen Elizabeth II had given her blessing. Clarence House hurriedly announced that the Queen had alerted Prime Minister Tony Blair, and that he would be formally consulted on the matter before the date was set. After the initial surprise, a raft of critical headlines followed, discussing everything from the legality of the marriage to the embarrassment of the venue being changed from Charles's preferred choice of Windsor Castle to the local civic hall.

Although privately he was at odds with his father's decision, William grasped the importance of being supportive in public. The following month, Charles celebrated his upcoming nuptials by taking off on his annual skiing holiday to Klosters, accompanied by his sons and an extended party, including Catherine. The trip would become notable for Charles's infamous exchange with former BBC royal correspondent Nicholas Witchell, when Witchell asked the heir about his feelings in the run-up to his wedding. Having been irked at the line of questioning, in the midst of a photocall with the travelling British media, Charles muttered, 'These bloody people. I can't bear that man. I mean, he's so awful, he really is', unaware of the microphones placed at his feet. William would also give a curt response to being asked if there was 'likely to be a second royal wedding soon', replying with a simple no. The tension was palpable, with Charles, William and Harry all keen to discharge the duty they had been cajoled into performing by the palace press team.

But that wouldn't be the last time that William spoke with the press that holiday. On 30 March 2005, having guessed William and Harry would be joining the après-ski crowd in one of Klosters' more exclusive venues, the *Sun*'s royal reporter

CHAPTER FOUR

Duncan Larcombe pitched up at the popular Casa Antica nightclub in the Swiss Alps. He found William's protection officers, and was speaking with them when the prince walked in and beckoned him over. Quite astonishingly, William – as the paper would suggest – 'opened his heart' to the journalist when questioned about whether, given his father's upcoming nuptials, his own engagement was on the horizon. 'Look, I'm only 22 for God's sake. I'm too young to marry at my age. I don't want to get married until I am at least 28 or maybe 30,' William said.

The prince's candid response would result in a world exclusive the next day. Then, just hours after the story hit the newsstands, another newsman asked William, who he had found with Charles and Harry, how Catherine 'was bearing up under the scrutiny'. William denied having seen the coverage, suggesting he was 'just gagging to get on the slopes'.

While they may not have thumbed through copies of the *Sun* during breakfast at their plush Swiss chalet, the party were certainly aware of the coverage. One former courtier suggested it caused an 'undeniable awkwardness' in the following days, adding, 'Kate undoubtedly was left bruised by the comments and had a face like thunder for most of the trip. She felt hurt, perhaps let down, and for all his paranoia over the press stirring up trouble, William was on this occasion the actual source of his problems.' Seven weeks later, on 9 April 2005, the Prince of Wales married Camilla at Windsor Guildhall, an event that had been postponed after the death, a week previously, of Pope John Paul II. It was a muted occasion, and neither Catherine nor Harry's then girlfriend, Chelsy Davy, attended. But celebration was still very much in the air. On 23 June 2005, William celebrated achieving an upper second-class honours degree in geography. The Queen and Duke of Edinburgh joined Prince Charles and Camilla, now Duchess of Cornwall, for William's graduation at St Andrews, with the royal party even making time to congratulate Catherine and meet her parents for the first time.

Following the ceremony, William visited the local police station to thank the Fife constabulary for its support throughout his time at his university. Closing the chapter on his Scottish experience, he said: 'I have thoroughly enjoyed my time at St Andrews and I shall be very sad to leave. I just want to say a big thank you to everyone who has made my time here so enjoyable. I have been able to lead as "normal" a student life as I could have hoped for and I am very grateful to everyone, particularly the locals, who have helped to make this happen.' William announced his intention to embark on work experience in the City, while also gaining experience in land management and spending time with a mountain rescue team. He was also continuing to consider a career in the military. William clearly wanted to keep his options before making his next move.

5

A PARTING OF WAYS

The dawn of post-university life would certainly present new challenges for William and Catherine. Through the ups and downs of their relationship, Catherine had remained steadfast in her belief that once William settled into a career of his choosing, whether that was joining the military or entering full-time royal duties, then his anxiety would pass. There was of course the added concern – again, mainly on William's side – over the expectations of others and the constant questions as to whether they were likely to settle down. They had become comfortable in their secret bubble, enjoying quiet nights in and walks in the countryside. Now they would have to navigate living apart from one another for the first time in three years, away from the protection that was afforded to them at St Andrews.

Those close to him at the time suggest William was 'lost' in those early days following the end of his university experience and already beginning to buckle under the weight of expectation he perceived was on his shoulders. The second in line to the throne seemed eager to explore more of the world before he joined the roster of engagements that senior members of the royal family were duty-bound to fulfil. But behind closed doors, palace aides felt William was lacking direction. One senior courtier said the prince had become 'disinterested' in engaging in meetings scheduled specifically to help him with the plethora of options he had at his feet. 'It was as if he wanted to be left alone and kept trying to distract from the issue, which, bluntly put, was that if he didn't get his house in order, questions would quite rightly start being asked about his privileged position as an idle prince that had no interest in either fulfilling some form of public duty or displaying some other purpose,' the senior aide said.

William hadn't always been this indecisive. During a visit to the Duchy farm with Charles in 2004, he had seemed certain he would join the armed forces upon graduating: 'I haven't really ruled anything out, but a career in the armed forces would be the best thing at the moment because it would be lovely to recognise all the hard work that the armed forces are doing,' the 21-year-old prince said. 'It is a risky business, but there's a lot of guys out there risking their lives.' Yet, a year later, he was having second thoughts about the direction he wanted to go in.

Perhaps the generational cycle of expectation was holding the young prince back. Queen Elizabeth II was Commander in Chief of the armed forces, a position William will one day assume as monarch. She had proudly served in the Auxiliary Territorial Service (ATS) during the Second World War, joining in 1945 as the first female member of the royal family to become a full-time, active member of the armed services. Her husband, the Duke of Edinburgh, had also enjoyed a distinguished military career with the Royal Navy from 1939 to 1951, serving during the Second World War, seeing action at the Battle of Cape Matapan and during the invasion of Sicily, where he was mentioned in dispatches. Charles also had a military career, spending most of it with the Royal Navy, with whom he served between 1971 and 1976, with his last ten months of active service being spent commanding the coastal minehunter HMS *Bronington*. William's uncle Andrew also enjoyed a decorated career in the Royal Navy, serving in the Falklands War of 1982 and returning to a hero's welcome. But Charles, the Prince of

CHAPTER FIVE

Wales, had made it clear to his son that he was under no obligation to choose the same path.

Though William was uncertain about his next step, others had more confidence in him. When the government proposed a royal tour to New Zealand, the Queen decided William should be sent on his first official solo trip. On 29 June 2005 he arrived in Wellington to represent Her Majesty at the 60th anniversary commemorations of the end of the Second World War in the Pacific. The 11-day trip was a deeply symbolic moment for William and lit a spark that would result in a life of duty to Crown and country. Here, William realised that, rather than being something to fear, he was actually quite at home with the role he had been born into. He enjoyed engaging with locals, visiting charities and being a figurehead for the monarchy. He joked to one aide on the trip that he felt like 'an apprentice for the family business'. The perfectly executed royal tour involved the prince attending a wreath-laying ceremony at the National War Memorial, and a visit to a primary school in the South Island, before he was invited by the British and Irish Lions rugby team to watch two Tests against the New Zealand All Blacks. For William it was evidence of the variety that service offered, at a time when he needed that evidence most. 'He rather enjoyed himself, which was quite a surprise to him,' a former palace aide said. 'Before he went, he was wracked with anxiety, but as soon as he was on the ground he threw himself into it. It's one thing to think you know how the family business works, but until you actually get under the hood, you don't really have an idea. That trip set something off in him, to make him realise it was something to look forward to in the future.' The local and international press jointly praised his down-to-earth demeanour, whether he was joining in with a game of rugby with schoolchildren or looking relaxed with sailors from the Royal New Zealand Navy. For the first time in months, the prince looked like he was enjoying himself.

Catherine had decided to base herself in London after graduation, moving with her sister Pippa into a flat in upmarket Chelsea, south-west London. She was content with doing some remote marketing work for her parents' business Party Pieces while she worked out what to do. Mostly, though, she was set on spending as much time as possible with William once he returned from New Zealand. The couple had a lot to catch up on, especially as the success of the tour meant that for the first time William was full of optimism about his future. The couple embarked on a romantic safari in Kenya, staying in a log cabin at the Lewa Wildlife Conservancy, near Mount Kenya, owned by the parents of his rumoured former flame Jecca Craig.

However, the subject of their future, including their living arrangements, remained on the agenda. William had passed the Regular Commissions Board (RCB) preliminary examinations, which would allow him to apply for army officer training at the Royal Military Academy Sandhurst. The previous year, together with Harry, he had secretly spent part of his summer holiday on training exercises with the Special Boat Service (SBS), the British Royal Navy's special forces unit. Even before achieving a B in art and a D in geography in his A-levels, Harry had decided he wanted a career in the military. He had been due to start his 44-week officer training course at the Sandhurst military in January 2005, but was forced to delay his entry due to a recurring knee injury, which he'd initially picked up after falling down a set of stairs during the SBS training. Once recovered, he was finally ready to start in May.

The brothers were aware of the comparisons that would inevitably be made if they were to join at the same time, yet William decided to enrol at Sandhurst in September 2005. He explained to Catherine that his time throughout the autumn and until the end of the year would have to be devoted to completing his officer training, as well as fulfilling his work experience commitments. The resulting schedule would prove another testing time for the couple, and would mean at least a further year of living apart. While Catherine started looking for work in the fashion world, William got to grips with working at the vast Chatsworth House estate in Derbyshire, renowned for appearing in the BBC shows *Pride and Prejudice* and *Peaky Blinders*, to learn more about land management. After his trip to Australia and New Zealand, William had a renewed sense of purpose. In addition to dedicating himself to the military, he had one eye on the vast Duchy of Cornwall operation that he would inherit from Charles on his father's accession to the throne.

In November, the prince completed a three-week stint at a variety of institutions in the City, including at the Bank of England, the London Stock Exchange, Lloyd's of London and Billingsgate Fish Market. The plan was to give William a deliberately varied overview of the financial sector, which he hoped to put to use when he was involved in charitable fundraising in the future. A month later he completed two weeks with an RAF mountain rescue team based in North Wales. William was able to gain flight experience in a jet, attend briefings on combat scenarios, join in with helicopter rescue techniques, as well as study mountaineering and sea drills. In secret, he also dedicated himself to visiting a number of the London locations for the homelessness charity Centrepoint. He'd first visited the organisation with his late mother in 1993, when he was 11. In homage to Diana's legacy, William accepted his first royal patronage for the charity in September 2005. The opportunities to combine his passions with his role as a senior member of the royal family came thick and fast. In the same month he was awarded the position of president-designate at the English Football Association, and the following year he would take over from his uncle Prince Andrew as president. The position meant he could further his love of football while actively helping the grassroots level of the game.

As William geared up for a change of pace as his military training began in January 2006, Catherine was struggling. Although the couple barely saw each other, a media feeding-frenzy had been in full force ever since they had graduated, with newspaper and magazine editors able to secure much easier access to them both since they had left the protection of St Andrews. The luxury of round-the-clock security for Catherine had gone and the tranquility of life in Scotland extinguished. Clarence House was maintaining an unofficial role in supporting her, counselling her to seek legal recourse in October after she was hounded outside her London home by paparazzi. Lawyers Harbottle & Lewis, who also represented Prince Charles, wrote to the editors of national newspapers and magazines, setting out a number of issues regarding press coverage of the 23-year-old's private life that they were unhappy with. Charles's senior aides also personally called the Fleet Street editors to appeal for a change in direction. But protection was now only offered when Catherine was with William or visiting the royal family, whether that was for high tea at Windsor Castle or dinner with Prince Charles at Clarence House or Highgrove.

The Queen had met privately with William and his girlfriend on several occasions throughout 2005, and had become very fond of her, even making a point of consulting Charles as to whether she was being prepared by his staff for what lay ahead. Although mindful of her grandson's unwillingness to commit his future prematurely, the Queen expressed concern that, if Catherine did not join the family, she would fall into the trap of being consumed by the attention. Catherine was being strategically followed across London by freelance photographers in cars, and William's ability to protect his loved ones, as he had sworn to do in the country pub 18 months beforehand, was already waning – a situation that would not improve, the prince thought, when his focus shifted to Sandhurst.

The couple enjoyed another trip to Klosters in the first week of January 2006, where they were pictured embracing and kissing, signalling that their relationship was going well, but the holiday was a brief relief from an otherwise strained period, thanks to the press attention and William's other commitments. When they returned, William immediately started his 44-week course at Sandhurst in Berkshire. In a statement ahead of his first day, William spoke of his excitement at finally starting the journey to becoming an officer in the armed forces, saying, 'I am absolutely delighted to have got over the first hurdle, but I am only too well aware, having spoken so much to Harry, that this is just the beginning.' Lieutenant Colonel Roy Parkinson, spokesman for the academy, insisted that neither prince would be afforded preferential treatment, meaning that William was not permitted to leave for the first five weeks of the course. At weekends, Catherine decided to seek solace in the comfort of the family home, almost in limbo as she waited for William to be allowed to join her.

On 12 April, it was Harry's turn to take centre stage, at his passing-out parade. Aptly described in reports as 'blushing deep to the roots of his red hair', the 21-year-old had cause to beam with pride as his grandmother, the Queen, flashed her unmistakable smile as she faced him while inspecting the newly inaugurated troops. It was the first time in 15 years that the monarch had attended the 'Sovereign's Parade' in the quadrangle of the college in Camberley, Surrey. Senior officer Major General Sebastian Roberts said it was 'eminently possible' that Cornet Wales, as

Harry was to be known, could find himself serving on the front line in Iraq or Afghanistan within six months, boosting his transformation from party prince to potential war hero. As an heir in the modern age, William was unlikely to be afforded the same chance, but he was on hand at the parade as part of the military to celebrate and congratulate his brother alongside the Duke of Edinburgh, Prince Charles and Camilla. Harry had taken great delight as William took his place among the other cadets standing to attention in navy blue uniforms and white gloves, joking with his older brother that their roles had reversed.

Harry's glamorous South African girlfriend Chelsy Davy had been absent for his passing out, but when William's turn came on 15 December 2006, Catherine made her first official attendance at an event alongside the royal family. Earlier that year, on 6 May, Catherine had accompanied the prince to the wedding of Camilla's daughter, Laura Parker Bowles, to Harry Lopes, their first big society occasion together – and had also been invited into the royal box by Camilla during the Cheltenham Gold Cup race meeting on 17 March, perhaps a case of one former outsider offering advice and comfort to another. But this occasion was a true elevation. As William marched alongside 232 other graduating cadets, photographers' lenses darted between the prince and his girlfriend. It was telling that William also chose to invite Carole and Michael Middleton, having established a deep bond with them over the previous year. Most Friday evenings, when he was granted leave for the weekend, he decamped to their house in Bucklebury for home-cooked meals. The Middletons' home had provided sanctuary for both Catherine and William. Catherine was still dealing with press interest, with reporters and photographers camping outside her flat. Despite the best efforts of palace staff, the attention had not abated. William's three months at Sandhurst had been a baptism of fire but had

CHAPTER FIVE

cemented his decision to pursue a full-time career in the military. Seated next to her parents, as well as William's close school friends, James Meade and Thomas van Straubenzee, Catherine was the picture of perfection for her royal debut, her attendance described by Tina Brown in *The Palace Papers* as a 'thrilling public show of commitment'. Keen for any new angle possible, broadcaster ITV News employed the services of a lip reader to pore over Catherine's every utterance, apparently capturing her muttering, 'I love the uniform – it's so, so sexy,' before breaking into fits of giggles.

The media were already speculating endlessly about whether William would propose. Some publications would label Catherine 'Waity Katie', while royal commentators cruelly mocked her for appearing to be 'desperate' or for 'waiting around'. Even the Queen, who had been supportive of William and Catherine's relationship, commented to her senior advisers that Catherine appeared to be resting on her laurels.

One of Prince Charles's former senior aides said the palace was 'full of sympathy' for her, but at a loss on how to advise her.

> She [Catherine] was in a completely unenviable position. On one hand she was being criticised to the point of abuse that she did not have a proper job, which was almost impossible given the media circus around her that had been created, and on the other she was being left hanging by William, who kept reiterating he was in no rush to get married, all the while essentially leaving her to fend for herself.

Catherine had in fact fully applied herself to getting a job, and in November 2006 she started as an accessory buyer for the high-street store Jigsaw. Inevitably, photographers started following her to her place of work. Still, while William – now a second lieutenant in the Blues and Royals Regiment, the prestigious cavalry regiment of the Household Division – was away in Devon for four months, Catherine wanted to fully immerse herself in London life. She was enjoying going to bars and clubs in the West End of London, despite the fact that even the threat of legal action could not discourage unwanted attention from the dozens of freelance photographers and news cameras who continued to pursue her every move.

On the day of her 25th birthday, on 9 January 2007, with speculation over an engagement announcement at fever pitch, Catherine emerged from her London flat to a scrum of more than 20 press photographers and five television crews. The resulting footage made for uncomfortable viewing. Amid the dizzying flashes of photographers' cameras, some sprinting across the road to get in front of her, some almost stumbling over each other, Catherine struggled to get to her navy Volkswagen Polo, before the media continued to take pictures through the windows of her car as it sped away.

Shaken and deeply distressed by the incident, Catherine called William in floods of tears. A source close to the couple said the situation and resulting conversation was 'incredibly distressing for both of them', adding, 'She [Catherine] said, "I can't do this any more." The situation was intolerable and William felt entirely helpless.' For the prince, as for many casual observers, this specific pursuit was an unwelcome echo of the time when Princess Diana had been constantly hounded, with the press wildly out of control. William demanded immediate action. One senior courtier revealed, 'This aggravated him [William] the most. He understood and recognised that the family were subject to interest from the press and the public because it came with the territory, but when friends and their family were targeted, he thought it was beyond the pale.' In a statement, Clarence House said the prince was 'very unhappy at the paparazzi harassment of his girlfriend', adding, 'he wants more than anything for her to be left alone. Miss Middleton should, like any other private individual, be able to go about her everyday business without this kind of intrusion.' Princess Diana's former press secretary Patrick Jephson said the media's behaviour had become 'utterly reprehensible' and needed addressing immediately. In *Catherine, the Princess of Wales: The Biography*, Robert Jobson revealed that Diana's former personal protection officer even contacted the Middleton family, offering to work for free until the chaos subsided.

The unabating pressure and provocation was only part of the problem. William's military commitments continued to keep him stationed far from London, often at Bovington Camp in Dorset, with the couple barely managing to snatch the odd weekend together. Catherine again retreated to her parents' home, telling friends that despite the advice and public statements from Clarence House, she felt abandoned. A crumb of comfort appeared with the public response to the moving footage of Catherine being pursued by dozens of photographers, who were almost exclusively men. There was huge sympathy at the idea of her being hounded in such a manner.

Then, lawyers Harbottle & Lewis, representing Catherine, issued a 'final warning' rebuke to the newspapers, with the further threat of officially engaging the industry watchdog, the Press Complaints Commission. The threat worked, and publications such as the *Sun* and *The Times* newspapers, and *Hello!* magazine, hoping to claw back some favour with the palace, announced they would cease to use paparazzi pictures of Catherine, in any situation.

A friend of Catherine's told how she had been 'deeply disturbed' by the birthday incident, prompting William to travel to Berkshire to be with her at the first opportunity. The conversations at the Middleton family home that followed were as tense and upsetting for Catherine as they were for William. The prince took counsel from his advisers, who could clearly see the effect Catherine's state of mind and the constant pressure from the press was having on him. Those close to him suggest over the Christmas period, just days after his passing-out parade, he had begun to think differently about the relationship. He had previously agreed to spend the New Year with the Middleton family, who had rented a house in Perthshire, north of Dundee, but cancelled at the last minute. Traditionally, unmarried couples did not join the Queen and her family at Sandringham (until an exception was made for the newly engaged Prince Harry and the American actress Meghan Markle in 2017), meaning William and Catherine had to spend the festive season apart. When William chose to stay on with his family instead of joining the Middletons as expected, it was a body blow to Catherine. She too began to re-evaluate her situation.

In parallel, William had, for the first time, engaged his beloved grandmother and grandfather, Prince Philip, as well as his father, on matters of the heart. He reiterated his belief that he was too young to get married and told them he wished to concentrate on his military career. Sensing his nervousness, all three counselled him to consider his future. For Charles, the idea of being pressured into marriage based on a relationship that didn't have cast-iron foundations felt all too familiar. He comforted his son, while speaking of the difficulties he experienced in his own marriage. The conversation struck home. A source close to William at the time said, 'It was clear he didn't want to make the same mistakes as his father. He had already voiced his concerns over history repeating itself in terms of the paparazzi, and that also applied to his relationship and any future marriage.'

CHAPTER FIVE

In March 2007, William and Catherine who had barely seen each other since Christmas, were pictured decked out in matching tweed, appearing frosty with each other at the Cheltenham horse racing festival. Sources claimed the relationship had 'soured beyond repair'. Days later, William heaped further embarrassment on Catherine when he was pictured in the *Sun* appearing to grope an 18-year-old Brazilian student he met on the dancefloor of Elements nightclub in Bournemouth. Looking wide-eyed, sweaty and clutching a pint of beer as he stood between two young women, William seemed to have temporarily abandoned his senses. Was this the normality he craved? Or was he simply a young man letting off some steam after finishing a tank commander course, while continuing to exist in a pressure-cooker situation? Catherine was upset and admonished him for his behaviour, questioning whether the light of their four-year relationship was about to be extinguished forever.

In the days after the Cheltenham Festival, deeply unhappy and at a loss to describe how their relationship had faltered in such a short space of time, Catherine delivered an ultimatum to William. While she did not explicitly demand an engagement or even a promise of marriage, she did break free from the gentle and arguably submissive persona that had typified her relationship with the future king. A long-standing friend who she confided in at the time said, 'Catherine was distressed. She was miserable, but she certainly wasn't desperate. She felt as though she had nothing to lose and for the first time she probably relayed her true feelings to William. She wasn't demanding an engagement, but she wanted a commitment, and if he couldn't deliver that, well, then she left him in no doubt that it was best they go their separate ways.' On many levels, the conversation was the clearest sign of the changing dynamic of their relationship. Catherine was no longer a shy student finding her way in the world, nor was she willing to be portrayed as the long-suffering girlfriend of a prince who had other priorities. Either they were a team, or they weren't.

Those who know Catherine well point to that exchange as a seminal moment in both her and William's lives. It's the source of the steely resolve she has demonstrated in recent years, whether that's facing her diagnosis with cancer, her key role in the monarchy's response to the furore caused by allegations of racism by the Duke and Duchess of Sussex, her deep influence in her children's upbringing, or the wise counsel she gave to William during King Charles's own battle with cancer.

But, blinded by his own insecurities, William did not react in the way Catherine expected. In a subsequent 30-minute phone call he laid out his reasons for believing they were on 'different pages' and said he could not offer her a guarantee of marriage. Catherine was understandably devastated. The couple agreed to give each other the space they needed. Secretly, Catherine wondered whether she would ever see William again.

In a shock move, William personally instructed Clarence House to confirm the news that he and Catherine were no longer together. But, behind the scenes, there was much going on that suggested this was more than just a difference of opinion. It's telling that William confided to one senior courtier that, 'at least she is free.' Sources suggest this was perhaps the most significant moment in his life since his mother had passed. William revealed a deep distress and anxiety over what a relationship with him represented in the real world. The attention, the constant pressure and expectation. He held these things responsible for contributing to the breakdown of his previous relationships, but now, when it mattered the most, he wondered if he was taking the right course of action, for Catherine or himself.

William and Catherine independently attempted to put on brave faces, despite both being stunned at what had occurred.

CHAPTER FIVE

Catherine and her mother flew to Dublin on 3 April to attend an art exhibition curated by one of Carole's friends, while William once again drowned his sorrows at the London nightspot Mahiki. On her return from Ireland three days later, Catherine also hit the city scene, partying with friends and being photographed wearing hotpants at a roller disco.

If her intention was to make William jealous, it had the desired effect. Once again, he sought his grandmother's counsel. The Queen had witnessed at first hand the toxicity that spilled over from Charles and Diana's relationship and the devastating effect of the Princess of Wales's tragic death on both William and Harry. And she knew that William was hurting from the attempt to reconcile so many competing expectations, demands and desires. During those initial days of hopelessness after the tragedy of Diana's death, Elizabeth's first reaction had been that of a grandmother, not a monarch. She refused to bow to pressure from the press and instead dedicated herself to comforting her suffering grandchildren. Now she would do the same. Sensing William was struggling, the Queen invited him to Sunday lunch to judge his mood. William was more than just crestfallen and worried about whether he was throwing away the one constant in his life. He was, according to one well-placed source, 'completely broken'. 'In that moment the Queen advised her grandson that the only certain path is the one supported by faith. It was all she had to say,' they said.

William had spent years agonising over whether he was making choices that would make his mother proud. At the forefront of his mind were her words concerning the choices that existed when it came to finding a long-lasting love. The day after the Prince of Wales's extraordinarily candid interview with broadcaster Jonathan Dimbleby on 29 June 1994, where for the first time he admitted his infidelity with Camilla, Diana raced to comfort the 12-year-old William. 'I went to the school and put it to William, particularly, that if you find someone you love in life you must hang on to it and look after it, and if you were lucky enough to find someone who loved you then one must protect it,' she said in her *Panorama* interview the following year.

What followed was an intense, albeit short, period of reflection for William. Ever since he was old enough to remember the turmoil and chaos that existed in his parents' relationship, he had been quietly determined to break the cycle of misery. Now he faced a decision.

6

A ROYAL ENGAGEMENT

Catherine had presented William with a simple choice: if he couldn't commit, their relationship would have to come to an end. To her, the response that followed from Clarence House had been definitive. Catherine told friends that, although she was not ready to move on, she would not wait around for William. If he wasn't ready, she couldn't put her existence on hold. She needed to get on with her life, and if that was to be without William, she was fully prepared to move in a new direction.

At only 24, William was struggling to process the break-up, as well as the concept of his own identity as a soldier and the expectations of him as a future monarch. In one sense he had convinced himself that the best course of action would be to focus solely on his role in the military. In another, he was secretly heartbroken. The situation was made more difficult by the press, who were filling the void left by the split with news of Catherine's movements. Her social diary was now the subject of almost daily coverage.

On 30 May 2007, Catherine was pictured walking into Boujis nightclub in London with estate agent Charlie Morshead and later leaving with Henry Ropner, the son of a multi-millionaire British businessman. Not only were the two men part of Catherine's wider social group, they were also close friends with William's pals from Eton, including two of the prince's closest confidants, Guy Pelly and James Meade. The pictures resulted in stories suggesting that Catherine had moved on and was now engaged in a new affair with William lookalike Henry, who, to add to the narrative, had dated William's ex-girlfriend Jecca Craig at Edinburgh University. 'They [the press] couldn't have been further from the truth,' one friend said. 'It was friends having fun. Although we did have a good laugh at the utter nonsense that appeared on a daily basis.' Headlines such as 'Wills is the real loser', and 'William who? Kate all smiles on girls' night out at Prince's favourite drinking den', appeared, as Catherine began to enjoy herself within London's social scene.

But the people who seemed to be enjoying themselves most were the press. Bookmakers were delivering odds on who the prince's 'new girl' would be, with suggestions ranging from the society figures he'd previously been linked with, to some of the attractive young women who were normally the subject of diary pieces in the more upmarket newspapers. Other columnists cruelly declared it had been Catherine's 'commoner' background that had finally convinced the heir to the throne to end the relationship. Carole Middleton also became the subject of brutal taunts and snobbish stories, mocked for apparently using the word 'toilet' instead of 'lavatory'. In more spiteful commentary, Catherine and her sister Pippa were dubbed the 'Wisteria Sisters', an apparent sobriquet from their schooldays, when photographed enjoying nights on the town. One particularly barbed newspaper piece explained the notion behind the slur: the sisters were 'highly decorative, terribly fragrant, with a ferocious ability to climb'.

The prince, by contrast, was painted as a lonesome figure. One story detailed how he had sloped off to the cinema to see the comedy *Blades of Glory* with just his personal bodyguard for company. It wasn't far from the truth. William had seen the pictures of Catherine out on the town with his friends and

CHAPTER SIX

wondered whether he had made the right call. The Queen had meanwhile urged Charles to keep an eye on his son, suggesting William should focus his energies on his military career.

Although equally heartbroken, Catherine had decided to stick to her guns. Throughout the most testing times of her relationship, Catherine had leaned on a group of close school friends, and now she did so again. She told them of her lack of direction and how she felt she had been cheated by putting her life on hold for William. If William wasn't ready to commit, then she was ready to explore her options as a beautiful, young single woman, who by now was known throughout the world.

Because they were no longer communicating, both William and Catherine carried on their lives unaware that they were each equally affected by the idea that their relationship might be over. They had both decided a period of no contact was for the best, but, in truth, it was torture. The breakdown was not caused by infidelity, confrontation or embitterment, but rather was the result of two young people navigating their first serious relationship at the same time as being thrust into a spotlight whose power had been magnified beyond comprehension.

Diana had always believed that William was a deep thinker, capable of assessing situations in ways that were wise beyond his years. Within weeks of his split from Catherine, he was having second thoughts, mindful perhaps of his father's decision in his twenties not to marry Camilla Shand, the love of his life. William did not want to make a similar mistake and yet he was still wracked with doubt. His grandmother's advice was also ringing in his ears. Did he have faith that Catherine was 'the one'? Could he see a future with her?

While Catherine was on holiday in early June with her family on the Balearic island of Ibiza, staying at 'Le Maison de Bang Bang', the villa owned by Carole's flamboyant, tattooed brother

Gary Goldsmith, William decided to make his move. At first, he texted and asked to speak, wondering if Catherine would even reply. With Catherine unsure of William's motives and unwilling to let her guard down just yet, the initial exchanges were tentative, if a little frosty. A few days into the holiday, though, she agreed to a call. William explained that he was missing her and floated the idea of them still attending a party that had been in their diary for months. Reluctant to commit over the phone, Catherine said she would consider the proposal, although she did agree they should talk, if only to clear the air.

On her return to the UK, Catherine agreed she would go. The party would be at the family home of Sam Waley-Cohen, a 17th-century manor house in Oxfordshire, and the theme of the evening was the rather risqué 'Freakin' Naughty'.

Keen to make an impression, and perhaps to help break the ice when he saw Catherine for the first time in months, William dressed in tight black hotpants and a plastic policeman's helmet. Catherine also turned heads when she arrived in a showstopping 'naughty nurse' outfit, complete with fishnet tights and a short dress.

Fellow guests said as soon as William and Catherine set eyes on one another it was clear their love had not extinguished. The couple peeled off from the rest of the party and spent hours locked in deep conversation. Catherine listened intently as William attempted to break the deadlock, laying out his reasons for doubting what they had. He talked of his fear of letting someone truly experience the world in which he lived, and also his fear of rejection if he did let himself get too close. Catherine, of course, knew that she still loved William deeply. That was why she had been so explicit in her demands. She was willing to agree to a future, if only he would stop allowing outside factors to affect his judgement.

CHAPTER SIX

After speaking for what seemed like hours, William's charm, it seemed, had worked. The couple returned to the party. As the cocktails flowed and the dancefloor filled, they only had eyes for each other. Sam Waley-Cohen later denied being the matchmaker that changed the course of history, saying in a newspaper interview a month after their April 2011 marriage: 'There's an idea that I was like Cupid with a bow and arrow. People love the idea that somebody put them back together, but they put themselves together far more.'

Reports of their reunion followed in the *Mail on Sunday* on 24 June, but William and Catherine were intent on keeping their decision to get back together a secret for as long as possible. They did not even confide in their closest friends. William also did not go to the trouble of confirming the news with Clarence House. The scoop left the press office to field a flurry of questions from reporters desperate to stand up the story that the royal relationship was back on.

Days later, on what would have been Diana's 46th birthday, William, flanked by Harry, had the responsibility of bringing some of the world's biggest music stars together for a special benefit concert at Wembley Stadium in London, to celebrate their mother's life and legacy. The day before, on 30 June, the brothers had joined soul singer Joss Stone on the Wembley stage to field questions from the media. They paid tribute to the artists for agreeing to be part of the charity gig and highlighted how their mother would have loved to have been part of the evening. After taking questions from BBC royal correspondent Nicholas Witchell and Sarah Hewson from Sky News, a reporter from the Seven News network in Australia dropped in a question about Catherine's rumoured attendance. 'I hate to ask it, but tell us about the friends you've got coming along to the concert, and how are things going with Kate?' William let out a loud nervous laugh before batting off the question by suggesting he had 'lots of friends coming'. Afterwards, Harry turned to say, 'Very well avoided, William!'

Catherine's name was, of course, on everyone's lips. At the concert a day later, as William and Harry took their seats in the royal box alongside a group of their close friends and Harry's girlfriend Chelsy, eagle-eyed photographers would have their story: Catherine was seated two rows behind William, beside her parents and siblings, Pippa and James. They all danced along to performances from Elton John, Duran Duran and Tom Jones, and William and Catherine were both seen singing along to Take That's rendition of their hit 'Back for Good', which seemed to be confirmation enough that things were back on.

William and Catherine knew full well the pressures that lay ahead. Getting back together would only intensify the questions over the future of their relationship, but this time they agreed to tackle it head on, together.

Two months later, in August 2007, William and Catherine booked a secret getaway to the idyllic Desroches Island in the Seychelles, using the fake names Martin and Rosemary Middleton. Catherine had come up with the plan and William jokingly told friends the names sounded like the sort of people you'd meet at the local golf club. The break was a time to reconnect, as well as to relax after the demands of the previous few months. In between daytime adventures snorkelling and kayaking, the couple sat down for the most honest heart-to-hearts they had ever had. This would be a new start, with refreshing honesty at its centre.

William made a promise to Catherine that, despite their previous troubles and his uncertainty over his future, she was the only person he could see himself spending the rest of his life with. He assured Catherine that an engagement and marriage would certainly happen, but now was not the right time. He had

CHAPTER SIX

to maintain focus on his career in the military, and somehow come to terms with the further pressure of what marriage would mean for both of them.

When Catherine had asked William to commit to her, she had never wanted to force him into a corner; she was merely protecting herself. If they were to move forward, she needed to know that they were a team. This was another leap of faith. Could she trust William to not have a full-blown crisis of confidence again? Catherine robustly told him that if she was to wait for him and take on everything that marrying a future king would mean for them both, they had to be on the same page. Whether that meant marriage or just a commitment that they were both in it for the long haul didn't particularly matter at that stage to Catherine, but William had to at least let her in. A source close to the couple said: 'they came back clear that they would face the future together. That's all Catherine had ever wanted and now that William was fully on board and recognised that it was not solely about him, everything seemed to fall into place.'

Towards the end of 2007 Catherine decided to step down from her Jigsaw role to return to the Middleton family business, where she was helping with web design and photography for the Party Pieces brand. It would give her the freedom to maintain a career while having the flexibility to see William whenever he was granted leave. At Jigsaw, she'd felt incredibly nervous whenever she needed to ask that her unusual schedule be taken into consideration.

William and Catherine managed to keep a low profile, and gossip about their relationship status largely waned. They resolved to spend time at the Middleton family home or at Highgrove with a trusted and very select group of friends, which took them both out of the public eye almost entirely for a while. In March 2008, the couple went back to Klosters. On the third day of the trip they were pictured together on the slopes, confirming they were an item once again. A month later, on 11 April, Catherine attended a ceremony where the Prince of Wales proudly presented his son with his Royal Air Force wings, after William had completed his training at RAF Cranwell in Lincolnshire. It was her first engagement with members of the royal family since the Diana tribute concert. The occasion was a huge moment for William, not only having qualified as a pilot – thus following in the footsteps of his great-grandfather King George VI, grandfather Prince Philip and father Prince Charles – but also having Catherine by his side for such a public moment. It was a clear sign of her growing importance in his life.

A month later, on 17 May, Catherine would be pulled even further into the heart of the monarchy, joining the Queen at the wedding of William's cousin, Peter Phillips (who was, at the time, 11th in line to the throne) at St George's Chapel, Windsor. Significantly, the prince was not at the event as he had travelled to Kenya to attend the wedding of his former girlfriend Jecca Craig's brother, Batian. It was a huge show of support for Catherine, not only from William but from the palace as well. William's aides at the time suspected it would not be long before an engagement was on the cards.

Those who observed Catherine that day suggest she was perfectly poised and not one bit overawed without William by her side. She was seated beside Chelsy Davey, who was attending with Harry, in the 15th-century church, and reports mused over whether this would be a precursor to their own weddings to the princes. Both women were astute enough not to get carried away; they elected to step out of shot when photographs were taken with the extended royal family. This included the Queen and Duke of Edinburgh, who waved the couple off as they left in a horse-drawn carriage towards Frogmore House for a reception and dance for 300 guests.

CHAPTER SIX

During the couple's eventual engagement interview in November 2010, Catherine said the wedding was her first meeting with Her Majesty, although this was not strictly true. This was her first meeting at an official royal engagement, of course, but the Queen had taken an interest in her grandson's relationship for some time, inviting the couple to meet and even dine with her on several occasions. Sources say the Queen had become intent on keeping a watchful eye over her heir and, as a result, had even considered bringing Catherine closer into the fold. One former senior courtier revealed that William had approached his grandmother with an unofficial request, asking if anything could be arranged to provide security for Catherine. After all, she had been hounded by the press, all but forced to give up her job at Jigsaw, and had almost walked away from her relationship with William. The Metropolitan Police Royalty Protection Command, which in April 2015 became Royalty and Specialist Protection (RaSP), investigated its own jurisdiction to determine whether police protection could be provided.

When the message reached the palace that taxpayer-funded police officers could not be used in such a manner, William asked the Queen whether it would be possible to privately fund security for Catherine. A decision was taken by the royal household that until the prince was engaged, no arrangement could be made. A former senior courtier said, 'The Queen was incredibly fond of Catherine. She found her polite and engaging and understood why William was so taken with her. William was desperate to protect her and did seek advice from the Queen, but the message was there was nothing more that could be done other than to advise at arms-length until they were engaged.' Despite William's request, the move was considered by all to be the right one.

The couple had been fortunate enough to have an extended period of time together, but the next stage of William's career as an

RAF search and rescue pilot was on the horizon. First though, he would have to complete five weeks' training with the Royal Navy, before joining an attachment in the Caribbean with the HMS *Iron Duke*, a Type 23 Duke Class frigate and one of the Royal Navy's most versatile warships. Rather than dwell on their time apart, William and Catherine were looking forward to one last blowout, to celebrate the prince's 26th birthday, and there were also royal duties to fulfil. This time, Catherine would be at their centre.

On 14 June Catherine would attend her most high-profile royal event to date: the annual Garter Day at Windsor Castle, a grand procession of the knights and officers of the Order in grand ceremonial dress. While Catherine had attended Peter Phillips' wedding and William's passing-out ceremony, both in the company of the Queen, the public nature of the event was an entirely different experience and one that created a profound sense of nervousness for Catherine. 'She asked a lot of questions,' said one former royal aide. 'She wanted to know where to stand, what to expect, whether she would be able to see William. And she also asked a lot of questions about the history, which was very interesting, she wasn't there just to turn up, she certainly took an interest in the nature of the event.' At the event marking the Order of the Garter, the country's oldest order of chivalry, founded by Edward III in 1348, William walked alongside the Prince of Wales, and was feeling nervous at the thought of Catherine seeing him in his 'fancy dress' robes. He did his best not to crack a smile while, dressed in an ostrich-plumed cap and velvet cape, he was inducted as a Royal Knight Companion. The honour from the Queen was a clear sign of her faith in William and further evidence that a public role within The Firm was approaching.

While he has full respect for the traditions of the past, William considers himself a modern man in an ever-changing world, and

CHAPTER SIX

he felt fairly uncomfortable walking through the grounds of Windsor Castle before the service at St George's chapel. He has, quite controversially, not worn a kilt in Scotland since he was a child and has staunch, though discreet, views on how he envisages his own Coronation and its numerous traditional elements including the requirement to dress in several pieces of ornate regalia. Those close to him say that, while he would not dismiss such occasions as 'dressing up', he is much more at ease presenting himself without costume and may seek to dispense entirely with elements of the ceremony.

On 21 June, at the Beaufort Polo Club in Gloucestershire, where he celebrated his birthday, William opted for a simple open-necked check shirt and jeans. Having consumed several drinks, from pints of cider to punch cocktails, William was seen throwing dubious shapes on the dancefloor, described by one onlooker as 'more hip-op, than hip-hop', as he jived to R&B and rock anthems. The onlooker in question was a national newspaper journalist who, with a colleague, had gained access to the ticketed event. Posing as a couple, they joined revellers who watched as William pestered the DJ with requests for American rock group Nickelback, R&B icon Rhianna and pop rockers Bon Jovi. Pictures of the night appeared in the *Daily Mirror* two days later, under the headline 'Rock 'N Royal', with William seen pulling Catherine in for a slow dance at the party's end. Still, it was clear that the couple, who had been through so much, were closer than ever.

Throughout the rest of 2008, William continued with his Royal Navy placements, undertaking survival courses, navigation training, and exercises aboard ships, while Catherine split her time between London with her sister, Pippa, and their parents' house in Berkshire.

While Catherine longed for the time when the two of them would be back living together again, the distance fortified their relationship and cemented their desire to build a solid foundation for their future life.

By 2009, William had decided to return to the RAF to complete an intensive training course that would enable him to qualify as a search and rescue pilot. Like all trainees, he was asked to provide two preferences for his first posting. He chose Lossiemouth, in north-east Scotland, and Valley, on Anglesey, the island off the north-west coast of Wales. In September 2010, William joined C Flight, 22 Squadron, supporting both military operations and civilian emergency services across Anglesey. And this time Catherine could join him on this new adventure. William first settled in at the barracks before the couple moved to an old, white-stoned farmhouse on the Newborough estate, a rural area on Anglesey's western coast. The remote location was a world away from the paparazzi-stalked London streets, and the couple at once fell in love with the beauty and charm of the rugged Welsh coast. Speaking at the time, William said, 'This island has been our first home together, and it will always be an immensely special place for us both. Catherine and I look forward to returning again and again over the coming years with our family. I know that I speak for Catherine when I say that I have never in my life known somewhere as beautiful and as welcoming as Anglesey.'

The 50,000-strong population of the island was fiercely protective of the couple. Any journalists who thought of pitching up to see if they could find a story were routinely sent on their way, giving Catherine the freedom to shop in the local supermarkets and go for walks with William after dinner on sun-soaked evenings around the bay. It was the anonymity they craved and that brought them closer than ever, united for a future in which one day they would be king and queen. What Catherine did not know was that William was finally ready to propose.

CHAPTER SIX

Five months before, in April, the prince had met with his private secretary and close confidant, Jamie Lowther-Pinkerton, to inform him that he was ready to pop the question. Jamie was aware of the global interest that would follow news of the prince's engagement. He also wanted to keep a respectful distance from the subject that had been on everyone's lips since William and Catherine had finished university in 2005. So he had simply suggested to William that, were he considering asking Catherine to marry him, a 'slight heads-up' would be welcome. The prince had intimated that a proposal would come following the completion of his naval training, and after he and Catherine were settled in at his first RAF posting. A group of just four royal aides was sworn to secrecy and quietly began to prepare for the moment when they would need to announce to the world that Prince William, the second in line to the throne, was to be married. A former senior courtier said, 'It was quite an exciting time considering there was a tiny group who knew it was coming. It was our duty to make sure nothing leaked, mainly to protect Kate, but also because it would have made our jobs a lot more complicated.'

William made arrangements for a romantic getaway to Kenya, returning to the 55,000-acre Lewa Wildlife Conservancy the couple had visited in 2005 after graduating. Kenya had been a place of sanctuary for William; it was where he had travelled as he struggled to come to terms with the death of his mother. Anyone who has prepared to ask a loved one to marry them will know the intense nervousness that comes with arranging the perfect moment to propose, but also the incredible responsibility of carrying the ring around with you until you finally find that moment. William was no different. For this most special of trips, he chose a remote log cabin along the shores of Lake Rutundu. They would be in an off-grid location approximately 165 miles north-east of the capital, Nairobi, that was extremely hard to reach unless by helicopter. Their cabin was fitted with a basic radio system that communicated solely with the Lewa rangers, there was no electricity, and hot water was supplied by a basic log burner outside.

Kenya did not just have special significance for the couple, it was also deeply meaningful for his grandmother and the history of the monarchy. It was where Princess Elizabeth discovered she would become queen at the tender age of 25, following the sudden death of her father, King George VI on 6 February 1952. Catherine's engagement ring was also of huge importance to William, having belonged to his late mother. Created by former Crown Jeweller Garrard & Co, the ring featured a spectacular 12-carat oval Ceylon Sapphire surrounded by 14 diamonds, all set in 18-carat white gold, and was a showstopper of epic proportions. It was William's way of including Diana's spirit, which still guides him in so much of what he does, in the most important moment of his life.

Although the couple had discussed marriage at length, Catherine was pleasantly surprised at the proposal and the effort William had put in to make it special. The next morning, after just 24 hours at the lodge, the couple thanked their hosts in the visitors' book. Signing himself as 'William', the future king wrote, 'Such fun to be back! Brought more warm clothes this time! Looked after so well. Thank you guys! Look forward to next time, soon I hope!' Though William still called her Kate, Catherine decided to sign with her full name, Catherine Middleton, a further sign that her future had now changed for ever. She wrote, 'Thank you for such a wonderful 24 hours! Sadly no fish to be found but we had great fun trying. I love the warm fires and candle lights – so romantic! Hope to be back again soon.'

In their engagement interview, which followed on 16 November, William said:

CHAPTER SIX

> I had been carrying it [the ring] around with me in my rucksack for about three weeks before that and I literally would not let it go, everywhere I went I was keeping hold of it because I knew this thing, if it disappeared, I would be in a lot of trouble, and because I'd planned it, it went fine. You hear a lot of horror stories about proposing and things going horribly wrong – it went really, really well and I was really pleased when she said yes.

While the couple agreed to savour the moment and keep the news out of the public domain until they returned home, Catherine called her parents from Kenya to tell them William had proposed. Carole and Michael were delighted for the couple, speaking to both to offer their congratulations. The Middletons were sworn to secrecy, with the couple still needing to tell the Queen and the rest of the family before going public.

Somewhat surprisingly, William had not followed the tradition of officially asking his partner's father for permission to marry his daughter. In the engagement interview, the prince joked how he was torn about asking Michael beforehand, but worried he might say no. 'So, I thought if I ask Kate first then he can't really say no. So I did it that way round. I managed to speak to Mike soon after it happened, really, and then it sort of happened from there,' he said. In truth, William had already spoken to both Michael and Carole about his intentions, after he and Catherine had got back together. Carole was straightforward with William about her fears about him stringing their daughter along. She was extending a protective arm around her daughter, but also around William. The Middletons naturally wanted their daughter to be happy, but the prince was someone they had grown fond of and welcomed into their lives, and they appreciated the pressure he faced even at such a young age.

On the way back from Kenya, William and Catherine discussed how they would break the news to the world. William was reassured that, having been given the time they needed, the palace would be prepared.

The couple returned to Highgrove on 23 October, in time to attend the wedding of their close friend Harry Meade, the son of Olympic gold medal-winning equestrian Richard Meade, to primary school teacher Rosie Bradford. Catherine was described in news reports as having a smile only surpassed by the bride. Sporting glowing tans and looking relaxed as they strolled to the church together, William and Catherine were bursting with happiness yet still determined to keep their news a secret.

Almost a month later, at 11am on 16 November, Clarence House announced to the world that the couple had become engaged during their romantic trip to Kenya. While William and Catherine had managed to keep the news a secret from the world, they had shared their joy with their friend and trusted journalist, the then ITV News political editor, Tom Bradby. Now a senior news anchor with the broadcaster, the couple presented the opportunity of a lifetime, offering him the chance to broadcast their first interview, recorded at Clarence House before they faced the world's media for the first time. Bradby had built up a strong relationship with the prince during his time as ITV's royal correspondent between 2001 and 2005. Their closeness was revealed later, when it emerged in court proceedings that Bradby alerted William to the possibility that their private communications had been intercepted. He was prompted to do so when a story appeared in the now defunct *News of the World* newspaper containing information that only he, the prince, and two other people had known about. The resulting police investigation led to the jailing in early 2007 of the *News of the World*'s former royal correspondent Clive Goodman, for phone hacking.

CHAPTER SIX

The interview was Catherine's first and, for millions of royal fans around the world, the first time they had heard her speak. With incredible modesty and self-awareness, she and William reflected on the tougher times that had led to this moment. They talked about how those early days as friends had given them a solid foundation as partners, which they believed would benefit them in the long term, not only as a couple but in cementing their future role within the monarchy. Posing for photographs at Clarence House, William made a considerably better impression than his father had in 1981 when interviewed on the day of his engagement at Buckingham Palace. When the interviewer asked if they were in love, Diana replied, 'Of course,' while Charles awkwardly said, 'Whatever in love means.' Diana's face immediately contorted, conveying an inner unease. She later said the engagement interview had left her 'traumatised'.

There would, of course, be comparisons with the late Princess of Wales, something Catherine expertly faced head on. Asked by Bradby whether it was intimidating entering the royal family, given Diana's status, she paid tribute to her legacy. 'I would have loved to have met her and she's obviously an inspirational woman to look up to. Obviously on this day and going forward and things, you know it is a wonderful family, the members who I've met have achieved a lot and are very inspirational.' William asserted there would be 'no pressure' on his bride, confirming, 'No one is trying to fill my mother's shoes. What she did was fantastic. It's about making your own future and your own destiny, and Kate will do a very good job of that.'

Finally able to share their joy at the news, Michael Middleton later read a prepared statement outside the family home, paying tribute to his new son-in-law. 'We all think he is wonderful and we are extremely fond of him. They make a lovely couple, they are great fun to be with, and we've had a lot of laughs together. We wish them every happiness for the future.'

The Queen and the Duke of Edinburgh were also 'absolutely delighted', Buckingham Palace said. During a reception that afternoon at Windsor Castle for leaders of British overseas territories, the Queen spoke for the nation when she told a guest who congratulated her, 'It is brilliant news. It has taken them a very long time.' There was no doubt that large sections of the country were delighted at the announcement, confident the young couple was capable of leading the monarchy into a new era.

7

THE WINDSORS AND THE WEDDING

Immediately after it had been announced to the world that William and Catherine's eight-year relationship would finally be sealed with marriage, the full mechanism of the palace institution was thrown into action.

On 17 November 2010, just 24 hours after posing for pictures and sitting down for their first joint interview, which was watched by more than 12 million people in Britain and many more millions around the world, the couple entered a succession of back-to-back meetings at St James's Palace. The meetings would be with the four royal aides who had previously been sworn to secrecy about William's intentions to propose – namely William and Harry's private secretary Jamie Lowther-Pinkerton, their press secretary Miguel Head, the Prince of Wales's press secretary Paddy Harverson, and Helen Asprey, the princes' personal private secretary, responsible for organising their individual activities and schedules – who now had the job of guiding the couple through the plan of executing the biggest royal event in 30 years.

Naturally, William was accustomed to courtiers creating a hive of activity around the big state occasions. But this was an entirely new experience for Catherine. Having been prevented from seeing much of the inner workings of the palace machine until her engagement to William was announced, and having had the sparsest of contact from the palace communications team, even as she had struggled with life in the spotlight, she was now faced with the reality of the world she was entering. A team of twenty aides was immediately assigned to the palace to help with the planning, while every element of the British state, including teams from central government, the Metropolitan Police, the intelligence services and the military, was mobilised. Catherine's nervousness was evident. The palace team took charge of facilitating everything from the venue to the reception, to Catherine's choice of dress designer and flowers, right through to liaising with the government and police to ensure the public would be able to join in the momentous national occasion. One former courtier said, 'It's fair to say she looked like a rabbit in headlights. We did our best not to bombard them with information, as much would be taken out of their hands anyway, but I think the speed at which the whole operation had to get off the ground was a surprise to both of them.'

Following some initial pleasantries and a promise that everything would be done to make their special day as true to their wishes as possible, the couple was presented with some potential dates and venues to consider. In reality, there were only two real possibilities, due to the size of the event and sheer number of guests who would be invited from all over the world. The first was St Paul's Cathedral, which in 2011 would be reopened after a £40 million renovation project. The second was the equally iconic and historic Westminster Abbey. In his book *Our Queen*, Robert Hardman recounts how William and Catherine were also presented with a list of 777 names of dignitaries and governors from all over the world, leading the prince to remark that he didn't know anyone on it. William called his grandmother up the next day and questioned whether he needed to concede to the courtiers' requests. To his delight, the Queen told him to 'bin the list' and start again, making sure to put down his friends first and go from there. A source quoted in Hardman's book noted that, 'She made the point that there are certain times when you have to strike the right balance. And it's advice like that, which is really key, when you know that she's seen and done it before.'

A flurry of early bets with bookmakers had already been placed on a summer wedding, but after eight years together, the couple did not want to delay the big day any further. They wished to get married as early as possible, and on a Friday, aware that the prime minister would most likely declare a bank holiday to allow millions around the country to join in the celebrations or at the very least get a day off work.

For years, William and Catherine had talked about the day they would marry each other. Throughout their discussions, William had been careful not to intimidate Catherine by drawing too much attention to the wider questions involving the country and the institution. Now that the wedding and, by extension, these conversations were happening, he was eager to help guide her. William placed a reassuring hand in Catherine's palm, relaying their excitement and even joking that they had 'got there in the end'. He revealed to the aides that Westminster Abbey was his and Catherine's preferred choice, describing the setting as 'a more intimate venue' than the grandeur of St Paul's. But just how intimate it would be with nearly 2,000 guests, many of whom they would have little say in inviting, including foreign royals, heads of state and hundreds of representatives from dozens of charities hand-picked by royal aides, remained to be seen.

The palace team agreed the Abbey would be an excellent choice. It had been chosen for its staggering beauty as well as its place in the monarchy's long history – with the Abbey having hosted the coronations of 39 English and British monarchs, including William the Conqueror in 1066 (in 2023, Charles III's coronation would take that number to 40), and been the burial site for 17 English, Scottish and British monarchs. There was also the personal connection William had to the venue: for him it was a place of both celebration and sadness. His grandparents Queen Elizabeth and Prince Philip had married there on 20 November 1947, but also ingrained in his memory would have been his mother's funeral on 6 September 1997, as well as that of the Queen Mother, his great-grandmother, on 9 April 2002. William had always believed that marrying at the Abbey would allow his mother to be somehow present on the most important day of his life. In an interview in 2017 for the documentary *Diana, Our Mother: Her Life and Legacy*, William reflected on his mother's passing and her absence from that happy occasion, saying, 'Beforehand, I had a lot of time to think about it. When it came to the wedding, I did really feel she was there. There are times when you look to someone or something for strength, and I very much felt that she was there for me.'

Like so many couples wrapped in the glow of planning their wedding day, once the venue was chosen, there was excitement in the air. At one point, as they ploughed through the exhaustive list of points to be covered, Catherine turned to William to whisper, 'I can't believe this is happening.' Decisions had to be taken urgently on Catherine's wedding dress, her flowers, her choice of transport to and from the church. One former courtier said, 'It was a baptism of fire for both of them, but from the off they were both very much in the driving seat. It was a mixture of very formal, very official and very institutional, everything had to be run like a military operation.'

Even though she was being asked to quickly make personal choices, Catherine also realised that this would not be a normal

CHAPTER SEVEN

wedding. The couple already had an abundance of ideas about everything from the wedding reception, to how the public could join in the celebrations. Talk in these meetings even moved on to a public party in London's Hyde Park and a UK tour after their wedding to officially introduce the couple to the country. It was a lot to take in, and Catherine frequently looked to William for reassurance. The courtiers came away from the final meeting of the day concerned that many of the couple's ideas were centered on the wedding itself, rather than the occasion, leading to a collective agreement to give them some space to consider what would actually be required of them. 'Catherine, especially, had to get used to the idea that their wedding wasn't a normal wedding. It was a grand state occasion and one which would be showing off the country to millions of people around the world, which is a pretty big thing to get your head around,' a palace source said.

William and Catherine's forthcoming marriage presented a chance of renewal for the royal family. For the first time in a generation the monarchy, whose very existence had been questioned in the wake of Princess Diana's death, had a genuine and relatable couple who could connect with the country and the Commonwealth. William was acutely aware of his position and that his marriage had the capacity to bring together communities around the world, as well as shoring up the position of the institution. Almost as soon as William had given his tip-off to his senior team, conversations had begun about where the newlyweds would travel to on their first official tour. William had recently been to Australia, New Zealand and southern Africa on official visits, so government advisers were keen to send the couple to Canada to demonstrate the monarchy's support for the country considered to be the premier realm, owing to its history and proximity to Britain. William understood that a lot would be expected of him and Catherine, and so was keen that everything must be done to support his bride. One former courtier said, 'William recognised that Catherine could become quite overwhelmed by the whole process, so a few days after those conversations, he made it very clear that everything had to be done to make her feel comfortable. It wasn't so much a request but an instruction to be circulated.' During meetings the following week, William continued to hold Catherine's hand as aides discussed the meticulous planning, which would have to balance all aspects of security, the church, the ceremony and the couple's personal wishes, alongside the global media interest, which was bound to reach fever pitch. Catherine's eyes widened when they were told initial crowd estimates from the Metropolitan Police, which suggested that more than one million people would flock to London on the day, meaning safety was absolutely paramount. One source said it was 'as if everything was just beginning to dawn on her at that moment'.

Catherine was briefed that as she and William were now engaged, her status would be elevated within the royal household and she would immediately be granted round-the-clock security, with her own dedicated team of personal protection officers. A ring of steel was placed around the Middleton family home in Berkshire, with armed officers stationed outside her parents' home. These were accompanied by a team from the royal protection squad that included two female police officers, quickly dubbed Cagney and Lacey by the press, after the 1980s US police drama. The team was led by Inspector Karen Llewellyn, who previously ran operations protecting Prince Andrew's daughters, Princesses Beatrice and Eugenie. Alongside her was Sergeant Emma Probert, the younger of the two women at just 39, who was trained in martial arts and licensed to carry a 9mm Glock pistol and Taser stun gun at all times. Catherine bonded straight away with the accomplished officer, who was among the first on

CHAPTER SEVEN

the scene after the 7 July 2005 attacks in London. Emma also shared an unlikely connection with Carole Middleton, having been an airline stewardess before her career in the police.

The Middleton home in Bucklebury was swept for bugs and the perimeter was searched for suspicious devices. Carole made a point of contacting the neighbours to apologise for the sudden appearance of police officers and assured them it was nothing to worry about, but it was clear that all their lives were rapidly changing.

Exactly a week after the engagement announcement, Buckingham Palace confirmed the couple would marry at Westminster Abbey on 29 April 2011. The then prime minister, David Cameron, declared it would be 'a happy and momentous occasion', confirming a national holiday across the United Kingdom, while the Scottish government followed suit. The press almost universally declared the event 'The People's Wedding', even as some left-leaning publications questioned just who would pick up the eyewatering £32 million bill, equivalent to nearly £50 million today.

With orders for souvenir china cups and commemorative tea towels already being placed around the country, just a week after the wedding announcement William returned to work as a search and rescue pilot at RAF Valley, leaving Catherine to get to grips with the planning. The schedule was punishing, and a little overwhelming. Immediately after the engagement announcement, Catherine split her time between her parents' home in Berkshire and the couple's Anglesey farmhouse, owing to the need to attend almost daily appointments in London. A palace source said, 'It was a huge graduation from simply being William's girlfriend to now being pretty much solely responsible for planning the biggest royal wedding in decades, while William was only on the end of a phone.'

In December 2010, Queen Elizabeth invited Catherine to Buckingham Palace. Although billed as an informal catch-up, it was the first time Catherine had met the monarch on her own and she was understandably nervous. Even though Catherine had by now met the Queen on several occasions, she sought advice from aides on what to wear and say during the meeting. In the car on the way over to Buckingham Palace, she adjusted her hair and touched up her makeup before being met by the Queen's private secretary and taken to a room where afternoon tea had been laid out.

Her Majesty had requested to be kept up to date with the preparations of the wedding committee, formed of her senior staff and representatives from both Prince Charles's household at Clarence House and William's private secretaries. But during the light buffet of tea and finger sandwiches, the Queen eschewed questions about the finer details of the production and instead looked to comfort the young woman she hoped would successfully shape the institution for the next generation. According to one former courtier, the Queen offered words of encouragement to Catherine regarding her future role as a senior member of the family, as well as guidance in how to deal with 'headstrong' husbands. William had a reputation among his staff and family for being down to earth and thoughtful, preferring to be addressed by his first name instead of His Royal Highness or Sir, but he could also be direct and plain-spoken when he wanted things done a particular way. The Queen's husband, the Duke of Edinburgh, was similarly forthright, and so she was well placed to advise Catherine; after all, her marriage had lasted more than 70 years, with a fair bit of compromise required as a foundation.

In a lighter moment, the Queen also advised Catherine to not get too bogged down with the details of the guest list, telling her not to worry about how many people would be there – there were many she wouldn't know and many she wouldn't

CHAPTER SEVEN

see again – and insisting there would be plenty of room for her loved ones to share in the event. In a startling gesture to the young bride, the Queen also generously offered Catherine the opportunity to consult with royal jewellers over borrowing an item from her personal, priceless jewellery collection. The source said, 'It was a lovely gesture and typical of the Queen to think of how Catherine would be feeling.'

Catherine left the meeting with the Queen with a spring in her step, later that day relaying the details of the audience with his grandmother to William. The couple agreed that, although they wanted their wedding to bear the imprint of their own personalities, they had a responsibility to respect the traditions of the past, while also making the Queen proud. William had intended to wear the frock coat uniform of an Irish Guards officer, as he had been appointed a colonel in that regiment earlier that year, his most senior military position to date. However, the Queen insisted that he wear the regiment's full dress uniform, complete with scarlet tunic. Royal author Robert Hardman reported, in *Our Queen*, a conversation that he had with William concerning his grandmother's choice of uniform. 'I was given a categorical: "No, you'll wear this!" So you don't always get what you want, put it that way ... But I knew perfectly well that it was for the best. That "no" is a very good "no". So you just do as you're told!'

Courtiers were also surprised when Catherine announced her wish not to travel in the traditional horse-drawn Glass Coach, as used by Diana, Princess of Wales as well as Queen Elizabeth. As much as tradition was at the forefront of her mind, Catherine wanted a modern slant on the proceedings and was of the view that she was not yet a 'princess' who would use such a mode of transport. Instead, she opted to travel to Westminster Abbey in a 1977 Rolls-Royce Phantom VI that had been gifted by the manufacturer to the Queen on her Silver Jubilee in 1977.

This prompted panic at the palace, who feared that an alternative vehicle might be necessary: in December 2010 vandals had splattered the car with white paint and smashed a rear window as Prince Charles and Camilla were heading to the Royal Variety Performance. An immediate review was undertaken by the Metropolitan Police, with extra briefings to all officers to remain vigilant for similar protests.

In a further sign of modernity, on 5 January 2011 Clarence House published details of the wedding on the social media site Twitter. It was a huge break in tradition for the palace and one that caught the world's attention. William and Catherine had been fully behind the idea, suggesting it was a way of delivering details to the public with speed and ease.

As with every wedding, there were controversies over the guest list. In a sign of his growing stature, and with an eye on his future position within the family, William decided his aunt Sarah Ferguson would not be welcome at the wedding. Sources claim that his decision was based on an anxiety that the Duchess of York, who had been embroiled in numerous misdemeanours following her exit from the royal fold, would be an embarrassment. Fergie, as she had come to be known in the press, had been excommunicated from the family following her 1997 divorce and subsequent attraction to scandal. Most notably, in May 2010 she was exposed by a *News of the World* sting operation by the journalist Mazher Mahmood in which she promised access to her ex-husband for £500,000. The subsequent furore forced her to take refuge in the US and to record a public apology on *The Oprah Winfrey Show*. By contrast, Catherine had insisted, after conversations with her mother, that her controversial uncle, Gary Goldsmith, should be included. The millionaire property developer, and Carole Middleton's younger brother, had been cut off by the couple after being filmed, in July 2009, offering to arrange cocaine deliveries (he denied taking drugs) for an undercover reporter from the *News of the World* he had invited into his Ibiza home.

Catherine had given considerable thought to the special touches she could bring to the occasion. Like most brides, she wanted both her wedding dress and flowers to be personal and full of meaning. Britain's fashion industry was abuzz when it was rumoured that Catherine had chosen the British creative designer of fashion house Alexander McQueen, Sarah Burton, who had taken over at the company after McQueen tragically took his own life in 2010, to create a wedding dress for the ages, a fact not confirmed until she stepped out of the car before entering the Abbey. The label's wedding dresses were already praised for being the epitome of elegance and exquisite tailoring, and Catherine's became one of the most iconic bridal gowns in modern history, incorporating incredible lace work created by the Royal School of Needlework, and featuring hand-cut lace appliqué of roses, thistles, daffodils and shamrocks – each representing the four nations of the UK – England, Scotland, Wales and Northern Ireland.

Catherine asserted that all-British flowers should be used, to make the ceremony as sustainable as possible in a gesture to her new father-in-law, Charles, who had long been a champion of the environment. The result was a stunning spring-garden-themed creation, with everything grown in the UK or cut from the royal estates. Her bouquet, made almost entirely from lily of the valley, was unusual in its modesty but so seasonal it could have been plucked from gardens on the way to the service.

Due to the apolitical nature of the royal family, it is often the subtle signs that carry the most impact. With this in mind, Catherine, with the help of florist Shane Connolly, who had designed the flowers for Charles and Camilla's wedding in 2005, decided to follow a theme informed by the 'language of flowers',

Prince Charles, Prince of Wales, and Diana, Princess of Wales, leave the Lindo Wing of St Mary's Hospital, London, with baby Prince William on 22 June 1982.

Diana taking William on his first day to Wetherby School in Notting Hill, London, on 15 January 1987.

Five-year-old Prince Harry (left), joining his brother Prince William, seven, on his first day at the Wetherby School with their mother on 25 April 1989.

Catherine (front row, centre) in a hockey team photo during her time as a pupil at St Andrew's School in Pangbourne, Berkshire.

William aged 13 on his first day at Eton on 6 September 1995, with Diana and Harry, alongside House Master Dr Andrew Gailey (centre).

William walking down The Mall during the funeral service for Diana, Princess of Wales, 6 September 1997.

William and Harry stand outside Westminster Abbey at the funeral of Princess Diana.

Catherine on an expedition with Raleigh International to Patagonia, Chile from January to March 2001. William took part in a similar programme in October 2000.

William arrives for his first day at the University of St Andrews, 23 September 2001.

William and Catherine on graduation day from St Andrews, 23 June 2005.

Prince William is greeted by Major General Andrew Ritchie, the Commandment of Sandhurst, while his father, the Prince of Wales, (now King Charles III), looks on, 8 January 2006.

Catherine and William attend day one of the Cheltenham Horse Racing Festival, 13 March 2007. Clarence House would days later confirm they had split up.

William and Catherine at RAF Cranwell after William received his RAF wings from his father, 11 April 2008.

Catherine arrives at the Renaissance Rooms in South London for the Day-Glo Midnight Roller Disco, 18 September 2008.

Attending her most high-profile royal event to date, Catherine, alongside Harry and the Duchess of Cornwall, watches the Most Noble Order of the Garter ceremony at St George's Chapel, Windsor Castle, at which William was installed into the order on 16 June 2008.

William and Harry on military helicopter training courses at RAF Shawbury, 18 June 2009.

William and Catherine pose for the media at St James's Palace in London, after announcing their engagement on 16 November 2010.

Prince William, Duke of Cambridge, and Catherine, Duchess of Cambridge, leave Westminster Abbey, London, following their marriage on 29 April 2011.

William and Catherine share a first public kiss on the balcony of the East Wing, Buckingham Palace, London, following their marriage.

Catherine and Prince William visit Province House in Charlottetown, Canada, during their royal tour of the country, 5 July 2011.

William and Catherine attend the Calgary Stampede Parade in Canada on day nine of their tour of North America on 8 July 2011.

Catherine accompanies Queen Elizabeth II during a visit to Vernon Park in Nottingham during the Queen's Diamond Jubilee tour of the UK on 13 June 2012.

Catherine and William celebrate Team GB success at the cycling velodrome on day six of the London 2012 Olympic Games, 2 August 2012.

Catherine and William dance at a Vaiku Falekaupule Ceremony in Funafuti, Tuvalu, during their tour of the Far East on 18 September 2012.

The Duke and Duchess of Cambridge leave the Lindo Wing of St Mary's Hospital in Paddington, London, with their newborn son, Prince George, on 23 July 2013.

William and Catherine in Anglesey on 30 August 2013, during their last public engagement in the coastal town where they lived from 2010 until 2013.

a floral code made popular by Queen Victoria. Entwined with sweet William, a clear nod to her beloved, the signature lily of the valley denoted 'trustworthiness', myrtle 'hope and love', hornbeams 'resilience', and field maples 'humility and reserve'.

As the weeks went on, Catherine grew in confidence, which was a joy to see. She grasped very quickly that this would be a celebration for family but also the country and she recognised that she had a real opportunity to make her mark on many things. At the time she may not have completely understood their value, but those individual characteristics have shaped the role that she has taken on, especially in respect to her love and appreciation of nature and the social environment in which we live.

Even the wedding cake was chosen with care. The couple opted for an eight-tiered traditional fruitcake decorated with floral motifs that mirrored the flowers used in the Abbey. William's personal touches made it into the day too: on the reception menu was a chocolate biscuit cake. It had been a favourite of his mother's, and he recalled memories from his childhood of the two of them enjoying it together.

In keeping with the tradition of the bride wearing something borrowed, Catherine took the Queen up on her gracious offer and chose a piece from her personal jewellery collection. The thought of wearing a tiara had not occurred to her at first, but after she was shown one of the most iconic royal wedding pieces in history, she was overcome with emotion. Known as the 'Halo' or 'Scroll tiara', the exquisite Cartier-designed piece, made up of 739 brilliant-cut diamonds and 149 baguette diamonds, was first gifted to the Queen Mother, in 1936, by her husband, King George VI, just weeks before his brother's abdication. It was then given to Queen Elizabeth II on her 18th birthday in 1944. The Queen, who was never pictured wearing it in public, had loaned it to her sister Princess Margaret, and then daughter

CHAPTER SEVEN

Princess Anne, who last wore it in the 1970s, and had given her blessing for Catherine to wear it. Many believe it to have been a symbolic gesture of not only her fondness for her grandson's bride but also a recognition of her future status within the family. To complement Catherine's look, Carole and Michael commissioned Robinson Pelham jewellers to create a pair of custom-made earrings for their beloved daughter. Derived from a coat of arms granted to the Middleton family before the wedding, the earrings featured a stud portion designed to resemble a curving oak leaf, while also mimicking the shape of the scroll elements of the tiara. Three acorns proudly displayed on the coat of arms represented the Middletons' children, Catherine, Philippa and James, and were chosen as a long-established symbol of both 'England' and 'strength', and the oak-tree-filled Berkshire countryside.

In the final weeks leading up to the wedding, William and Catherine learned they would be granted new titles as they started married life, becoming the new Duke and Duchess of Cambridge. In March 2010, having arranged the majority of the grand affair in just four months, they left the final details to their army of aides, who were working round the clock, and celebrated their stag and hen dos. No stranger to a party, Prince Harry approached his best-man duties with vigour, organising a weekend away at Hartland Abbey, the 12th-century North Devon family home of his friend George Stucley. Twenty of William's closest confidants, including Eton school friend James Meade, Thomas van Straubenzee, the prince's friend from Ludgrove Prep School, and Hugh van Custem, one of Prince Charles's godsons, spent the weekend learning to surf near a secluded cove called Speke's Mill, while Harry later organised shooting on the estate and a range of drinking games. William was even forced to dress up in a wig and apron with fake chest hair.

Catherine, unsurprisingly, opted for a somewhat more subdued occasion. Her sister, Pippa, organised a gathering at her Chelsea flat, inviting a small selection of Catherine's old school friends for cocktails and karaoke. The details of the party would emerge the following year in the memoir of the singer Cheryl Cole, *Cheryl: My Story*, who recounted how on meeting the royal couple at the Queen's Diamond Jubilee celebrations in 2012, 'William looked at Kate and they both started laughing before Kate confessed that she dressed up as me on her hen night, in a body suit and split trousers and sang "Fight for This Love". She even learnt the dance routine and was considered step-perfect by all.'

The night before the wedding, Catherine was joined by her parents and sister at the Goring hotel in London, just a mile from the Abbey. London had been transformed for the occasion: streets along the procession route were decorated with flags and closed to cars to deal with the huge crowds expected. Giant screens were installed in Hyde Park, Trafalgar Square and other public spaces around the capital, so that spectators could watch the ceremony live. Hundreds of hotels had been booked months in advance, and there was a throng of international news crews already delivering round-the-clock coverage from temporary studios erected near Westminster, broadcasting to an estimated 2 billion viewers worldwide.

After enjoying a light supper, Catherine retired to her room with Pippa. Her last night as both a single woman and a 'normal' girl from the Home Counties. By dawn the next morning on 29 April 2011, the capital was already buzzing with excitement. More than a million and a half people packed into the city to witness the historic occasion. Guests had been ordered to arrive at the church by 8.15am, almost three hours before the scheduled start, to help the police deal with such a huge operation.

CHAPTER SEVEN

After months of planning and attention to detail, the time had come. At 10.50am, Catherine stepped out from the hotel and into the waiting Rolls-Royce Phantom VI, accompanied by her father, Michael. If she was nervous, she did not show it. Far from being the rabbit in headlights of the start of the process, Catherine had shown that she had the capacity to not only learn quickly on the job, but to lead with authority, bringing different elements of the institution together. 'She was great to work with,' a former courtier said. 'She was fun and vibrant, self-deprecating and thoughtful, and cared about working in a happy environment, which certainly couldn't be said for all members of the family.' The thumping buzz of news crew helicopters tracking the car's five-minute journey was only broken by the throng of the crowd noise, which moved like a Mexican wave as the car travelled down the Mall outside Buckingham Palace to Parliament Square and, finally, Westminster Abbey. Catherine could be seen beaming as she intermittently broke off conversation with her father to politely wave to the crowds flailing Union Flags and screaming cheers of good luck.

Catherine arrived at the Abbey to the sounds of the chorus of church bells. As she stepped out of the car, there were audible gasps from the crowds as her dress was revealed for the first time. Catherine's sister, Pippa, was led out to greet her sister and support her incredible 2.7-metre train as she made her way into the Abbey. Catherine looked both ways as if to savour the moment, waving to the crowds who had queued up patiently to catch a glimpse of the bride, before stepping forward.

Those who have been inside Westminster Abbey, especially those who have been lucky enough to witness a royal event, will tell you it is a spine-tingling experience to hear the reverent sounds of the choir. The juxtaposition of the silence as Catherine walked up the aisle and the huge cheers from thousands of people outside the church as the couple completed their vows to one another was spine tingling.

After the service, the happy couple departed the Abbey in the open-top, horse-drawn 1902 State Landau carriage that had transported Charles and Diana back to Buckingham Palace following their wedding in 1981. Catherine could be seen on television cameras asking William 'Are you happy?' to which the newly married future king replied, 'So much', before they were led off on the five-minute journey back to royal HQ. The streets along the route back to the palace, at least 40 people deep in some parts, erupted in cheers, as a sea of flags, flowers and smiling faces greeted the newlyweds.

Back at Buckingham Palace, and moments after jets from the Royal Air Force flew over it, the couple emerged to seal the day with a kiss in front of the nation. A little over two minutes later, William nervously looked over to Catherine to ask, 'One more kiss?' before his beaming bride tilted her head for the prince to lean in once more, creating one of the most iconic moments in royal history.

In a further sign of the couple's individuality, they opted to have two receptions, one after the other, in order to carry on the celebrations. Immediately after the balcony moment, the Queen hosted a formal lunchtime reception for around 650 guests, where dignitaries were served canapés and champagne, while later that evening the Prince of Wales hosted a smaller, more intimate dinner and dance for 300 of the couple's closest family and friends. The new Duke and Duchess of Cambridge danced the night away, enlisting friend and British chart-topping singer Ellie Goulding to sing a version of Elton John's 'Your Song' for their first dance together as husband and wife.

When the couple emerged the next day, they sent a message of thanks to the nation, remarking on the 'most wonderful day

CHAPTER SEVEN

of our lives'. William had to report back to the RAF base in Anglesey, putting off their honeymoon to the Seychelles for two weeks, meaning that the couple spent their first married weekend privately in the UK. The country rejoiced throughout a weekend that had gone without a hitch, celebrating a couple who would become the future of a very modern monarchy.

8

MAPPING OUT

The white sand beaches and crystal-clear waters of the Seychelles held a special place in the hearts of William and Catherine. In 2007 it had been the destination for their make-or-break holiday, and the site of their most honest conversations about the possibilities and pitfalls of a future together. Four years later, after a wedding that had captured global attention and set the monarchy on a new path of optimism, the new Duke and Duchess of Cambridge were returning as newlyweds.

When they touched down on 10 May 2011, there was a feeling of possibility in the air. Their wedding had left them both on cloud nine and had sparked a wave of sanguinity across the country and the Commonwealth that palace aides were determined to capitalise on. Yet there was an undeniable feeling inside palace walls that while William and Catherine were hugely significant to the future of the institution, they would need to be guided through the complexities of royal life.

While courtiers were au fait with William's hankering for a 'normal' existence, which most recently had been a deciding factor in choosing to study in Scotland and later to live in Wales, there was a distinct feeling in the palace that whatever he and Catherine did next would break the royal mould. William's immediate dismissal of the guest list handed to him for his wedding had shown that he was prepared to challenge the status quo, and his desire to create a life outside of the royal

CHAPTER EIGHT

bubble would challenge the more traditional courtiers' views of how the royal family should operate. Some senior aides privately disapproved of his choices, mainly to do with the pace at which he was prepared to enter the royal fold. His grandmother had taken the throne at just 25 and his father had maintained a solid foundation of royal engagements even before retiring from the armed forces aged 27 in 1976. But William knew he had the Queen's backing, as well as that of his father, for delaying his entry to royal duties for as long as possible, especially while the Queen, Duke of Edinburgh and Prince of Wales were still performing them full time.

In a one-on-one meeting with his grandmother before his wedding, William had reiterated his desire to take advantage of the freedom of living in Wales after marriage, while also giving Catherine the opportunity to make her first tentative steps into a world that was almost completely alien to her. Catherine's life would now be managed and judged in a wholly different way. It was no longer a question of just turning up at the odd royal engagement or royal wedding; she was now a fully fledged member of The Firm. There would come a time when Catherine would be expected to take on causes of her own, to develop lifelong associations with charities, organisations and the military. But in William's view, that time did not need to be now. In response, the Queen shared her own profoundly personal experiences as a newlywed with Prince Philip. Between 1949 and 1951, the Duke of Edinburgh's service with the Royal Navy's Mediterranean fleet had provided the couple the opportunity of a lifetime. They had the chance to experience living in Malta, away from the watchful eyes of the courtiers who believed in the absolute structure and tradition of life within the institution.

In a decision that might today be seen as controversial, Elizabeth left a young Prince Charles and Princess Anne behind in the care of their grandparents and nannies at Buckingham Palace to enjoy what she considered to be one of the happiest periods of her life. It was her and Philip's only real experience of living as a relatively ordinary couple – the intimacy of the small island providing a haven of privacy away from the expectations of royal duties. The couple were able to attend parties, enjoy picnics and serene boat trips around the island, while neighbours would think nothing of strolling up to their front door to deliver fresh oranges each morning. The young princess even felt comfortable enough to drive herself around in a humble Morris Minor and, for the first time in her life, to visit the hairdressers on her own.

The Queen felt there were deep parallels between her cherished time in Malta and William's determination to live in Wales for longer. 'The Queen certainly had sympathy with his [William's] situation. Her direction was very much "go and live your life", but also to have one eye on the future, as you never know when things will change,' one former courtier said. Indeed, those cherished days of freedom for Elizabeth and Philip came to an end in July 1951, when they were forced to return home due to King George VI's failing health. Before long, Elizabeth was crowned Queen.

William drew much comfort from his grandmother's words and felt emboldened to make the most of the opportunity that lay in front of him and Catherine, for as long as they could make it last. In what was considered a precursor to moving permanently to Kensington Palace, plans were made for him and Catherine to establish a London base in Nottingham Cottage, on the Kensington Palace estate. To help them with the transition into a more structured involvement with royal life, they would take on a light programme of duties when required, while still being able to enjoy married life out of the spotlight

CHAPTER EIGHT

in Anglesey. William believed they would stay in North Wales for at least two to three years. After that he would be required to take on public duties full time. The couple and Prince Harry had set up their own royal household, and their office would be based in St James's Palace, with close links to the Prince of Wales's team at Clarence House. The setting up of the separate office created a point of focus for William, Catherine and Harry, giving them their own team who could help them schedule and execute their public duties in support of the monarch and the family. It would also signify that the young royals were ready to move out of the shadow of the Queen and Prince of Wales and begin to forge public futures of their own.

Catherine had shared a deep bond with her younger brother, James, and immediately struck up a playful friendship with Harry. In his memoir, *Spare*, Harry reflected on his first meetings with the young woman who would go on to become his sister-in-law, describing her as 'carefree, sweet and kind'. The prince reminisced about how he enjoyed making her laugh as his 'transparently silly side connected with her heavily disguised silly side'. In his best-man speech at William and Catherine's wedding, he endearingly described her as the 'sister I never had', paying tribute to Catherine for making his beloved brother so happy. William and Harry at that time remained incredibly close and the trio were hugely looking forward to being part of a team of royals who could, they believed, accurately portray and develop the reputation of the monarchy for a younger generation. The idea of working together like this, partly to give Harry direction and a supporting cast, was a break from tradition. For instance, Charles, Anne, Andrew and Edward operated very much in silo.

The first engagement for their joint household came just a week after William and Catherine returned from their honeymoon. On 24 May 2011, together with Prince Harry, they met

President Barack Obama and the first lady, Michelle Obama, during the US leader's three-day state visit to Britain. The job demanded personality and likeability, characteristics that Catherine would call upon in most of her public duties in the future. The 20-minute chat was in private, but royal aides later briefed that their conversation in Buckingham Palace's 1844 Room was both engaging and filled with mutual affection. It was an introduction for Catherine to the soft diplomacy wielded by the royal family.

An unexpected consequence of the meeting, at least for Catherine, was the incredible interest in her fashion. The dress she wore for the audience, a cap-sleeved, caramel-coloured item by British high-street brand Reiss that retailed for around £200, sold out online hours after photos of the gathering were broadcast. One of her former dressers and stylists remarked,

> It was a surprise for her and something we had to gently suggest that she would have to get used to. Her initial feelings were that she had so much more to offer than simply what she was wearing, but once the emotion was taken out of it, she realised that she did have her own style and way of presenting herself, which was a great advantage in being comfortable in such situations.

Before long, Catherine started to become excited about how she could use her own sense of individuality, and profile, to raise vast sums of money for charity. The willingness to help others came naturally to her – she had always recognised the privileged position she was born into, running cake sales for charity throughout her days at school. And the opportunity to act as a convening force had been a significant factor, other than her obvious love for her husband, in her decision to join the

CHAPTER EIGHT

royal family. In the month before their wedding, William and Catherine had set up a gift fund to allow well-wishers, in lieu of gifts, to donate money to charities the couple cared about. The fund raised more than £1 million for 26 charities, including the armed forces, children, the elderly, art, sport and conservation.

It was with that same iconic sense of style and individuality that on 9 June 2011 Catherine made a dazzling entrance at the tenth annual Absolute Return for Kids (Ark) gala dinner. The dinner was to support Ark, a charity that helps children around the world, and saw rich benefactors invited to rub shoulders with royal and celebrity guests. Most of the 900 attendees paid £10,000 each to be part of the evening in a specially erected marquee in the grounds of Kensington Palace. At the event, all eyes were on Catherine, as she wowed in a £3,835 floor-length Swarovski crystal-embellished gown by designer Jenny Packham. 'She was modest and down to earth, or perhaps still a little naive,' suggests one former aide.

> Despite the wedding, which was obviously absolutely massive, Catherine still had little idea of how her profile had now shifted into the stratosphere. Everyone would be poring over what she said, how she acted, who she spoke to, and of course how she dressed. It came with the territory and that was something she had to get used to quickly, but while she was frankly terrified of public speaking, which we were very mindful of, she was a quick learner.

Notwithstanding her previous puzzlement at the immense interest from the media in her sartorial choices, she was beginning to accept it as a way through which she could highlight the causes she was most interested in. Most important of all, the charity event raised an astonishing £17 million on the night. Courtiers said Catherine mentioned the amount for weeks on end during meetings with staff, clearly astounded at the sum that had been possible. One former palace aide said, 'It was very clear that she had very little idea that this was a part of the role that was immediately identifiable as a tangible product of her involvement.'

It was quickly apparent that active engagement in charitable causes was going to define William and Catherine's approach to royal life. Catherine became joint patron of the Royal Foundation set up by William and Harry in September 2009 and, according to another former aide, was fascinated with the foundation and its capacity to raise money for good causes. Jamie Lowther-Pinkerton, former private secretary to the Prince William and Prince Harry from 2005 and then the Duke and Duchess of Cambridge and Prince Harry until 2013, said,

> Catherine really bought into it and wanted to know everything from how it was run, to how the charities were chosen and where the funds were allocated to. From day one she saw this as her future. Some members of the family might see their role as purely ceremonial, but Catherine wanted to be very hands-on and saw it as a vehicle she could engage in with real purpose.

Catherine also had a deep respect for soldiers and would mention the plight of families and children of servicemen and women regularly, especially those serving in overseas military operations. 'Being a military wife, she saw this as a real opportunity to get involved very early on. She was very ambitious and full of ideas. She wanted to help people and use her platform to do that in any way she could,' said one royal aide. On 25 June, William and Catherine celebrated the third annual British Armed Forces Day, William's first engagement as Colonel of the Irish Guards. He

CHAPTER EIGHT

and Catherine presented operational medals to the Irish Guards, including Elizabeth Crosses to the families of three servicemen who were killed during a six-month tour of Afghanistan. It was Catherine's first personal taste of engaging with the military and lit a fire inside her to do more for the community.

It was around this time that Catherine was first introduced to David Manning. Manning had first joined the royal household to advise William and Harry, and now had the duty of guiding the Duke and Duchess of Cambridge on their first royal tour, which would begin in Canada and end in Los Angeles. As a former diplomat, and foreign affairs adviser to Tony Blair, he was incredibly well set up for the job, and the tour went without a hitch.

The schedule was designed to play to William and Catherine's strengths. They visited veterans' institutions and publicly recognised the value of public service by interacting with the military as well as the voluntary and emergency services. By following Manning's guidance, the couple would draw praise from across the political divide. Upon William and Catherine's return to the UK, part of Manning's brief was to guide the young royals, as well as Prince Harry, through the next stage of the Royal Foundation's existence, designed to keep it fresh and active, which was to prove a much more challenging affair.

Before then, though, there would be a momentous event that showed how much of an asset the princes' closeness could be: the upcoming Olympic and Paralympic Games. In December 2011, the Duke and Duchess of Cambridge and Prince Harry were recruited as official ambassadors to promote Britain's athletes in the run-up to, and during, the London 2012 Games. It was a huge honour and an indication of how they could combine their individual passions for sport and supporting the country for the collective good. William, Catherine and Harry greeted the Olympic torch at Buckingham Palace. They also attended the glittering opening ceremony, where the Queen got the event off to a thrilling start, with a special cameo alongside Daniel Craig, in character as James Bond. The young royals attended athletics, hockey and tennis events, taking part in a Mexican wave on Wimbledon's Centre Court as they cheered British hero Andy Murray on his way to Olympic gold. Images of William and Catherine caught up in the emotion and hugging each other as the cyclist Chris Hoy won a record-breaking sixth gold medal, showed they were not afraid of engaging in public displays of affection. A far cry from generations of royals before them.

But what had started as a loosely formulated launch pad for their ideas would, over time, have to become more structured in order to give each of them a clear plan for their future roles within the institution. This shift suited William's mindset. He believed that the royal family had to evolve in order to stay relevant. The institution could not afford to repeat the same tried and trusted methods of members of the family backing causes, raising money, or turning up to the odd charity event or high-society dinner. They had to be effecting change. However, this resulted in conflict around a perceived landgrab, as both brothers sought to claim ownership over the particular areas in which they'd be engaging. The source of much of their contention was their role within the military. Following his first tour of Afghanistan, in late 2007, where he served for ten weeks as a forward air controller in the notoriously brutal Helmand Province, Harry had formed a deep connection with the military and the veteran community. What he hadn't considered was that William would one day be Commander in Chief of the armed forces and was therefore quite likely to take an active interest in the field. Harry had been the one who had seen active duty and felt he had earned the right to be an authoritative voice on such matters. 'Harry was put out,' said a palace source.

CHAPTER EIGHT

He felt he was having to play the little brother role again, and basically wanted to tell his brother to get lost, to put it mildly, but that's not the sort of thing you can do when your brother is the future king. But it did hurt him, having fought for his country, especially in such a place as Afghanistan. He felt he had the right to be pissed off that he was essentially being told he couldn't step on William's toes when it came to the military.

For years William had shown an interest in the environment and conservation, especially across Africa, and was keen to follow in the footsteps of both his father and grandfather, who had used their global standing to campaign on such matters. It was an area that William felt a deep passion for, it connected his love of the countryside to the wider environment, and was somewhere he could use his profile to push for change. Again, Harry regarded this as confrontational. 'You don't just get Africa,' Harry told William in one meeting at St James's Palace. Ed Perkins, who served as press secretary to the Duke and Duchess of Cambridge and Prince Harry from 2012 to 2014, felt that something was emerging in the brothers' relationship that went beyond sibling rivalry: We had to sit them down and say, "Listen, you have to help each other, be on the same team." There's no point going around trying to lay claim to things that aren't going to work for you down the line, but in the same breath, if you're smart about it, then things can work out in ways that suit everybody.' Patrick Jephson, private secretary and equerry to Diana, Princess of Wales from 1988 to 1996, also held the view that the brothers had to be shown the door to harmony at a young age.

The princes were the same as young men, especially William. He possessed a desire to just live a normal life. It came up frequently. The trouble is there isn't such a thing as normal when you're born into the monarchy. Do the basics right, go to places people want you to go, support the causes you are interested in and give people what they want. The other things you are interested in will follow, but there has to be harmony for the whole operation to work.

The true disintegration of William and Harry's bond would not occur until many years later, but Catherine witnessed their competitive nature and often acted as a peacemaker. Her upbringing in a close-knit, loving family environment, where supporting each other was almost an unofficial family motto, spurred her actions. Whether counselling William or having a quiet word in Harry's ear, she saw it as her duty to keep the two brothers on the same team, as did their senior aides.

Before long, though, it became clear that William and Catherine could soon be striking out on their own. On 6 November 2011, in a move that was seen as a precursor to William and Catherine starting a family, it was announced that the couple would be making Kensington Palace their permanent London residence after Prince William's RAF training came to an end in late 2013. The grand apartment they'd move into, 1A, complete with 20 rooms incorporating a huge entertaining space for private functions and high-level meetings, had been the long-term London residence of Princess Margaret and her husband, Lord Snowdon, from their marriage in 1960 until her death in 2002.

One of the more unenviable roles of a courtier is the requirement to have, on occasion, difficult conversations regarding personal matters with members of the royal family. This might be to offer counsel or guidance, or perhaps help them navigate the minefield of personalities within the royal fold. Or it might be to discuss the subject of children. While friendly with all of his staff, William was not a fan of courtiers prying into his personal life, and certainly not in intimate matters, no matter how they were framed, and so aides had been careful to not explicitly raise the subject of children with the couple since their marriage.

In late 2011, Catherine decided to bring the subject up with them herself, in a meeting with an aide, shortly after their intention to move before the end of 2013 was announced. 'Catherine was very clear from the off that she wanted to do the job. She didn't want to sit back and although it wasn't explicitly said, the impression was that children would come into the equation whenever they were blessed with it happening. In the meantime, she wanted to crack on.' For the next two years, she hoped to spearhead meetings with aides, with the idea of taking on a range of royal patronages that would demonstrate the full range of her interests. Catherine had expressed an interest in helping the most marginalised in society and focusing on children, and so these patronages included Action on Addiction, the National Portrait Gallery, Place2Be, SportsAid, and the Natural History Museum. All of this would culminate, in 2021, in the founding of the Royal Foundation Centre for Early Childhood.

William and Catherine's determination to do things differently extended beyond their duties. While Christmas was a time for the royal family to let their hair down and spend time with each other in a less formal setting, there were still many of the festival rituals that William believed were archaic and did not fit with his view of how the family should operate. Christmas 2011 would be the first time Catherine would spend the festive season with the royals for their traditional gathering at Sandringham, and away from her family. In line with their Germanic roots, the royals have carried on the tradition of celebrating the festival with a black-tie dinner on Christmas Eve, which is preceded by the sharing of small gifts, often with a humorous slant. Catherine had been worrying about what to get the Queen. In previous years, William and Harry had tested the boundaries of the tradition, with Harry reportedly gifting the Queen a shower cap emblazoned with the phrase 'Ain't Life a Bitch', which, perhaps surprisingly, was a big hit with the monarch. Another time he gifted his grandmother a Big Mouth Billy Bass, a singing toy fish that was said to sit proudly at Balmoral. One year, William reportedly gifted the Queen a pair of slippers that were emblazoned with a picture of her face. As he grew older, William believed the order of distributing the gifts, where the Queen had stood at a trestle table and handed out the joke presents to guests in strict order of seniority, was not in line with his vision of harmony within the family. On learning of the process, Catherine had been keen to avoid offence with a joke present that had the capacity to go terribly wrong, and decided to make the Queen a homemade jar of chutney, using her grandmother's recipe. It was a typical gesture that the Middleton family had carried on for decades, choosing not to buy expensive Christmas gifts for one another, but instead present something heartfelt and with meaning. The Queen was delighted with the thoughtful gift, leaving it on the table for Christmas lunch the next day. In an ITV documentary to mark the late Queen's 90th birthday in 2016, Catherine reflected on Her Majesty's reaction to the homemade gift, saying:

> You would expect a lot of grandeur and a lot of fuss, but actually what really resonates with me is her love for the simple things. And I think that's a special quality to have. I can remember being at Sandringham for the first time at Christmas, and I was worried what to give the Queen as her Christmas present. I was thinking: 'Gosh, what should I give her?' I thought: 'I'll make her something,' which could have

CHAPTER EIGHT

gone horribly wrong, but I decided to make my granny's recipe for chutney.

I was slightly worried about it, but I noticed the next day that it was on the table. I think such a simple gesture went such a long way for me, and I've noticed since she's done that on lots of occasions and I think it just shows her thoughtfulness, really, and her care in looking after everybody.

It was the start of a deep bond between the two women.

William and Catherine's support for each other when it came to changing the status quo would go on to bring them closer as a couple when crises hit. In September 2012, ahead of a major nine-day tour to South-East Asia, as part of commemorations for Queen Elizabeth's Diamond Jubilee, William and Catherine decided to take a mini-break in the south of France. The couple stayed at the Château D'Autet, a stunning 19th-century hunting lodge in the Luberon hills of Provence, owned by Viscount David Linley, Princess Margaret's son. The holiday was a chance for the couple to recharge their batteries before setting off on the tour, which would be widely covered by the international media.

The trip that followed started off positively, with Catherine delivering her first overseas speech at a hospice in Malaysia, highlighting the role played by palliative care in delivering transformative experiences for children receiving end-of-life care. Never the most confident of public speakers, she was relieved it had been received well. But the couple's world came crashing down when they were informed that the French magazine *Closer* had decided to publish intrusive photographs of Catherine sunbathing topless. One former aide said it 'was as if time stood still' when they were confronted with the news. There was an eerie silence before William was the first to react.

The pictures were believed to have been taken covertly, while the couple were sunbathing on the balcony of the private home. The prince was incandescent, instructing their staff to issue legal proceedings at once. For years he believed he had toed the line with the press, giving access at key moments of his life, but this was 'an utter violation'.

William made frantic calls to his father and the Queen, informing them of his determination to release a statement and sue the magazine. A statement was prepared, castigating the publication for a 'gross breach of privacy'. Royal aides said William knew immediately he was prepared to take legal action 'all the way', suggesting the publication of the photographs was an attack on him and his wife. This would be the first time William had personally engaged in taking legal action against the press, and he was determined to draw a line in the sand over the 'monstrous behaviour'. Catherine was deeply upset over the incredible invasion of her privacy but remained determined to carry on with the tour. She was happy for William to respond in the strongest terms but wanted to carry on showing a united front that did not detract from what they were there to do: to honour the Queen and to carry out their duty.

While lawyers were engaged in a race against time to take out injunctions preventing any further publication of the pictures across Europe, William and Catherine attended a reception at the British High Commissioner's residence in Kuala Lumpur. It was hours after *Closer* had hit the newsstands but Catherine's reaction typified her calmness under such pressure. Without the slightest indication that something was amiss, she smiled and engaged in meaningful conversation with her hosts, shook hands and worked the room. Aides marvelled at her professionalism. Palace insiders told how, as the story blew up around the world, Catherine displayed a quiet reassurance. One palace

CHAPTER EIGHT

source said, 'What was very evident during that episode was Catherine was incredibly calm and measured and seemingly in complete control. Her life had been firmly intruded upon by the press for years but it was very different facing these issues with William by her side as a married couple and the fact he was prepared to take such a stand.'

William, whose anger was palpable, appeared to be under unimaginable stress, demanding to be kept abreast of every action being taken thousands of miles away by the royal lawyers working in London and their colleagues across Europe.

In the days that followed, as William and Catherine attempted to put the situation to one side, further images were published in the Italian magazine *Chi*, a gossip magazine owned by controversial former prime minister Silvio Berlusconi's Mondadori group, which also publishes *Closer* in France. A 26-page photo spread of the couple included the topless shots.

The Irish version of the British *Daily Star* newspaper followed suit, claiming that the British royals should be treated like any other celebrity couple. Palace staff reacted furiously, suggesting the clock had been turned back 15 years to the dark days of Princess Diana being hounded to her death by the paparazzi. Aides, describing the publication as 'grotesque and totally unjustifiable', said the couple were 'livid' and felt 'violated', and would pursue full criminal proceedings. Years before, William had gone against the grain when he warned the Fleet Street photographers that he would not tolerate a life of intrusion. This time, he was ready to go to war with the press.

9

THE NEXT GENERATION

The text message came early in the morning, summoning the senior team to an urgent meeting. The fact that a message had been sent was not out of the ordinary. Prince William would often contact courtiers in his household by text. Sometimes these texts would contain ideas he had about charity work or about facilitating links to people he wished to bring together for new projects, but this time the tone was different.

The Duchess of Cambridge was pregnant. Catherine had discovered the news in early November, when feeling under the weather. While the couple had insisted to courtiers that they were intent on moving forward with their public roles, they had secretly hoped to start a family. Plus, when William had been asked of his intentions by senior courtiers soon after the marriage, he had bluntly suggested that such private affairs were not to be raised. William was of course over the moon, yet he was nervous at what he predicted would be a months-long onslaught of media attention and commentary. The prince was still consumed with the ongoing legal proceedings against the French magazine and photographers that had published pictures of Catherine. He was quietly determined to see the court case through to a potential criminal prosecution, while also instructing lawyers to pursue the highest damages available, which would be donated to charity. Sources close to the prince suggest he felt a deep sense of personal responsibility over the issue, questioning whether

CHAPTER NINE

he had offered too much of his life to the press, and whether the event would have happened if he had previously taken a stronger stance with the media. The couple wanted to extend this moment of complete privacy, where they could share in the elation of being prospective parents, for as long as possible.

In a life of public service, these intimate episodes where time can pause, and nothing else matters, can be few and far between. The couple only shared the news with Catherine's parents, who were naturally elated, but within days, Catherine became seriously unwell, unable to eat or even drink for hours on end. Believing these were the first signs of morning sickness, she sought comfort from her mother, who advised her to try and keep hydrated and attempt to eat dry crackers. Determined to not cause alarm and hoping that the symptoms would pass, on 31 November she put on a brave face and returned to her old prep school, St Andrew's in Berkshire, for a royal engagement. Despite feeling nauseous, and the presence of the royal press pack, she grabbed a hockey stick and played with the year six children before sharing an endearing tale from her childhood about how she and her sister Pippa used to keep guinea pigs, named Pip and Squeak, which led to their classmates passing the nicknames on to them.

By 3 December, though, Catherine's condition had worsened. William called royal doctors to her parents' home in Berkshire where, still unable to eat and barely drink, Catherine had begun to feel delirious after vomiting. William was advised to take her to hospital as soon as possible, where she could be given an intravenous drip. It was recommended that she would likely be admitted for a period of observation.

As Catherine was not yet 12 weeks into her pregnancy, the time when the risk of miscarriage is highest, the couple, like the majority of prospective parents, had still hoped to be able to keep the news to themselves, but this now began to feel less tenable. William at once made arrangements to call his father, Prince Charles, and the Queen and Duke of Edinburgh, to tell them the news before it inevitably broke, and instructed aides to send a message to Prince Harry in Afghanistan, where he was serving as an Apache helicopter pilot with the Army Air Corps, during his second tour of duty in the country.

He then arranged a call with the most senior members of his and Catherine's communications team, where the prince told them of his wife's pregnancy and that she would likely be admitted to hospital for an unspecified amount of time. Discussions quickly moved to whether the team could facilitate Catherine entering the hospital without being seen. Aides voiced their concern that any plan was not guaranteed; a member of the public or hospital staff might recognise her, which could lead to a leak and potentially create unnecessary speculation as to why she was in hospital. Ed Perkins, the couple's press secretary at the time, said: 'The risks were too high and to make Catherine go through the stress of sneaking into a hospital given the gravity of her condition was too much. William's overriding concern was for his wife, so suggested to the team to make the call [on whether to tell the press].' Catherine was taken to hospital immediately and smuggled in a back entrance so as not to be seen, with medical staff on hand for her arrival, before she was taken to a private room on the third floor. Typically, health conditions of members of the royal family are not broadcast, to protect their privacy, but as speculation as to whether Catherine was pregnant had already begun, a decision was taken to announce that she was in the early stages of pregnancy and suffering from an acute condition.

Once admitted to the King Edward VII hospital in central London, a clinic with a long history of treating members of the royal family and senior politicians, Catherine was diagnosed with hyperemesis gravidarum, a severe form of morning sickness. The condition can cause debilitating nausea, vomiting, dehydration and weight loss. As Catherine was between eight and ten weeks pregnant, the Queen's surgeon-gynaecologist, Alan Farthing, and his predecessor, Sir Marcus Setchell, deemed it essential to ensure the baby was supplied with enough vital nutrients. William dutifully stayed by Catherine's bedside, leaving his communications team to draft a press statement that would be released to the world. Both he and Catherine knew they would be the subject of round-the-clock coverage once the news broke, but the prince's concern was only for his wife and making sure she was adequately cared for. At 4pm that day, St James's Palace released a statement: 'Their Royal Highnesses the Duke and Duchess of Cambridge are very pleased to announce that the Duchess of Cambridge is expecting a baby. The Queen, the Duke of Edinburgh, the Prince of Wales, the Duchess of Cornwall and Prince Harry and members of both families are delighted with the news.' It said the duchess was suffering from hyperemesis gravidarum, which requires supplementary hydration and nutrients. 'As the pregnancy is in its very early stages, Her Royal Highness is expected to stay in hospital for several days and will require a period of rest thereafter,' it added. The evening bulletins led with the news, while the next day's newspapers were filled with a mixture of celebration and concern for the future queen. William and Catherine's baby was due in the summer and, in a break with tradition, would immediately be third in line to the throne. For hundreds of years, under the ancient rules of primogeniture, first-born daughters born in a direct line to the throne were leapfrogged by their younger male siblings. That would all change in October 2011, when the prime minister David Cameron announced that the 16 Commonwealth countries for whom Queen Elizabeth II was head of state had agreed to give female royals the same succession rights as their brothers. This move to change a system that had been widely viewed as outdated and discriminatory was not the work of politicians or campaign groups, but rather Prince William himself. In the lead-up to his wedding with Catherine, he had raised the issue with his grandmother, saying that if they were to have a daughter, he believed that she should maintain the right to become Queen if he and Catherine then went on to have any sons.

'William was the driving force behind the change, which he knew the Queen ultimately had no power to change,' one former senior courtier said. 'But from those initial conversations it was made clear to her advisers that it was her sincere wish and that of her family for the government to lead the way for the Commonwealth countries to agree to the change.' Since the rules were first fixed in 1668 there had been at least 11 recorded attempts to amend them. That Queen Elizabeth II and Princess Diana both gave birth to boys first had made any proposed alterations during recent generations hypothetical and took the urgency out of the issue. William, however, was a man with a modern, or perhaps more realistic, view of the world, and did not wish to take chances.

On 6 December 2011, Catherine left hospital with William by her side, announcing she was feeling 'much better' before getting into a waiting car. Catherine was looking forward to getting home and being in the comfort of the small sanctuary they had created, while William was relieved to be leaving the hospital where, he told one aide, he had 'felt like a spare part' during his wife's stay. The couple released a statement later that day, thanking the medical staff who had cared for her, and the well-wishers from around the world, who included Barack Obama and his wife Michelle.

CHAPTER NINE

During Catherine's stay an investigation had been launched over a lapse in procedure when two nursing staff were duped by Australian radio DJs Michael Christian and Mel Greig, who called the hospital posing as the Queen and the Prince of Wales. Jacintha Saldanha, the nurse who took the call at 5.30am on 4 December, transferred the callers through to the duty sister, who was tricked into divulging details of Catherine's condition. The call was aired a day later, making headlines around the world and leaving the hospital at the centre of a media storm. The hospital was quick to denounce the hoax as 'deplorable', suggesting it was considering legal action against the Sydney-based radio station 2Day FM, and immediately contacted the royal household to offer their apologies. William and Catherine were notified, but neither they nor the household requested any further action be taken.

Tragically, mother of two Jacintha, who had sent a series of distressed emails to colleagues in the aftermath of the prank to offer her apologies for putting the call through, was found dead at her nursing accommodation just yards from the hospital on 7 December. Though both she and the duty sister had breached protocol, bosses had made no mention of disciplinary action, on the basis they had fallen victim to 'a nasty trick'.

William and Catherine were left stunned and deeply saddened when told that Jacintha, who they had both met during her stay at the hospital, had taken her own life. Immediately after he returned to his RAF base shortly after Christmas, William penned a handwritten note to her husband and family to express his profound sorrow. In the heartfelt letter offering his condolences, William said how devastated he and Catherine were to learn of Jacintha's death. He explained how they had been thinking of Jacintha and made reference to how many of her colleagues spoke so highly of her. 'I am just so sorry that someone who cared for others so much found themselves in such a desperate situation. This letter comes with my thoughts and prayers to you all,' William wrote.

'It was typical of William, and Catherine for that matter,' Ed Perkins said.

> Behind everything people think they know about them, they are human. Everyone was devastated for Jacintha's family when we heard the tragic news, it was a dark episode and put into context once more the lengths that certain people are prepared to go to access their lives and the effect that potentially has on others. William didn't tell anyone he planned to write to Jacintha's family and nor should he. It was a personal moment to offer his sympathies and something that speaks to both of them as people who care.

With Christmas approaching and arrangements being made for the royals to gather at Sandringham, William and Catherine informed the Queen that they planned to spend the holiday with the Middleton family. The break would give Catherine an opportunity to recover and regain her strength away from the spotlight.

William and Catherine joined the Middletons from 22 December until Boxing Day. It was the perfect refuge for them. On Christmas morning the family, alongside Catherine's siblings Pippa and James, attended a service at the local St Mark's Church, a ten-minute drive from their home, before returning to the house to prepare lunch. William was jokingly ordered to stay away from the kitchen and instead took the role of helping to prepare the table with Pippa and James. In the afternoon the family sat round the television and watched the Queen's speech, where the monarch spoke of the 'excitement and drama' of the London Olympics, paying tribute to Team GB athletes

CHAPTER NINE

for providing a 'splendid summer of sport'. The Queen also reflected on those forced to spend time away from their families. William had managed to get a message to his brother, who was still serving in Afghanistan, and who had himself celebrated Christmas by putting on a Santa hat to cook breakfast for his crew, then later joining his fellow soldiers for a Christmas dinner at their Camp Bastion base in Helmand Province.

William and Catherine joined the Queen and the rest of the royal family on 27 December, before the prince reported back for duty at his RAF base in Anglesey on 30 December and Catherine returned to her parents' home to see in the new year. From the moment Catherine was discharged from hospital, the palace maintained a policy of not providing a running commentary on her condition, suggesting that she would be given all the time necessary to recover with adequate rest and privacy away from royal duties for the foreseeable future. Royal aides had personally advised Catherine to undertake a lighter schedule of public engagements, but she insisted on keeping busy to alleviate the stress over her symptoms, which had continued, although not as severe as in her first trimester.

Within 24 hours of returning to his RAF base, the prince was involved in a daring rescue mission in gale force 8 winds. In rain-lashed skies, William and three of his crew scrambled aboard their Sea King helicopter just after midnight on 31 December, responding to an emergency call reporting a man being blown from a promenade near the Blackpool coast into the ferocious sea. Working in tandem with local lifeboat crews, police and coastguard units, William spent over an hour and a half searching for the man who had plunged into icy waters when walking his dog with a friend. Both men had been blown into the sea, with the friend somehow managing to scramble out to raise the alarm. Tragically the man could not be found, despite William battling 50-mile-an-hour winds while lifeboats crashed through 5-foot waves in total darkness.

The loss of life was something William had sadly become used to throughout his three years in the RAF, but he had also experienced on many occasions the elation of saving someone's life. With a child on the horizon, William was deeply conflicted as to how he could pursue his vocation, commit to increasing royal duties and maintain the family life that he deeply wanted. A former royal aide said:

> When he spoke about the job, he was as enthusiastic as you'd ever seen him be about anything. He said there was 'no greater calling' than working with the search and rescue team and having the ability to use your skills to save someone's life. It had a profound effect on him and reinforced his view that he wanted to carry on in the job for as long as possible. How that fitted in with a transition to royal duties was considered to be a bit of an issue, but considering the Queen had given him the green light to be out of the spotlight for a bit, he was definitely going to take full advantage.

Catherine carried out 19 days of public engagements before going on maternity leave in the middle of June. Her schedule, normally planned at least six to nine months in advance, was rearranged to provide a balance of different activities: support for her patronages, the Queen, children's charities and a bit of fun. Catherine's first engagement of the year involved a rather unique proposition when on 11 January she, alongside William and her parents, viewed a portrait of herself by Paul Emsley at the National Portrait Gallery. A month later, on 19 February, she visited the kitchens at Hope House residential centre, run by Action on Addiction

CHAPTER NINE

for recovering addicts, a charity that was quickly being recognised as a central pillar of her work. The association had already drawn comparisons with Princess Diana's use of her position to highlight the experiences of some of the most marginalised groups in society. On 17 March, Catherine accompanied William, a Colonel of the Irish Guards, to attend the annual St Patrick's Day Parade at Mons Barracks in Aldershot. Three days later she was pictured in fits of laughter when presented with a 'Baby on Board' badge during a visit to Baker Street Underground Station, accompanying the Queen and Prince Philip to celebrate the 150th anniversary of the London Underground.

Now five months pregnant and experiencing fewer episodes of the nausea that had left her bedridden for days on end in the earlier stages of pregnancy, Catherine appeared to be relaxing. She had undergone numerous ultrasounds to monitor the baby and had begun purchasing baby clothes – strictly keeping to neutral colours as she and William had agreed to keep the sex of their baby a surprise until the birth.

One thing they couldn't concur on was a name. Catherine had her heart set on Alexander for a boy or Alexandra (also Queen Elizabeth's middle name) for a girl. Several of Catherine's close friends had already had children and she revelled in the process of swapping baby name ideas with them over text as the birth drew closer. William had privately voiced his preference for having a girl, and was keen to incorporate a tribute to his late mother, most likely in the form of a middle name. The couple had been given a book of baby names by a close friend, which they spent hours thumbing through – they often ended up in fits of laughter after one or the other had presented a more left-field suggestion. One royal source said that William would often start meetings with his press team by blurting out suggestions such as, 'What do you think about Rodney for a boy, or maybe

THE NEXT GENERATION

Graham?', pausing for their stuttered response before roaring with laughter. In fact, the future king, who favoured a more traditional route for his heir, settled on a shortlist of two names for a boy: George and Louis.

On 29 April, William and Catherine had a quiet celebration at home to mark their second wedding anniversary, a break from the seemingly endless plans for the upcoming arrival that were being ticked off. Catherine's final engagements saw her visit a children's hospice in Winchester during Children's Hospice Week in April. In the same month the law allowing the Duke and Duchess of Cambridge's first child to become monarch, whatever its sex, passed its final hurdle after the House of Lords gave the green light to the bill, which had been fast-tracked through both Houses of Parliament. William and Catherine did not feel the need to make a personal statement or any reference to the ruling, but 'quietly celebrated the next stage of their vision to create a truly modern monarchy', according to one royal source. Entering the final stages of her public duties, in May Catherine, along with the Prince of Wales and Duchess of Cornwall, attended a Buckingham Palace garden party where thousands of members of the public working in the charity sector were celebrated for their service. On 4 June, William and Catherine joined senior members of the family to attend a service at Westminster Abbey to mark the 60th anniversary of the Queen's coronation, with a final public appearance before the birth at the annual Trooping the Colour parade on 15 June.

As Catherine's due date approached, a cascade of activity was unleashed across the royal household. William and Catherine's child would be the most significant royal birth in 30 years, since the birth of Prince Harry in 1984. William and Catherine did not have a preference for how the birth would be announced, choosing to leave it up to their press secretaries to manage. But

CHAPTER NINE

one issue for the small team now based at Kensington Palace, and the wider royal households, was the lack of experience in dealing with such a monumental announcement. A former courtier said: 'On the surface they were both incredibly relaxed, which actually made us all slightly more nervous. We genuinely had no idea how the birth should be announced, so proceeded to get some old documents and newspaper cuttings from the archives, which only complicated matters. The weight of expectation was extraordinary. There was no doubt in our minds that this would be a global event, so everything had to be right.' Watertight security arrangements were put in place, with just four people privy to the information, as on a daily basis the press office fielded hundreds of calls from news organisations around the world.

Two weeks before the birth, security barriers were erected outside the Lido Wing of St Mary's hospital in Paddington, where Prince William and his Prince Harry were born. Dozens of journalists and photographers started to camp outside, some broadcasting 24 hours a day as they waited for news of Catherine's arrival at the world-renowned maternity unit. The 'Great Kate Wait', as it became known in the national press, had started.

Late into the evening on 21 July 2011, the couple's aides assembled at Kensington Palace on being told the Duchess was in the early stages of labour. William and Catherine were spending the weekend at the Middletons' home when they summoned a royal doctor, who after examining Catherine told them to stay put and monitor the contractions. In the early hours of the morning a decision was made to take Catherine into hospital, where she arrived by car at 6am on 22 July. Catherine was taken to a private room to be monitored under the watchful supervision of a top medical team led by Marcus Setchell and Sir Alan Farthing, who Catherine had seen on numerous occasions throughout her pregnancy.

A royal source who spoke to William on the day said he was 'as stressed and nervous as any expectant parent is in that situation', but stayed by his wife's side throughout. At 4.24pm that day, Catherine safely delivered a beautiful baby boy weighing 8lb 6oz, with a gorgeous scrunched-up nose and a light dusting of brown hair. William had decided not to appear outside in front of the waiting press, instead deciding to share this first experience as a family. William and Catherine had been preparing for the moment for weeks, even practising placing their new car seat into the back of their black Range Rover – a trial run for their big moment in front of the world's media.

In her 2020 interview with the author and podcaster Giovanna Fletcher on *Happy Mum, Happy Baby*, Catherine admitted to feeling 'terrified' at the prospect of facing the press outside the hospital. The couple certainly had mixed emotions about the act of showing their baby to the world, especially as they had not yet had the opportunity to introduce him to their wider families. While they were hugely grateful for all the support they had received from around the world throughout Catherine's troubled pregnancy, they were as nervous and overwhelmed as any new parents are during those first few hours of bringing a new life into the world. The moment they would need to present themselves to the press, however, arrived a little over 24 hours later when, at 7.14pm on 23 July, exhausted yet looking radiant, Catherine, with William alongside her, emerged from the hospital doors holding their baby to the blistering sound of hundreds of camera shutters. 'It's very special,' William said in front of the waiting broadcast cameras, whose live pictures were already being beamed around the world. While the couple acknowledged the immense interest in their child, they were keen to get going. For months there had been rabid speculation as to when the royal baby would be born, with estimates suggesting Catherine was beyond her due date when she was finally admitted to hospital, and William appeared to confirm the lateness of his son's arrival, saying, 'I'll remind him of his tardiness. I know how long you've all been standing here, so hopefully the hospital and you guys can go back to normal now and we can go and look after him.' Wishful thinking perhaps, as the juggernaut of interest in his young new family was only just beginning. The couple returned inside briefly as they waited for their car to be brought out to the front to meet them. William and Catherine re-emerged from the hospital, this time with their baby boy strapped to a car seat. Suddenly, all William's practice was about to come to fruition. As Catherine gently slid into the back seat on the passenger side, William carefully placed his son into the back of the car for the first time, ensuring the safety locks were engaged. He turned back around to face the press, giving out a sigh of mock relief before getting in and driving off with a police escort following behind.

The new family would spend the night at Nottingham Cottage before leaving to spend William's two-week paternity leave from the RAF at the Middletons' home in Berkshire. William had kept the press and the public guessing on the name they had chosen for their firstborn, suggesting that 'we're still working on a name' when asked by one of the BBC royal correspondents outside the hospital. In fact, he and Catherine had decided several weeks beforehand but chose to keep it between themselves. The next day, at 6.18pm on 24 July, Kensington Palace released a statement confirming: 'The Duke and Duchess of Cambridge are delighted to announce that they have named their son George Alexander Louis.' William and Catherine were delighted to have the opportunity to introduce their son to the Queen before she left for her summer break at Balmoral, after she had joked during a visit to a primary school in the north-west of England that she hoped her great-grandchild would arrive soon as she was going on holiday.

A month later, as they prepared to make the move into their new family home, William and Catherine began the search for a nanny to help them with their new arrival. William maintained a fantastic relationship with his childhood nanny, Tiggy Legge-Bourke, whose son Tom Pettifer was a page boy at their wedding in 2011, and sought her guidance about individuals and agencies to consult and how to conduct the right kind of interview for prospective candidates. He also reached out for advice to another former nanny, Jessie Webb, who by now was 71. She had looked after William and Harry during the 1990s and left an immense impression on the young princes. To William's surprise, Jessie agreed to help out on a part-time basis, although she insisted she would not be a long-term solution. In early 2013, William and Catherine would welcome Maria Teresa Borrallo into their lives to be George's nanny, a position she still holds, helping to care for and educate George and his siblings. Marie, who was 43 at the time she was appointed, was educated at the prestigious Norland College in Bath, England. The academy, described as 'Hogwarts meets Mary Poppins meets James Bond', trains nurses decked out in their distinctive bowler hats and brown and yellow matron-type-uniform in everything from defensive driving to escaping paparazzi and even self-defence moves. Maria would become a much-loved fixture in their new home.

The period coincided with a great deal of professional change for William. He had spent three years as an RAF search and rescue pilot, but Kensington Palace announced on 12 September 2013 that he would leave the military to explore his charity interests, particularly in the field of the conservation of endangered species. Courtiers dressed the announcement up as William entering a 'transitional year', while carefully explaining that the prince would not necessarily take on any more royal duties. But, behind the scenes, William's attitude had begun to frustrate his staff, with senior aides challenging him over the risk that he might be seen as lazy, given the Queen and the Duke of Edinburgh were still carrying out royal duties into their tenth decade. One former senior aide explained:

> William seemed to have the attitude that his grandmother had given him a free pass to take his time in deciding what he wanted to do, which was not the reading of the situation from anyone else involved in trying to map out his affairs. We would gently ask him to consider taking on more duties or specific engagements, but he would immediately push back. There was an intense worry in the camp that he had no strategy for his long-term future and was continually putting off decisions over what direction he should take. When the annual list of engagements completed by members of the family would be published at the end of the year, it was pretty embarrassing, but it didn't seem to affect him one bit.

It is true that William did not shy away from the fact that his focus was on his young family. Reeling from a childhood in which he often felt abandoned, it was beyond question that he wanted to be there for his children and give them the childhood he wasn't able to have. Furthermore, he believed that the Queen had given him the green light to pursue his outside interests before he entered The Firm full time. But that did not stop the detractors, especially the British press, who began to launch a campaign that openly questioned what he was doing. Although William had been troubled by negative coverage in the past, his decision to forge his own path was becoming increasingly important to him, especially when it came to defending his family. His own childhood had been blighted by warring parents and separate homes. He was the product of a broken home and an institution that didn't adequately address his mother's mental state or the difficulties she faced when joining the family at such a tender age. Those close to him say he was on a mission to ensure that history would never repeat itself.

William's son was christened on 23 October. It was certainly a more modest affair than that of his or his brother's, with the Duke and Duchess inviting just a handful of guests to the intimate ceremony at the Chapel Royal in St James's Palace. The Queen and Duke of Edinburgh attended alongside the Prince of Wales, the Duchess of Cornwall, Prince Harry and the Middleton family. William and Catherine chose a mixture of close friends and family to be godparents, including Oliver Baker, who attended the University of St Andrews with the Duke and Duchess, and Emilia Jardine-Paterson, who attended Marlborough College with Catherine. William's childhood friend William van Cutsem and Hugh Grosvenor, now the Duke of Westminster, were also chosen. The list of godparents was completed by William's private secretary, Jamie Lowther-Pinkerton (a sign of their immense closeness), Julia Samuel, a close friend of the late Princess Diana, and Princess Anne's daughter Zara Tindall.

Prince George, who behaved impeccably throughout the 30-minute service, was dressed in a handmade replica of the royal christening robe, created by the Queen's dresser Angela Kelly. The traditional Lily Font and water from the River Jordan were used during the baptism, before the guests retreated to Clarence House, where Charles and Camilla hosted a private tea, with guests enjoying slices of the christening cake, taken from a tier of the Duke and Duchess of Cambridge's wedding

CHAPTER NINE

cake. The couple were determined to do things differently to the royal generation before them – and plans would soon be in motion for them to take Prince George with them on their first major international tour to Australia as a family. Kent Gavin, the legendary *Daily Mirror* photographer who captured Prince William's christening in 1982, reflected on how this period started to show the new face of the modern monarchy. 'It was clear from so many of their actions that this is what William and Kate wanted to present and we were seeing it evolve in real time.' From the formation of their office to the way in which they were already choosing to structure their family life, William and Catherine believed that simplicity would not only give them more control over their futures, but also make them more relatable in a modern world.

10

DRIFTING APART

Following a transitional year, in which he took on more royal duties while Catherine was on maternity leave with Prince George, William announced in August 2014 that he intended to join the East Anglian Air Ambulance service (EAAA) and donate his £40,000 annual salary to charity, making him the first member of the royal family to earn a salaried job outside of the armed forces. The new job meant the family were on the move again, this time from their home in Kensington Palace to Anmer Hall, a ten-bedroom Georgian mansion on the Queen's Sandringham estate, the sprawling 20,000-acre property dotted with churches, parishes and country houses. Anmer Hall had been gifted by the Queen to the Cambridges on their wedding day, and it had recently undergone a £1.5 million, privately funded, refurbishment to accommodate their growing family.

The following month, in September 2014, Kensington Palace announced that Catherine was pregnant with her second child. This time, she and William were more prepared for the sickness that had left her hospitalised during her first pregnancy. The Duchess was immediately put under the watchful eye of royal doctors, and William was able to be far more present while he was undertaking his training with the EAAA, where he would complete a civilian pilot course and dedicated 999-response training. The training would allow William – now with a toddler at home and a new baby on the way – the opportunity to foster

CHAPTER TEN

the close-knit family environment that had been lacking from his own upbringing.

William's view of how the monarchy should position itself in the modern world was also being formulated. Instead of racking up a list of engagements throughout the year, attempting to service the hundreds of patronages previous generations of the royal family had taken on, the prince believed he would be better suited to taking on a handful of key causes that would not only typify his personality, but also have a greater impact around the world.

So, for instance, William was presented with the opportunity to become the most senior member of the royal family to visit China since the Queen's tour of the country in 1986, something that would also allow him to demonstrate his passion for the natural world. During his solo tour between 26 February and 4 March 2015, the prince met the Chinese president, Xi Jinping, and the pair discussed wildlife protection and the need for stricter controls on the ivory trade as well as their shared love of football. The visit was seen as a triumph, with commentators suggesting it symbolised an improvement in the relationship between the two countries. Prince Charles had never visited China and was seen as a divisive figure in the country after describing Chinese officials as 'appalling old waxworks' in a leaked diary, written at the time of the Hong Kong handover in 1997. The heir had furthermore hosted the Dalai Lama at Clarence House – the exiled Tibetan spiritual leader is viewed by China as a separatist threat. William's solo tour also saw him travel to Japan, being greeted by thousands on the streets of Tokyo in a further sign of his international appeal.

On completing his training, William took up a post in the EAAA in March 2015, agreeing to a full-time, four-days-on, four-off rota, so he could accommodate a light schedule of royal duties. In choosing to continue to postpone his entry to full-time royal life, William made clear that his future role would be shaped by the fact that he was also raising the next generation of royals. Even before Princess Charlotte's birth on 2 May 2015, William and Catherine were in staunch agreement that their family should remain their highest priority. As much as possible they would do the pick-ups and drop-offs to nursery and school. While William's childhood had been shaped by numerous courtiers, the Cambridges wanted to create a home life that centred on giving their children a rounded upbringing away from the trappings of royal palaces. William and Catherine believed that before they could start introducing their family to their public roles, they first had to create a solid foundation at home. Only then, slowly, would they reveal to their children the world they were to inhabit. William and Catherine had seen how life in the palace could become stifling for both members of the royal family and palace aides if the right atmosphere wasn't created from the off.

As the Queen approached her 90th birthday in April 2016, senior members of her family agreed to take part in interviews that celebrated her role as head of state, a mother, grandmother and great-grandmother. As heir to the throne, there was as much interest in what William had to say about Elizabeth's life and legacy as there was over his own decisions to further delay entering the family business. When the BBC put in a request for Nicholas Witchell to conduct a sit-down interview with William, the prince knew there would be no easy questions. However, it would present an opportunity to explain to the public the reasoning behind his decision to delay taking on a full-time public role in favour of gaining experience in areas other than royal engagements. William gave Witchell and the BBC complete freedom. Instead of demanding a prepared list of questions or at the very least an agreed set of topics, 'his attitude was "ask me anything",'

Witchell said. 'And it was very refreshing. He certainly went up in my estimation.'

The prince knew he would have to address the criticisms that he was a somewhat 'reluctant royal' head on. The pressure from the press had been increasing in recent years, with many labelling him as 'work shy'. The fact that he was taking part in fewer official royal engagements than the Queen and his father Prince Charles had also not gone unnoticed by his own household. 'He was not immune to the criticism,' a former courtier said. 'The team made it very clear after he finished his posting in Wales with the RAF, he really had to come up with a plan.'

It was with this in mind that William delivered the most insightful and candid interview of his life. William had signed a contract with the EAAA until March 2017, and insisted that by then he would be ready to enter royal duties full time. He stressed that he would be the 'first person to accept' duties when the moment came for his grandmother to hand over responsibilities, but for now was focused on making the most of time doing another 'worthwhile job', while he could, and his family was supportive. 'I take duty very seriously. I take my responsibilities very seriously. But it's about finding your own way at the right time and if you're not careful, duty can weigh you down at a very early age. I think you have got to develop into the duty role,' he told Witchell. The prince highlighted the support both his father and grandmother had given, making clear that he had given careful consideration to his future, with the Queen being 'the best role model I could have in front of me'. 'The Queen's duty and her service, her tolerance, her commitment to others – I think that's all been incredibly important to me and it's been a real guiding example of just what a good monarch could be,' he said. The plan, when in place, seemed to get people to lay off him for a while.

One courtier said, 'The trouble with breaking the mould, as William was doing by balancing his roles as a father and air ambulance pilot, is that you can't please all of the people all of the time. But from the moment he and Catherine started a family they were absolutely steadfast in their commitment to doing the best they could for their children, and I think the public have been very supportive in that view overall.'

Witchell said:

> William showed he was clearly a man who thinks with his head. He was considered and sharp, acknowledged the criticism that had come his way and said, 'Hey, look, these are my reasons, I believe they are the right ones and I stand by my decisions.' It helped that he had the backing of the Queen and his father, who were no doubt hugely sympathetic to his plight having grown up in the glare of some of the institution's most troubling times. I was left thinking, here is a young man who wants to prove he is a person of worth outside of being handed the role of a prince and my feeling was the general public would recognise that too. He was in a period of transition and the acceptance of him having to step up at some point in the future was a considerable turning point.

William has always been different: different to his brother, which became more pronounced in later life, certainly different to his father and from an entirely different generation to his grandmother. Those who have worked closely with him over his formative years tell an almost universal story of how he viewed the world and his place in it. Almost since birth, he had been made aware of his place in the line of succession and his future role in the world, and he was often left feeling deeply uncomfortable about it. It had been a burden that weighed heavily on him ever since the Queen Mother showered him with affection in a clear sign of favouritism over his brother.

It would be unfair to suggest that Queen Elizabeth and the Prince of Wales, now King Charles, were not modernisers in their own way, but William comes across as a man who understands the pace of the modern world and the royal family's place within it. In the BBC interview, William outlined the need for the monarchy to 'modernise and develop' in order to survive. 'As it goes along and it has to stay relevant, and that's the challenge for me, how do I make the royal family relevant in the next 20 years' time, it could be 40 years' time, it could be 60 years' time, I have no idea when that's going to be,' he said. One former courtier gave an intriguing insight into the importance to the heir of modernising the monarchy:

> It has guided his principles, perhaps even before university. Look at most millennials, their world has changed more rapidly than any other generation, birth of the internet, social media, everyone rushing around, the world is literally on fire every way you turn. In one way it's harder to be heard than ever and in another it's never been easier with everything at our disposal, so perhaps it's about balance. William and Catherine have been very good at that, taking their time, finding their feet on what matters to them. They recognise their own foundations need to be rock solid before they can deliver for anyone else, much more so than anyone in the family before them.

The most important thing, for William as much as Catherine, has always been the welfare of their children. Asked by Witchell if he recalled when he had an 'inkling' that he was not from an 'ordinary' family, and when he might prepare George, William's demeanour visibly changed.

> As far as we are concerned within our family unit, we are a normal family. I love my children in the same way any father does, and I hope George loves me the same way any son does to his father. We are very normal in that sense. There'll be a time and a place to bring George up and understand how he fits in, in the world. But right now it's just a case of keeping a secure, stable environment around him and showing as much love as I can as father.

This balance of normality above all else was William and Catherine's guiding light. Central to this was being at home as much as they could, making sure one of them did the school run and not working weekends, outside of observing major events in the royal calendar such as the sovereign's birthday or Remembrance Sunday.

The Middleton family, who had become a constant presence in their lives, were crucial to this. William appreciated their involvement beyond measure, enjoying their company and the normalcy of the environment, whatever the circumstance. 'More room to breathe', he once told an aide. Michael and Carole enjoyed visiting the couple in Norfolk and would often stay for weekends, providing much-needed extra support for the young family. Of course, William would have to explain why people bowed or curtseyed to his grandmother, why on occasion they went to visit her in a castle, or who the men in the front of their cars and outside guarding their houses were, but the time to address George's future certainly wasn't now.

In this interview, William made the shape of his future clear: he wanted to be more in tune with what ordinary people were

CHAPTER TEN

thinking, feeling and living though in their everyday lives. 'It was an announcement for many things, most of all the direction of the monarchy as he saw it. For all the criticism that was thrown his way he hadn't had pity or cried "why me", he knew what he was doing. I was very impressed, and I expect the public were too,' Witchell said. Evolution, more than revolution, would be the guidance given by courtiers, both inhouse and in external off-record briefings to the press.

In May 2016, William, Catherine and Harry united to launch what would be their most celebrated joint achievement. At the Queen Elizabeth Olympic Park in east London, which had hosted the incredible 2012 Olympics, the trio unveiled the Heads Together campaign. The plan was to bring together eight charities to change perceptions about mental health. In order to give each of them their own space, the three royals would focus on a different component of mental well-being. William would target young men at risk for suicide, while Catherine would focus on childhood mental health. Harry would help serving soldiers and veterans cope with the mental health challenges they often face, while highlighting the 'invisible injuries' of their service. The plan, in practice, seemed a logical way of using their combined star power while also giving them individual platforms to shine but, behind the glossy video and successful launch day, William and Catherine were already sowing the seeds of their new direction.

They were not the only ones charting a new path. Just a few weeks later, in July 2016, Harry was set up by a mutual friend on a blind date with the glamorous American television actress Meghan Markle. Three weeks later, after two back-to-back dates, they were camping out under the stars in Botswana, and Harry was smitten. Meghan was beautiful, intelligent, articulate and already in the public eye through her role in the popular legal drama *Suits*. Not only that, but she had spoken eloquently at the United Nations on women's rights and flown to Afghanistan to support US troops. The perfect combination, Harry thought.

Harry had not so secretly longed for a successful relationship for many years, but had had a succession of girlfriends who, for one reason or another, had decided that the scrutiny that came with being with him was too much to bear. He was now 31 and had grown tired of being lumped with William and Catherine on their public engagements. Cracks had been beginning to form behind closed doors. The two princes had been at loggerheads over their desire to establish their own way of working, which courtiers diplomatically described as a 'clash of personalities'. William was thought to be more considered, someone who saw the bigger picture and the potential to play the long game, whereas Harry wanted to do things that had immediate results so he could move on to the next thing or the next project.

In an interview with Roya Nikkhah of the *Sunday Times* two months before he met Meghan, Harry spoke of his efforts to 'stay relevant' at a time when it was perceived that he feared being surpassed in popularity by his nephew and niece. 'I'm in this privileged position and I will use it for as long as I can, or until I become boring, or until George ends up becoming more interesting,' Harry said. 'There's nothing worse than going through a period in your life where you're making a massive difference and then suddenly, for whatever reason it is, whether it's media or the public perception of you, you drop off. You want to make a difference but no one's listening to you.'

After leaving the army in 2015, Harry had been at a crossroads, not only with regard to considerations about how he could combine his career with his attachment to duty, but also his capacity to have a romantic relationship, with his relationships with Chelsy Davy and Cressida Bonas having failed. In the

CHAPTER TEN

clearest indication of where his thinking lay, he said, 'I'm not putting work before the idea of a family, marriage and all that kind of stuff,' but went on to reveal the 'massive paranoia that sits inside of me'. He was desperate to settle down and have a family, and the Duke and Duchess of Cambridge were capturing media headlines with theirs. On 24 September 2016, they embarked on a highly anticipated tour of Canada, accompanied by their three-year-old son, Prince George, and one-year-old daughter, Princess Charlotte. From the moment they stepped off the plane to a rapturous welcome in Victoria, British Columbia, any rumblings about the Canadians considering a different relationship with the monarchy seemed to disappear. The die had been well and truly cast when it came to the future of the institution, and Harry knew it.

He and Meghan kept their relationship secret, meeting covertly in both Toronto, Canada – where Meghan lived – and London – where Harry lived – but on 30 October 2016 that changed. In a world exclusive, Camilla Tominey, the then royal editor of the *Sunday Express*, wrote that Harry was 'secretly dating' Meghan Markle, a US actress, human rights campaigner and, controversially, a divorcee. The story was immediately followed up by news outlets around the world.

Not long before the story broke, Harry had plucked up the courage to share his secret with his brother and sister-in-law. 'Fuck off!' was William's initial reaction. In his memoir, *Spare*, Harry talked of his surprise when William and Catherine confessed they were 'regular – nay – religious viewers of *Suits*'. Meghan had later met the Queen during a chance meeting in Windsor, when Harry popped in to see his cousin Eugenie, and had been introduced to William at his Kensington Palace home. Both meetings had gone well. She had pulled off a perfect curtsy to the Queen and managed to charm William, even if he felt a little awkward after receiving a hug on arrival. According to one source, Catherine described Meghan as 'friendly', albeit erring on the side of somewhat over-friendly, with a 'touch of California' about her. Yet the course of true love never did run smooth and the onslaught of the media interest changed things overnight. Journalists and photographers were dispatched to camp outside Meghan's house, descend upon the set of her show and knock on her mother's door. They tracked down estranged family members and ex-boyfriends and offered huge sums of money to her ex-husband, American film producer Trevor Engelson, who she was married to for three years between 2011 and 2014.

The granular details of Meghan's life were suddenly Fleet Street currency, and the boundaries of taste and decency became blurred. Outlandish headlines began to appear, such as a story in the *Sun*, headlined 'Harry's girl on Pornhub'. The article in question detailed how scenes from *Suits* featuring Meghan in her bra or in a steamy clinch with a co-star, which could hardly be considered pornographic, also appeared on an adult website. Another article on the *Mail Online* containing blatant racial undertones ran, 'Harry's girl is (almost) straight outta Compton: Gang-scarred home of her mother revealed – so will he be dropping by for tea?' Ofcom, the UK's communications regulator, received hundreds of complaints about the piece but no action was taken against the publisher.

Harry's reaction was furious and swift. A source quoted in *Courtiers: The Hidden Power Behind the Crown*, by the former *Times* journalist Valentine Low, suggested that this might have had a lot to do with Meghan's insistence that if he didn't publicly defend her, she would finish the relationship: 'She was saying "If you don't put out a statement confirming I'm your girlfriend, I'm going to break up with you."' Without consulting his father or brother, as the hierarchy of a constitutional monarchy

CHAPTER TEN

would normally dictate, he instructed the Kensington Palace communications team to respond at once. On 8 November 2016, a statement was issued highlighting 'a wave of abuse and harassment ... the racial undertones of comment pieces; and the outright sexism and racism of social media trolls and web article comments' that Meghan has been subjected to. Harry had taken a stand, but he had left his father and brother utterly furious. A royal source said, 'The feeling was that Harry had made them both look bad. Granted, he was rightly outraged about the treatment his girlfriend was receiving, some of the coverage was utterly disgusting, but the royal family have a specific way or process of doing things. This wasn't it.'

The media's tone may have dampened in response to Harry's broadside, but the interest in their relationship did not. Harry was infuriated that his father and brother admonished him for his rash actions, and the tense conversations left Harry astounded that his own kin were refusing to offer their support, even after their spouses had endured years of being hounded by the media. William was angered that their shared communications team had not thought to consult him before issuing such a formal rebuke. He also, as Harry related in his memoir, questioned the seriousness of Harry's relationship to his face. Harry also says that William openly mocked him for suggesting that their late mother sent Meghan to him in some form of spiritual guidance, 'Well now, Harold ... I'm not sure about that. I wouldn't say THAT!' Harry did not like having his feelings challenged, nor did he appreciate being told what to do. It is not hard to sympathise with Harry here. Why should his older brother have any say over who he should date or how he should feel? Yet William's inference that his feelings were not valid did not settle well with Harry. A palace source close to the brothers told how this period did indeed mark an outward shift in their relations.

Suddenly it was harder to get them in the same room, each giving various excuses as to why they could not – or perhaps would not – be available to engage with meetings together.

Although William had told Nicholas Witchell that he was part of 'a normal family', they were all also part of the royal family. Just as Harry would discover a year later when discovering that he needed his grandmother's permission to marry, there were rules and protocols to follow that not only affected the individual, but the wider family and the institution. Was William simply looking out for his brother, or did he have an eye on the impact on the monarchy if Harry were to marry a woman who, at the time, he barely knew? While that may have been his obvious concern, the way he asked the question, and his audacity to ask it at all, would drive a wedge between the brothers that could possibly be seen as the precursor to the eventual demise of their bond.

William's questioning over the statement composed by Jason Knauf, who served as William, Catherine and Harry's communications secretary from 2015, in defence of Meghan also irked Harry considerably. While Knauf was not duty-bound to run statements like this past William, Harry feared that William would start micro-managing him and insisting on being kept abreast of any future interactions Harry might have with the media. Matters were complicated by the physical distance between the brothers: Harry was spending more time travelling back and forth to Canada to see Meghan. 'The relationship between them [William and Harry] was already tense and this didn't help,' said a former aide.

> Harry was intent on the palace doing more, he felt as though William wasn't backing him up and had already told him to slow down with the relationship and the criticism

CHAPTER TEN

of the media, which only served to anger Harry even more. Was William looking out for his brother or himself? Only he would know that, but it was clear even back then that things were heading in the wrong direction.

In July 2017 William finished his last shift as an air ambulance pilot, marking the end of an era and the start of life as a fully fledged senior working royal. The family moved back to London, and on 4 September 2017 Kensington Palace announced Catherine was pregnant with their third child. Meanwhile, Harry's relationship had continued at pace. By coincidence the September 2017 location for the Invictus Games – the international sporting event created by Harry in 2014 for wounded, injured and sick service members and veterans – was Toronto, Canada, which would provide the perfect backdrop for Harry and Meghan to put on a show of unity. As Harry celebrated the superhuman exploits of the brave ex-servicemen and women, and Meghan, dressed in a fashionable oversized white 'husband's shirt', flashed her trademark smile, the couple looked as though they were capable of shutting out the negativity and taking on the world.

By October 2017, had Harry engineered a private conversation with the Queen during a hunt on her Sandringham estate, where she granted him permission to get engaged. Following the monarch giving her blessing, as is required for the first six in line to the throne, Harry approached William: he wanted to take two round diamonds from one of their mother's bracelets to create an engagement ring, which would also include a three-carat conflict-free cushion-cut diamond he had sourced from Botswana.

William again warned his brother about the speed at which the relationship had progressed, urging him to take his time. In *Spare*, Harry related how he took issue with William's description of Meghan as an 'American actress'. Lovestruck, he was in no mood to listen. A source said:

> It's easy to forget now, given everything that has gone on, but William did find Meghan quite refreshing at first. He was genuinely happy for Harry and only wanted the best for him. Meghan made him happy and if she had been prepared to take a chance on their relationship, then he certainly would have never stood in their way. If there was one thing he was uneasy about, it was a clash of styles. William was pretty down to earth but he did like a certain amount of deference, whereas when Meghan came in she was very upbeat and had a sense of that Americanised 'go get 'em' attitude, which was very alien to his world, or most other Brits for that matter. He definitely saw it as a potential problem on the horizon. But on the other hand, if Harry was married, he [William] would be able to concentrate on what he wanted to do, rather than worrying about his little brother.

Meghan and Catherine were two women from incredibly different worlds and very different backgrounds. Meghan had crafted a successful career for herself, while Catherine had essentially had one job. Perhaps two if you count working for the family business. They did not dress in the same way or act in the same way. But despite this – and at first the contrast between the two women was largely contrived by the media – Catherine was, according to sources, willing to give Meghan a chance. She adored Harry and had urged William to maintain his relationship with his brother despite their growing differences. Catherine and Sophie, the then Countess of Wessex and now Duchess of Edinburgh, had attempted to assist Meghan as she assimilated

CHAPTER TEN

into royal life, but their 'repeated attempts' were not responded to. Charles had also welcomed Meghan into the family, going on to give her the nickname 'Tungsten', in reference to the metal known for being tough and unbending under extreme pressure. A former courtier said, 'He [Charles] was very fond of her and in the early days found her charming to be around. Meghan was engaging, polite and was clearly in love with his son, so there were certainly no apparent issues he felt the need to address.'

On 4 November 2017, Harry created a makeshift romantic setting, laying out a blanket surrounded by electric candles in the garden of Nottingham Cottage. Meghan said yes. Sixteen months after their first blind date, she and Harry were engaged.

Planning a normal wedding has the propensity to bring out the best and worst in people; the stress created by a royal wedding – managed by the institution and the establishment, with a very public element – only serves to magnify that. Much coverage and commentary have been devoted to Harry and Meghan's behaviour throughout the planning, documenting rows around everything from Harry's treatment of royal staff (the journalist Robert Jobson reported Harry's insistence that 'What Meghan wants, Meghan gets') to Meghan's security.

Meghan became a target on social media owing to her biracial heritage and Harry demanded that action be taken. Royal aides informed him they were powerless to act, so he turned his attention to the royal protection teams funded by the Home Office. When told any such protection would not be provided until after he and Meghan were married, Harry was incredulous and appealed to his father and brother to intervene. The Prince of Wales rightly insisted he could not become involved in a government decision, especially one where any costs would be footed by taxpayers, but Harry was well aware that Catherine had not only received unofficial guidance from the palace when merely his brother's girlfriend, but that she had also qualified for round-the-clock protection as soon as they became engaged. One rule for him and another for me, Harry thought.

Prince Charles's decision was final, though, and William's subsequent unwillingness to help sparked a row that ignited a long-running and ugly feud. A source said: 'To say Harry wasn't happy would be an understatement. He was mightily pissed off. He wanted action taken immediately and while there was a lot of sympathy for him and Meghan, especially by anyone who had seen the sort of unhinged comments online, which weren't exactly isolated incidents, he had a point. But when he didn't get his way, things suddenly ratcheted up.' With this in mind, it's clear why Harry felt so much frustration in 2020, when he and Meghan announced they were stepping down as working royals to go and live in the United States, and subsequently discovered that they would no longer qualify for security. The subject would become a festering wound for Harry, especially after both he and his wife were the subject of death threats following their marriage.

This feud led to a distinct change in atmosphere in the run-up to the wedding, not only between the brothers but also in the household. William and Catherine had worked hard to foster a good working relationship with their staff, encouraging relaxed dress codes, a young and vibrant team, and creating a motivating culture. By contrast, one former staff member recalled how when Meghan was told she would be in line for a royal title her excitement was palpable. 'She started saying "I'm going to be a Duchess, can you believe it? I am going to be a Duchess" – she was almost leaping out of her seat.' Valentine Low, in *Courtiers*, recounts how at the Queen's request, the most senior member of her staff, the Lord Chamberlain, Earl Peel, spoke to Harry and Meghan about the inner workings

CHAPTER TEN

of the palace while Harry's private secretary Ed Lane Fox and David Manning worked in the background to present options to the couple for where they could best fit within the institution. These were the attempts at getting the newly engaged couple used to how things were run, how engagements and tours were decided and the overall hierarchy of a hereditary monarchy and everything that went with it. Yet it was not enough.

As the tensions around planning the wedding ratcheted up, so did complaints from members of the team – going right up to the top. In July 2025, the royal author Sally Bedell Smith, in her *Royals Extra* newsletter, claimed that Lady Elizabeth Anson, a cousin and close confidante of Elizabeth II, felt that the monarch had been left deeply hurt when Harry 'was rude to her for ten minutes' in a meeting in the lead-up to the nuptials. The Queen was upset that Harry had asked the Archbishop of Canterbury to perform the ceremony at St George's Chapel, Windsor Castle, instead of the Dean of Windsor, as tradition would dictate. Bedell Smith described how Meghan 'refused' to tell the Queen about her wedding dress and had insisted on wearing a veil, which the Queen privately disagreed with, due to her being a divorcee. Lady Anson, who died aged 79 in 2020, had helped plan many royal events, including the Queen's 90th birthday celebrations, the Queen and Prince Philip's 70th wedding anniversary, and William and Catherine's wedding. At the behest of the Queen, Lady Anson offered her assistance to Harry and Meghan, but Meghan told her she was not required. Lady Elizabeth said the fiery exchange with her grandson left the Queen 'hurt beyond belief'.

A source told how, upon discovering the nature of the exchange, William remonstrated with his brother for his 'unforgivable behaviour'. Just weeks earlier, Harry had launched into a tirade against the Queen's dresser of nearly 30 years, Angela

Kelly, over the delivery of a tiara that Meghan had chosen to wear on the wedding day. The source recalled:

> It was a very stressful time, tensions were high, people were running on empty and generally working themselves to the bone trying to get across all the detail for the wedding. [William] saw what was happening and apologised on behalf of his brother on more than one occasion. [William and Catherine] had spent a considerable amount of time fostering a really nice and relaxed working atmosphere and in those few months it was utterly extinguished, people were leaving all the time, it was horrendous.

Palace insiders suggest William and Catherine were fearful not only of the effect on team morale, but also their capacity to work with Harry and Meghan moving forward. 'In one camp you had the people who cared, wanted those working in the household to enjoy themselves while working there, and on the other side it was something different every day. Nothing was ever good enough, there were constant complaints. It was exhausting.'

The country was swept up in a wave of emotion and goodwill towards the couple on their wedding day on 19 May 2018. But relations inside the palace could not have been more different. By July 2018, William and Catherine had invited Harry and Meghan to their home to stage clear-the-air talks. The resulting exchange did not bode well for the future. Harry and Meghan were unwilling to concede they were responsible for the departure of two of Meghan's PAs, or for the general desperate atmosphere, in which members of staff reported they were sick with stress. William accused Meghan of being difficult and rude and according to Harry, pointed directly at his wife. A source said: 'The whole atmosphere was ugly.'

CHAPTER TEN

William had only just returned from a historic historic five-day tour of the Middle East, including the first official visit by a senior royal to Israel and the Palestinian territories. The trip focused on the themes of reconciliation and cultural heritage, and took in sites such as the Holocaust memorial Yad Vashem, the Mount of Olives, where his great-grandmother, Prince Philip's mother, Princess Alice, is buried, as well as poignant pilgrimages to the Old City of Jerusalem, and a Palestinian refugee camp in the city of Ramallah.

William has long been interested in world affairs, in particular the fractious political landscape that has plagued the Middle East for over a century. Although the visit was carefully designed to be 'non-political', his meetings with Israeli prime minister Benjamin Netanyahu and Palestinian president Mahmoud Abbas, acknowledging Israel's 70th anniversary while addressing Palestinian concerns, would normally be considered a diplomatic minefield but were successfully negotiated. Welcomed as a 'prince and a pilgrim' by the Israeli president, Reuven Rivlin, William did not appear fazed when was requested to convey a 'message of peace' to Abbas on the next leg of his journey.

It was the biggest diplomatic test of William's life. It would also strike a chord with him that endured beyond his visit. Indeed, his senior advisers at the time briefed that William saw his potential involvement in this part of the world as a 'lifelong mission'. William is acutely aware of the royal family's relationships with their counterparts in the region, and they are relationships that William continues to enjoy and take pride in. During the same trip, William met Crown Prince Hussein bin Abdullah al-Hashimi of Jordan, and visited the historical site of Jerash, where he posed at the exact spot Catherine had visited with her family when she was a child living in the country. William's relationship with the Crown Prince Hussein bin

Abdullah al-Hashimi, a young man who appreciates the expectations of him as an heir and future leader, continues to this day.

On his return to Britain, William instructed his closest aides to help him formulate a list of ideas for how he could further his interest and influence in the region. In July 2018, Tony Blair, who served as prime minister of the United Kingdom from 1997 to 2007, was invited to Kensington Palace to meet William, where for more than three hours the two men discussed ways in which the prince could engage with the Middle East in the future.

A former senior courtier who set up the meeting said:

> William came away from that visit incredibly inspired. From talking to the world leaders to engaging with refugees in the camp in Ramallah, he was engaged in personal stories and that's what stayed with him. It certainly sparked something.
>
> When Tony Blair came in, he was very direct. He said, 'The direction of progress is through conversations, it's difficult and requires a lifetime of engagement,' but he believed William could be an incredible ambassador. Blair said it was all about getting to know the people at the centre of any situation and William was very clear he was ready to engage. It was incredibly important to him and absolutely still is.
>
> There was a lot of talk at the time, and there had been even more since, of William growing into a statesman role. But this is what he has been doing all his life. He has been engaging with people at the very top of international relations for many years and will continue to do so throughout his whole existence.

Harry and Meghan, the new Duke and Duchess of Sussex, undertook a tour of their own in October 2018 to Australia,

Fiji, Tonga and New Zealand. On the face of it, it was a great success. Huge crowds greeted them wherever they went, Harry's Invictus Games were celebrated once more and the royal family's popularity Down Under was sky high. But behind the scenes a crisis was threatening to envelop the institution. On 26 October, when Harry and Meghan were flying back from Tonga, Kensington Palace press secretary Jason Knauf, who had missed the tour with a broken collarbone, wrote an email to his boss, Prince William's private secretary Simon Case, outlining a series of bullying allegations against the Duchess of Sussex – the same issues that William and Catherine had already tried to confront her about. The concerns outlined by Knauf, including that Meghan drove two personal assistants out of the household and undermined the confidence of a third member of staff, would not emerge until two and a half years later, in a report in *The Times*, prompting Buckingham Palace to launch an immediate investigation. What would happen in that period would question the core values and future of the monarchy like nothing before.

11
ALL CHANGE

The planning and execution of Harry and Meghan's wedding and the subsequent discussions over their future role pushed relations across the household they shared with William and Catherine to near breaking point. Harry and Meghan felt they were not being listened to and decided to establish themselves away from Kensington Palace. On 14 March 2019 they announced that the Queen had agreed to create a new household for them, which would be stationed at Buckingham Palace. The decision coincided with a move out of Nottingham Cottage and into the more family-orientated Frogmore Cottage. These were quarters that had, over the past two years, been renovated for Harry and Meghan at a cost of £2.4 million to the taxpayer (although a year later the couple paid the money back, following uproar over their decision to leave their royal roles). While the separation of the two households may have seemed a logical step behind the scenes – Harry and William were now married and well into their 30s – it was the first public sign of a crisis that was threatening to envelop the wider institution.

Harry and Meghan's distrust of their senior team had begun just months after their wedding, amid mounting concern over their treatment of royal aides. This was the context in which the communications secretary, Jason Knauf, had emailed Simon Case, appealing for guidance: he could sense that there might be further trouble ahead. A palace source described relations between

CHAPTER ELEVEN

Harry, Meghan and the staff as 'very, very bad'. 'It had reached an intolerable situation for so many of them, there were a lot of issues surrounding people needing time off work, not wanting to come in or be on engagements on duty with Harry or Meghan. Everything possible was being done at all stages to help them but nothing was ever good enough.' In *Spare* Harry claimed Meghan had gone out of her way to create a happy working environment, checking in on staff who were ill and brightening up the dark and cold office with lamps and heaters. He said: 'Despite what certain people were saying about her, I never heard her speak a bad word about anybody, or to anybody. On the contrary, I watched her redouble her efforts to spread kindness.'

At the beginning of 2019, William arranged to see his brother at his home to question him directly over Meghan's behaviour towards palace staff. While William's account of what happened that day has never been heard, sources close to the Prince of Wales insist that the Duke of Sussex's recollection of events was 'massively overblown'. The suggestion of an altercation at Nottingham Cottage in which Harry claimed his brother physically assaulted him has been questioned by several sources with knowledge of the incident. One said, 'It was a cheap shot [from Harry] to present such an argument. Tensions were running very high and yes there certainly were cross words exchanged that on reflection were regrettable, but the prince [William] is adamant there was no physical violence.'

The context of the fracas is, however, not debated. Harry claimed William echoed the narrative of the tabloid press, calling his wife 'difficult', 'rude' and 'abrasive'. Sources close to the future king suggest that, while they could not confirm the specific language William used during the exchange, 'it would have been a fair assessment if he did'. Another source said, 'To accuse William of peddling the tabloid narrative is ridiculous.

[William and Catherine] had assembled a happy team and cultivated a good working environment that was being actively destroyed on a daily basis. People were being ground down by both Meghan and Harry.' Another source said, 'It wasn't peddling a tabloid narrative to stick up for staff that were deeply unhappy to the point of walking away or having their mental health being affected.' Whatever the truth about the altercation, the stage had already been set for a parting of ways.

Sources suggest that Catherine, who had so long been a voice of reason in the brothers' previous squabbles, decided she could do no more to bring them together. Catherine has always favoured reason over conflict. It was how she had been brought up, in a household that resolved differences with dialogue rather than by bearing grudges. At first she had thought William and Harry's squabbles were rooted in immaturity or stubbornness, on both sides, but Harry and Meghan's attitude towards palace staff, who she and William cared about, set the couples on an entirely different course. Following Harry and Meghan's wedding, things were undeniably different. One source who knew both couples well at this time suggested William and Catherine felt the Sussexes had 'an agenda'. A source said:

> They definitely thought the Sussexes' behaviour stemmed from something more than being difficult. The whole atmosphere between them was pretty toxic. Meghan was being bullish, Kate found her abrasive. There was definitely a hope from her side [Catherine's] that William could try and talk to Harry and settle things but that didn't exactly happen … and at the end of the day, she had three young children, who were her focus and if anything she saw the inevitability of the parting of ways, although perhaps not to the extent of what eventually happened.

CHAPTER ELEVEN

Another former senior courtier said,

> William and Catherine had fostered a very nice working environment for everyone in their office, they made sure people had a decent amount of time off, they remembered birthdays and celebrated anniversaries, that sort of thing. They didn't need to work at this, it's just who they are. Then when they discovered that people were being treated badly, it had a direct effect on them because many of these people had previously worked for them, so they wanted to do something about it immediately.

The move to Windsor and the establishing of their private office at Buckingham Palace would take the Sussexes further away from the Cambridges both physically and metaphorically. But William and Catherine held on to the belief that starting a family and having some space away from the London royal bubble would at least give Harry and Meghan an opportunity to take stock of how things were playing out. They had endured the stress of planning a wedding, as well as the further drama of Meghan's father not being able to attend, ultimately due to his health problems, which brought even more press attention.

And, soon after, Harry and Meghan welcomed their first child, a son, Archie, born on 6 May 2019. The couple's unease about their relationship with the media was underlined when it emerged Meghan would not pose on the steps of the hospital after giving birth, as Princess Diana and Catherine had done before her; nor would they share details of their son's chosen godparents.

It is hard to disagree with this parental choice, but what irked members of the family was that it then emerged that Harry and Meghan had entered negotiations with the British television network ITV to have its news anchor Tom Bradby and a film crew document their tour of Southern Africa in September 2019. It is quite obvious how contradictory this stance appeared to others within the institution. 'Bloody ludicrous,' said one former aide. 'In fact, it was insulting and just incredibly foolish. If you want one thing, such as making a stand on privacy, then there will be a great deal of sympathy from the public where children are concerned ... but you can't parade around New York with your celebrity friends ... signing up for documentaries if you are actually serious.'

(Meghan's choice of venue for her baby shower in February 2019 had caused a great deal of controversy. Not only for its location and guest list, but for the complete lack of consideration she had given her communications staff. Friends including Serena Williams and Amal Clooney hosted a party at the exclusive Mark Hotel in the city, renting out the penthouse suite, at a reported cost of $500,000. Meanwhile, as revealed in Valentine Low's book, *Courtiers*, Meghan had also already lined up a tell-all interview with US chatshow queen Oprah Winfrey, which was scheduled for the autumn but then postponed to March 2021 for unconfirmed reasons.)

Tom Bradby had been friendly with both William and Harry since before he conducted William and Catherine's engagement interview. Bradby was well aware that the brothers' relationship was at breaking point, as was Harry and Meghan's future within the institution, and he and ITV saw the documentary as an opportunity to uncover sensational revelations.

It was billed as the moment that would set Harry and Meghan apart from the rest of the royal family: young, relatable, and engaged with Africa in a way no other member of the family had been before. Already, William as well as senior Kensington Palace aides were on the alert. 'Oh, we thought it would be nuclear,' said a former aide. 'It was collective tin hat time.' On the Sussexes' first engagement, in Cape Town on 23 September,

CHAPTER ELEVEN

Meghan, dressed in a striking black and white wrap dress by the ethical Malawian brand Mayamiko, delivered an emotional and rousing speech to teenage girls living in one of the most deprived parts of South Africa. Standing on a tree stump in the middle of a playground at the women and children's centre in the crime-ridden Nyanga township, Meghan said she stood with them 'as a woman of colour and as your sister'. For the royal family, it was a step into uncharted territory. To observers who witnessed the event at the time, though, it felt like a possibility of what the royal family could harness with Meghan as a central figure.

Meghan's introduction to the royal family had been anything but steady. She had endured the insatiable attention from a global media that had been captivated by her relationship with Prince Harry. Her background had been dissected and her fragile relationship with her father exposed. Prior to Meghan's wedding, Thomas Markle was exposed for colluding with a British newspaper to stage photos showing him being measured for his wedding suit, reading a book on British history and looking up reports about the wedding in an internet cafe. He pulled out of attending just five days before he was due to walk his daughter down the aisle, and in August of that year, Meghan had to write him a letter pleading with him to stop engaging with the media. The letter was subsequently given by Thomas to the *Mail on Sunday*, which published extracts of it in February 2019. Incensed at the invasion of her privacy, Meghan and Harry instructed royal lawyers to issue legal proceedings against the newspaper. But in *Courtiers* Valentine Low recounts a meeting with the palace's solicitor Gerrard Tyrrell, from the firm Harbottle & Lewis, and other advisers including the Prince of Wales's former communications secretary Paddy Harverson, who had taken on an informal advisory role at the palace. They all recommended that Meghan took no action.

The result was a secret severing of ties with the Buckingham Palace legal advisers: Meghan instead took her grievances to Schillings, a London-based legal firm with a fearsome reputation, favoured by celebrities and high-net-worth individuals. Unbeknown to the palace courtiers employed specifically to advise and protect the reputations of the royal family, the Sussexes had set out on a path that would see them confront the British media head on.

This was never more apparent than at the end of their ten-day tour of Southern Africa. The tour had produced acres of positive coverage, about everything from the Sussexes taking four-month-old baby Archie to meet the human rights activist Archbishop Desmond Tutu, to Harry following in his mother's footsteps by visiting an Angolan minefield to support the HALO Trust. Then, with a full day of engagements left to complete, the couple announced that Meghan was suing the *Mail on Sunday*'s parent company Associated Newspapers for publishing the letter from her father. Via a specially created single-page website, Harry then released a 500-word statement accusing the media of 'double standards' for covering their tour favourably while continuing to publish critical pieces about the couple, and announced that they would be taking a stand against what he called the 'ruthless campaign that has escalated over the past year'. Invoking the highly emotive use of his mother's legacy, Harry said, 'There comes a point when the only thing to do is to stand up to this behaviour, because it destroys people and destroys lives,' and spoke of his fear of 'history repeating itself'. He added, 'I've seen what happens when someone I love is commoditised to the point that they are no longer treated or seen as a real person. I lost my mother and now I watch my wife falling victim to the same powerful forces.'

Back in London, shockwaves reverberated around the palaces. Harry and Meghan had dropped a bombshell of monu-

CHAPTER ELEVEN

mental proportions, ignoring the advice from palace lawyers and their senior advisers. A former courtier said:

> If you think people were nervous before they went [on the tour], taking in the decision to bring a documentary crew along, then that atmosphere just ramped up to eleven. By this stage everyone was aware relations were already at near breaking point and that the Sussexes were a pair of loose cannons. No one in the wider household trusted them, and then they go and blow up their own tour after so much good work. The whole PR strategy, if you can call it that, seemed utter madness from the outside.

What's more, it was clear that Harry and Meghan had been planning this move for some time: the website used to deliver Harry's message had been registered on 14 March 2019, a whole five months previously. According to Valentine Low, Harry had called his grandmother to inform her of the impending legal action against the *Mail*. The Prince of Wales and William and Catherine were duly made aware too, and waited for the tsunami of attention to hit. Sources suggest William and Catherine, along with their staff, were at an utter loss to describe how and why the Sussexes had chosen such a course of action. Courtiers insist the palace had 'bent over backwards' to accommodate Harry and Meghan's impassioned feelings on media intrusion and to placate them when family relations appeared to become further strained.

Sir David Manning, the former British ambassador to the US and special adviser on constitutional and international affairs to the two princes, had, a year before the Sussex's tour, begun to mastermind a potential major international role for the couple that would enable them to escape Britain for half the year, while fulfilling their duty to the Crown. Details of the hybrid role would emerge on 21 April 2019, when it was leaked to the *Sunday Times*. The proposal, the newspaper said, would give the couple the chance to enjoy a break from the divisions within the royal household while 'harnessing' their global appeal for Britain. The arrangement, in part, stemmed from the precedent set by the Queen and Prince Philip, when they lived in Malta when they were first married, as well as William and Catherine's time in Anglesey. It was hoped it would provide Harry and Meghan some breathing space as a newly married couple to decide what they wanted to do next. Several options were suggested, including making Harry governor-general or deputy governor-general of Australia or Canada, or the couple becoming trade envoys in a post-Brexit world. A former courtier said, 'All of this clearly demonstrates they were hardly left fending for themselves in an environment that wasn't interested in looking after them.' Manning himself told Valentine Low that, 'I thought it was very important when they were starting out, Meghan and Harry should have a vision of what they wanted to do.' But when the financial and security constraints were deemed too great, Manning's plan for Harry and Meghan to be handed an international role was scrapped. 'I absolutely accept there were real problems with it, but it just seemed to me that we needed to try and think really differently about this couple and what role they could play, and particularly play to their strengths.' The failure of the plan was not welcomed by the Sussexes, who still felt aggrieved that they were not being listened to and believed they were being purposely stifled to safeguard William and Catherine's place in the pecking order.

On 18 October, just over two weeks after the Sussexes returned, ITV released a trailer for its documentary *Harry & Meghan: An African Journey* amid a blaze of publicity. Generally, a rule exists in the royal family: its members should refrain from doing anything that might overshadow, or interfere with, another member's important engagements or long-term projects. In the past, given Harry and William's competitive nature, the boundaries had sometimes become blurred when it came to laying claim to certain charitable endeavours, but this was now a decidedly different time. While the Sussexes claim they had little say in the scheduling of the promotional material and indeed the resulting documentary, the trailers were designed to cause maximum effect. William and Catherine were in Pakistan, riding high on the success of a five-day tour that had been celebrated for its sensitive diplomatic and cultural messaging. On their penultimate day, the trailer dropped. In it, Meghan, fresh from meeting Nelson Mandela's widow Graça Machel in Johannesburg, places her hands in the pockets of her affordable £95 dress and, occasionally biting her bottom lip, admits to feeling 'vulnerable' during her pregnancy – and says the experience was 'made really challenging'. When Bradby asks how she is coping behind closed doors, Meghan utters the immortal line: 'Thank you for asking, because not many people have asked if I'm OK. But it's a very real thing to be going through behind the scenes.' The comment would lay the foundations for some of the Sussexes' most remarkable allegations against the royal family, which struck at the heart of the institution.

The full documentary, which aired on 20 October 2019 and was watched by 2.8 million people in the UK, contained a number of damaging allegations for the palace to consider. For the first time Harry openly discussed the damaging rift in his relationship with William, admitting that they were on 'different paths'. In a further break from royal convention, Harry revealed he had come close to a 'complete breakdown' several times and had sought the help of a therapist as he struggled to deal with the devastation of losing his mother, and his troubled relationship with the media. Meghan would go even further, suggesting that her well-being was at a crisis point, and that she had pleaded to her husband, 'it's not enough to just survive something, that's not the point of life. You've got to thrive, you've got to feel happy.' Royal aides on the tour were caught in a state of disbelief and realised that when the documentary was aired it would heap further pressure on the couple. 'There wasn't much consultation with the wider staff,' said one former palace staffer.

> There was a set agenda, agreed with ITV, and Meghan and Harry had a loose plan of how it would play out. Obviously, almost exclusively, we believed it would end up not playing out well for them, but their intention was to show their side of the story, which was always going to be incredibly one-sided anyway because they knew the people they were criticising were very unlikely to respond publicly. The whole thing seemed to detract from everything we had worked on for months and the genuinely good work they were doing or had done on the ground throughout the tour, which just seemed bonkers.

Such a move was outside the parameters of how senior members of the royal family were expected to perform in public. Inside the palace, it delivered as much sadness as it did acute shock.

In the days before the screening, Harry had broken down in tears at the WellChild Awards ceremony for sick children, as he spoke about his journey to fatherhood. It was a concerning sight, leading William to contact his brother immediately to check that he was OK. Clearly, he was not. Speaking to *The Times* at the time, a source described the gulf between the two princes: 'One of them has had a pre-destined path, and the other hasn't. It is not surprising that in any family where you reach a new chapter, that [it] takes a little [time] to settle back in and

CHAPTER ELEVEN

figure out your new routine and your new relationship as it is growing, going forward. He is no longer the baby brother that is across the courtyard [when they lived at Kensington Palace together], and the third wheel to the two of them [the Duke and Duchess of Cambridge].'

William saw the decision by ITV and Bradby to participate in the documentary as having crossed a line. Until that point, some close to William suggest that Bradby, fifteen years older than the prince, had become almost like a father figure to him after they had bonded in the early 2000s during the journalist's time as royal correspondent for the network. On his return from Africa, Bradby contacted William to say he was concerned about Harry's well-being. A source with knowledge of the conversation said William was furious that, as he saw it, Bradby had taken Harry's side. He told Bradby he would speak to Harry to ensure he was OK, but ended the conversation abruptly. Deep down, William believed Harry was in a crisis and needed the support of his family, but that he was taking a course of action that was leading to further division. 'William felt betrayed and severely let down. He considered Tom a friend, they had always got on and Harry was close to him too, but [William] never thought [Bradby] would take a side like he did.' One of the main sticking points was, in William's view, Bradby's unwillingness to ask Harry or Meghan any questions about the true state of affairs in the royal household. The source added, 'Tom knew full well what Meghan was accused of and chose not to raise it in the documentary, while she ran roughshod over the family. As far as [William] was concerned the friendship was over there and then.' Another palace source close to William suggested that while he was perplexed at Bradby's willingness to be a conduit for Harry and Meghan, he never considered any public reaction.

Tom [Bradby] had spent the last couple of years prior to getting Harry and Meghan to agree to doing a documentary, asking almost every single member of the royal family to do one. There literally wasn't a month that went by where he wasn't lodging some form of request to work with him. Everyone knew the brothers were on different paths, as Harry said, and Meghan coming out and saying no one had asked her if she was OK, well that's complete nonsense, as most of the family had spent the last two years making sure she was being welcomed and able to feel comfortable coming into the institution, especially those who had followed the same path as her.

Sources close to William and Catherine suggest the couple became even more deeply concerned for Harry and Meghan's welfare after watching the documentary. A source close to William suggested he had also attempted to help his brother, saying, 'He [William] felt as though somewhere down the line, perhaps it is impossible to even say when, that he lost his brother. He became paranoid, angry, obsessive and firmly rooted in the past. There's no doubt, at that time at least, there was a lot of love and support available for Harry.'

As the fallout continued behind closed doors, the Queen appealed to Harry and Meghan to put aside their differences with the rest of the family and to attend the Royal British Legion Festival of Remembrance at the Albert Hall on Saturday 9 November. The Sussexes agreed but told the Queen they would not join the rest of the royal family for Christmas, instead leaving straight after the event to fly to California to join Meghan's mother, Doria, for Thanksgiving. Royal sources at the time confirmed the couple would take a six-week break from duties, described as a chance to reset following the scrutiny of the tour

CHAPTER ELEVEN

and the documentary, before they left for Canada, where they would spend Christmas. They would return in the new year.

As William and Catherine were still reeling from Harry and Meghan's documentary, another scandal started to emerge. On 21 October 2019, the night after the Sussexes' African travelogue aired, the Channel 4 investigative programme *Dispatches* dug deep into Prince Andrew's 12-year association with the convicted paedophile Jeffrey Epstein. Epstein's death in his prison cell on 10 August 2019 had intensified the spotlight on the duke, whose association with the sex offender was already creating significant harm to the institution. In the documentary, address books and flight logs belonging to the billionaire financier were compared with the duke's schedule, detailing a dozen meetings between them. A month before, the US network NBC News had aired an interview with Virginia Roberts Giuffre, where she alleged that she had been forced to have sex with Epstein and others in his orbit, including Prince Andrew, who she claimed she had sex with on three occasions in 2001, when she was 17 years old. Andrew had always vehemently denied the allegations, but the pressure was building.

Determined to present his side of the story, the duke decided to grant an interview to the BBC's flagship current affairs programme, *Newsnight*. Andrew had acted against the advice of his former press adviser Jason Stein, who later left the palace by mutual consent, and also the Queen's most senior communications chief, Donal McCabe, who had urged Andrew's team to rethink the interview. Instead, he relied solely on his own bravado and the willingness of his dedicated private secretary Amanda Thirsk, who had negotiated the introductions with the *Newsnight* team. Esme Wren, the editor of *Newsnight*, later revealed that following a meeting at Buckingham Palace with Andrew before the interview was agreed, he said he was going to 'refer up', adding 'one assumes that means checking with his mum'.

The extent of the Queen's knowledge of the interview and what it would cover is not exactly known, although sources suggest Andrew merely informed the monarch he was taking part in an interview without detailing the exact nature of the content or its presentation. Donal McCabe, who sat through the entire excruciating interrogation by the BBC's Emily Maitlis, would later deliver a report to the Queen via her private secretary on the full details. He gave a withering assessment that differed drastically from Andrew's evaluation that it had 'gone rather well'.

And so, on 16 November 2019, millions of viewers watched in disbelief as the Queen's son faced an unprecedented grilling for which he seemed hopelessly unprepared. As he squirmed on his chair inside the Blue Drawing Room at Buckingham Palace, Andrew failed to express regret over his relationship with the convicted sex offender or the plight suffered by his countless victims, and went on to not only deny ever meeting Giuffre, but also to give a series of wild and embarrassing explanations, which included being unable to sweat and attending a birthday party at Pizza Express.

The interview was a disaster, not only for Andrew, whose reputation was in tatters, but for the monarchy at large. Suddenly the palace was engaged in a full-scale fire fight, with deepening questions over its relevance in a modern world, even its survival. In the aftermath, William spoke to his father to implore him and the Queen to take immediate action, fearing not only the public backlash but for his own future. A source said,

> Once you understand the fact that everything that happens in the here and now, affects everything in the future, William's future, it is very easy to put yourself in his shoes. He never much liked his uncle and wanted him out of the picture immediately before the rot further set in. William's

CHAPTER ELEVEN

view was that he [Andrew] got himself into the whole mess, so he should be left to his own devices to sort it out away from the family.

Andrew was summoned by the Queen and the Prince of Wales to be told his royal life was over. He was stripped of his royal and military patronages and, in the days that followed, dumped from all his remaining charity associations. Four days later, Andrew announced he was stepping back from royal duties because the scandal had become a 'major disruption' to the royal family. He later said he deeply sympathised with Epstein's victims, and everyone who wanted 'some form of closure'. Andrew's responses and the fact that he had become subject to widespread condemnation gave Giuffre the confidence to give her first UK interview, to the BBC's *Panorama* programme, where, a week after the Maitlis interview, she repeated her allegations, saying, 'It was a really scary time in my life. He knows what happened, I know what happened. And there's only one of us telling the truth.'

The annual Christmas gathering in 2019 was therefore a decidedly quieter affair than usual. Prince Philip was discharged from hospital on Christmas Eve after spending five days receiving treatment for a pre-existing condition, Harry and Meghan were in Canada with Meghan's mum Doria, and Prince Andrew was forced to stay away from public view, even if he did attend the family lunch. In her traditional Christmas broadcast, the monarch presented an optimistic view of her hopes for the future after an extraordinary 12 months, saying, 'The path, of course, is not always smooth, and may at times this year have felt quite bumpy, but small steps can make a world of difference.'

Despite all that had happened, William and Catherine were hopeful that they could break the impasse with Harry and Meghan.

While that may arguably appear naive, considering how bad relations were and went on to be, William was not yet prepared to sacrifice his relationship with his brother and believed there was a chance that the situation could be improved. According to one palace source close to William, he decided over the Christmas period that he would meet with Harry to discuss 'a new direction' with his brother in order 'to keep him within the fold'. William believed that if Harry and Meghan were to take part in more interviews in which they criticised the royal family or any gave any indication that they were thinking of exiting their roles, it would have a potentially catastrophic effect on the institution. It would also have a direct effect on him and Catherine when, after the Queen had passed, they stepped up into new, elevated positions. What he and the rest of the family did not realise, though, was that Harry and Meghan had other ideas.

On 9 January 2020, just days after returning from Canada, and giving the Queen and the Prince of Wales barely ten minutes' notice, they announced in an extraordinary statement their plans to withdraw from their roles and divide their time between Britain and North America. Sources described the royals as being 'bloody furious' at the time, while newspapers carried quotes from insiders describing them as 'hurt and deeply disappointed'.

Harry and Meghan had concluded during their six-week sabbatical on Canada's Vancouver Island that their current way of life was untenable. In his memoir, *Spare*, Harry suggests while in Canada his father forced him to write to him outlining their desire to spend part of the year away from Britain, presenting various scenarios they had dreamed up – such as living and working in South Africa and visiting other Commonwealth countries – to satisfy the Crown. Harry was left despondent after being told by the Prince of Wales, in response to his letter, that they would have to discuss the details in person,

CHAPTER ELEVEN

and no sooner than the end of the month. This agitated him because he believed that their plans were being blocked. On 3 January, Harry called his grandmother to inform her that he and Meghan were returning from their break and wished to discuss their plans 'to create a different working arrangement'. Despite the Queen not being pleased, she agreed to see him in the days that followed to listen to the proposals. The meeting never happened. Harry surmised she had been blocked by the 'men in grey suits' once more, throwing him into a panic. On 8 January the *Sun* ran on its front page a leak of their plan, sending the Sussexes into overdrive. On 9 January, Harry and Meghan published on their Sussex Royal Instagram page and then in detail on a website of the same name, their decision to leave their royal roles to seek 'financial independence' away from the institution. How that would work, they were not entirely clear; outside of his inheritance from his mother's estate, Harry was entirely reliant on his father's goodwill to fund his lifestyle. A message from William's press secretary Jason Knauf to Sara Latham, Harry and Meghan's spokesperson, said it all, replying immediately, 'This is going to go nuclear.' A palace source said, 'Bewilderment is how best to describe it, and yet it was all quite inevitable. We all realised Harry and Meghan had the capacity to do something like that, it was their style. So, the best thing was to regroup and address what was in front of you.' Courtiers were outraged such a course of action had been taken without consultation or the courtesy of informing the palace. After weeks of speculation on their future, the couple had taken the most drastic possible option.

The message read:

> After many months of reflection and internal discussions, we have chosen to make a transition this year in starting to carve out a progressive new role within this institution.

The Duke and Duchess of Cambridge with Prince George, 21 months, during their tour of Australia and New Zealand on 25 April 2014.

Catherine alongside William after giving birth to Princess Charlotte at the Lindo Wing of St Mary's hospital in London, on 2 May 2015.

The Duke and Duchess of Cambridge visit India and Bhutan, 12 April 2016.

Catherine dances with Paddington Bear at the Charities Forum Event at Paddington Station, on 16 October 2017.

The Duke and Duchess of Cambridge and Prince Harry launch mental health campaign Heads Together, 21 April 2016.

The Duke and Duchess of Cambridge leave the Lindo Wing of St Mary's Hospital in Paddington on 23 April 2018, following the birth of Prince Louis.

William touches the Western Wall, 28 June 2018, during his tour of Israel and the Occupied Territories.

The Duchess of Cambridge pulls a pint of lager alongside Prince William during a visit to the Empire Music Hall in Belfast on 27 February 2019.

William and Catherine and their three children attend Trooping the Colour, Buckingham Palace Balcony, 8 June 2019.

The Duke and Duchess of Cambridge visit the north of Pakistan, 16 October 2019.

The Duke of Cambridge opens the new NHS Nightingale Hospital in Birmingham via video link in response to the Covid-19 pandemic, 16 April 2020.

William and Catherine and their three children join in the 'Clap for NHS carers' as the nation celebrated the heroic efforts of emergency responders during the Covid crisis.

William and Harry are separated by their cousin Peter Phillips during the Ceremonial Procession at the funeral of Prince Philip, Duke of Edinburgh, at Windsor Castle on 17 April 2021.

Catherine at the funeral of Prince Philip.

William and Catherine join in the carnival atmosphere in Jamaica following a visit to Bob Marley's childhood home at the Trench Town neighbourhood of Kingston, during the Platinum Jubilee Royal Tour of the Caribbean on 22 March 2022.

William and Catherine take their children to their first day at Lambrook School, near Ascot. on 7 September 2022.

The Prince and Princess of Wales accompanied by the Duke and Duchess of Sussex for a walkabout outside Windsor Castle on 10 September 2022 following the death of Queen Elizabeth II.

The Prince and Princess of Wales attend the Earthshot Prize Awards at the MGM Music Hall at Fenway, Boston, USA, on 2 December 2022.

The Prince and Princess of Wales attend the James Bond *No Time to Die* world premiere at the Royal Albert Hall in London on 28 September 2023.

Prince William, Prince of Wales, touches the St Edward's Crown worn by his father, King Charles III, during the King's Coronation Ceremony inside Westminster Abbey on 6 May 2023.

Catherine announces in a personal video message on 20 March 2024 that she has been diagnosed with cancer.

Catherine shares a sweet moment with Princess Charlotte as she makes a return to public life for the first time since being diagnosed with cancer, attending the Trooping the Colour military parade on 15 June 2024.

The Prince and Princess of Wales, alongside their three children, join King Charles and Queen Camilla on the Buckingham Palace balcony following the Trooping the Colour ceremony in London on 15 June 2025, marking the King's official birthday.

> We intend to step back as 'senior' members of the Royal Family and work to become financially independent, while continuing to fully support Her Majesty The Queen.
>
> It is with your encouragement, particularly over the last few years, that we feel prepared to make this adjustment.

Buckingham Palace rushed out a statement at 6.30pm saying the discussions were at an early stage and included 'complicated issues that will take time to work through'. The next morning the Queen, supported by the Prince of Wales and Prince William, directed all four household teams 'to work together at pace' to find 'workable solutions' to the Sussexes' desire to break free. The full mechanism of government at home, Canada and in the United States would also have to be engaged, owing to the enormous security implications of having senior members of the royal family living overseas. The path ahead was anything but smooth, and yet the monarch declared the negotiations would have to take 'days not weeks'. She did not believe that Harry and Meghan would be able to devise the hybrid role they craved. As far as the Queen was concerned, no one could be a part-time royal.

Negotiations continued round the clock between the three principal private secretaries to the Queen, the Prince of Wales and Prince William: Edward Young, Clive Alderton and Simon Case. A select few of the senior communications team from each household were also involved at a later stage, to draft the wording of five different scenarios that would be presented to the Sussexes to consider. In the meantime, Meghan decided to fly back to Canada with Archie, leaving her husband to face the music alone.

In his book *Courtiers*, Valentine Low described a positive atmosphere within the palace. At one stage, Clive Alderton suggested that if they could get this right then they would be solving a problem for future generations of the royal family who were also not in the direct line of succession. It was Alderton's

CHAPTER ELEVEN

view, and indeed that of William and Harry's foreign affairs adviser, David Manning, that Harry and Meghan could fulfil an international role. Another senior palace source who was part of the negotiations said:

> We'd spent months trying to work out a role for them and every time we thought someone had cracked it, there would end up being several reasons why it couldn't work. Harry being governor-general of Canada wouldn't happen because you need to be Canadian, various ideas of them working across Africa had security implications, or someone else was already doing the job, it was almost an impossible task. Plus, we already knew they were intent on signing commercial deals and that just wasn't going to work within the model. So we kept saying to them, how do you want this to work? Do you actually have a tangible plan that could help us, but we got nothing in return.

On 13 January 2020, five days after the Sussexes' initial statement, Harry was summoned to a meeting at the Queen's Sandringham home. Meghan would dial in from Canada. A source with knowledge of the event recalled that the atmosphere was strained. The optimism that had been shared by the three main households when drafting the five options had dissipated. The day before the meeting, dubbed by the media the 'Sandringham Summit', the *Sunday Times* suggested William had told a friend: 'I've put my arm around my brother all our lives and I can't do that any more; we're separate entities. I'm sad about that. All we can do, and all I can do, is try and support them and hope that the time comes when we're all singing from the same page. I want everyone to play on the team.' In the meeting itself, William was more than saddened; he was angry. A source with knowledge of the meeting said William faced down his brother for putting his 'self-serving' interests above those of the family: 'He accused him of plotting behind the Queen's back and said his behaviour was disgraceful.' William hit back at Harry's suggestion, made during the meeting, that the households had conspired against him and Meghan to create negative stories in the press. 'There was an appeal for calm by the Prince of Wales to bring the conversation back round to the business in hand, but overall it was very tense,' the source added. After an hour of discussions, where Harry was presented with the five options, ranging from option one – keeping the status quo to option three – Harry and Meghan's proposal, a 'half in, half out' model described as 'half-baked, at best' – to option five – a complete severance for Harry and Meghan, with total loss of funding and their security – it was deemed that only one could potentially work.

The Queen declared there could be no 'half in, half out' proposal. If her beloved grandson – who she had much sympathy for, for the pain he had endured throughout his life – or his wife – who she had tried to surround with guidance and good grace – could not agree to row back on their demands, then they would have to accept the consequences. She believed that their proposed hybrid role was at odds with what the job, and the privileged position of a senior member of The Firm, entailed. The Queen couldn't have been clearer. She was adamant that no member of the family could continue as a working member of the family and trade on that connection to earn money in the corporate world. At the meeting, William had joined the chorus of calls from the Queen and the Prince of Wales: he agreed that Harry and Meghan would be far better off staying within the fold. William had even directly appealed to his brother not to leave, to regroup and think again. But Harry was adamant. Despite the consequences of being cut adrift, they were out. The monarchy would be changed for ever.

12

ALL ALONE

The decision by the Duke and Duchess of Sussex to walk away from their duties meant the royal family was losing two of its youngest and most popular figures, who appealed to an international audience and had the capacity to help lead the monarchy in a new direction. Courtiers across the palaces were left scrambling, not only to regain the narrative over how Harry and Meghan's transitional year would look, but also to reassure the public that their departure would have little effect on the future appeal of the institution. Harry and Meghan had proposed pausing their roles as full-time senior working members of the family, in favour of creating a new hybrid way of working. It was their presumption that they would be able to continue taking on public royal engagements while also exploring their options in the corporate world, no doubt with the ability to earn millions of pounds in private deals. Unfortunately for them, those in the palace did not share their enthusiasm. At the Sandringham Summit, this and all other options were ultimately rejected in favour of a complete step back.

The first issue was working out how this could be implemented without further antagonising the couple. Harry and Meghan believed their time in the royal family had become so intolerable that they had no option but to break free, yet Harry was desperate to keep some affiliation with the family so that he would not be forced to walk away from the charities and organisations with which he had built up a genuine connection. Tensions were so high following the meeting at Sandringham that those in the 'no' camp – which included everyone besides Harry and Meghan – were on edge. A source close to William described an 'intense nervousness' following the summit. After the ITV documentary, the palace felt that Harry and Meghan had demonstrated they were not to be trusted. They had cut out their senior staff and colluded with a major broadcaster to torpedo their own royal tour. They had also, by allowing the trailer's release to overshadow the success of William and Catherine's major tour of Pakistan, shown little regard for other members of the family. Furthermore, the Queen, the Prince of Wales, and William and Catherine did not recognise Meghan's accusations about not having been supported. All were concerned that if the couple did not get their way, they would be ready and willing to immediately speak out about the injustices they believed had been visited upon them. The source said:

> The impression was that they [Harry and Meghan] had to be kept close, or they may feel they had nothing to lose and would just blow it all up, while things were still being worked out by the day. That intense nervousness, that if they didn't get what they wanted, could easily result in them suddenly doing an interview with whoever was going to give them maximum exposure totally fed into the pressure of trying to find a solution which would at least buy everyone some time.

The morning of the summit, *The Times* had carried a story suggesting the Duke and Duchess of Sussex felt pushed away from the royal family by the 'bullying' attitude of Prince William. Several sources confirmed that Harry and Meghan's senior communications officers had willingly repeated the allegation to royal correspondents covering the fallout. In an attempt to cool the situation, Buckingham Palace issued a statement that appeared to be signed by both William and Harry, dismissing reports that the Cambridges had been responsible for bullying the Sussexes out of the family. In his memoir, *Spare*, Harry denied he signed the statement, saying he was left 'stunned' after it was published without his knowledge. Harry's ignorance of the clarification is widely disputed. 'It was discussed and agreed with all parties,' a source said. What had started as an attempt to control the narrative had quickly turned into an ugly briefing war between the two households. One source with detailed knowledge of the summit said:

> At all stages, appeals were made for Harry to stay in the camp, that they were all better off together. The Queen, the Prince of Wales and William all said to him, whatever has happened, it can be worked out and we will all help you and Meghan find your way, but Harry wasn't prepared to listen. Of course they were upset at the way in which the Sussexes had gone about making everything so public but there was a willingness to help them and bring in other people to help mediate if needed. The forming of the statement was agreed and published by both brothers at the summit. But Harry simply wasn't interested, so there was little anyone else could do.

On 18 January the true extent of the bitter split was laid bare: a statement from Buckingham Palace announced that Harry and Meghan would step back permanently from their duties and enter a 'transitional year', where they stopped undertaking official royal duties on behalf of the Queen and would cease to use their 'Royal Highness' (HRH) titles. Harry and Meghan would not draw any public funding, but provisions would continue for their security, something that had been of the utmost importance to Harry. While all parties agreed to a 12-month review period, in order to give everyone more time to work through the arrangements, the same palace source said 'no one in the room' believed the Sussexes had any intention of returning to their public roles. On 21 January 2020, Harry returned to Canada to be reunited with Meghan, Archie and their dogs, as they prepared for their new chapter away from royal duties. In his memoir he spoke of his feelings of abandonment, by both his country and his family. 'My emotions are complicated on this subject. I love my Mother Country, and I love my family, and I always will. I just wish, at the second-darkest moment of my life, they'd both been there for me. And I believe they'll look back one day and wish they had too,' he said.

William and Catherine had added reason to be nervous about the Sussexes' departure. Sources close to the couple say William was intensely saddened at his brother's decision to quit. He and Harry had been drifting apart for years, but now he knew deep down that there would be no turning back. He would be losing his brother for ever and his children would lose their uncle and almost certainly not have a relationship with their cousins in the future. Fond memories of their childhood, from helping each other through the tragedy of their mother's death, to growing up in the public eye, were now tarnished by the division at the heart of the family. A former senior courtier said,

> The state of relations between the brothers had actually been strained between them for quite a few years and it goes back to this very, very odd problem in this family, just like every other royal family, which is, if you're born first there is

a path set out for you, and if you're born in any order after that, you're on a different path and it is almost impossible, barring family tragedy, to change those dynamics. That's actually a really unhealthy situation to be in, and so actually what had happened is the brothers as men, as adult men, were possibly artificially and certainly unhealthily bound together, not as brothers, but as workmates. Which was thought of as being fine, but the trajectory of them was always going to be different, so actually this story ends with the fundamental dynamics of the family.

As an 'outsider', Catherine had witnessed the deterioration of William and Harry's relationship. She had seen Harry and Meghan become ever more bitter at having to follow the rules of a hierarchical and hereditary monarchy, until they felt as if they could follow them no longer. Sources suggest Catherine had less interest than her husband in trying to persuade Harry to stay in his current role. She believed William and Harry's fundamental differences as the 'heir and the spare' had created the inevitability of Harry wanting more from his role than being a bit-part player.

Alongside all the issues between the two households, however, William and Catherine had to face the sudden reality that the Prince of Wales's vision of a slimmed-down monarchy was starting to look worryingly thin. The Prince of Wales had taken his lead from his father Prince Philip, advocating for the existence of a smaller pool of royals taking on official duties, which would therefore be less reliant on public funding. Already there had been the departure in absolute disgrace of the Duke of York. And there was little appetite to broaden the profile of minor royals such as Princesses Beatrice and Eugenie, due to them already having forged working lives for themselves outside of the institution. Add to that the age range of the existing working group of royals, of whom 7 of the 11 available were over the age of 70, and serious questions emerged about the monarchy's ability to perform its basic functions in the future. This became a source of angst for William and Catherine. A source said:

> The age of the working group of royals was definitely a concern. Most of them were, at that stage, in their mid-to-late seventies and eighties and the Cambridges had concerns over the lack of people they would be able to call on in the future to help with the workload. Of course, they had an awareness that if you have members of a family business who don't want to pull their weight, then there's little point in them being part of the team, but their concerns were pretty valid when you look at the bigger picture.

Both camps struggled to come to terms with the devastating fallout. William would not be swayed, even by his conviction that he would never see his brother again, while Harry and Meghan remained intent on extracting themselves from the family and taking a path of no return. But little did they know that the entire world would soon be plunged into a historic crisis that would result in even further isolation.

On 9 January 2020, a 61-year-old man was registered as the first death from a virus known as Covid-19, recorded in Wuhan, China. Within weeks, the virus had swept across Europe, and many governments made the unprecedented decision to close their borders and order their citizens into lockdown. On 20 March 2020, the Queen delivered a message urging the people of the United Kingdom to 'come together to work as one' in an attempt to defeat the coronavirus pandemic. The monarch, then 93, and the Duke of Edinburgh, then 98, retreated to Windsor Castle just hours before the United Kingdom entered its own

CHAPTER TWELVE

lockdown, on 23 March. The same day, Prime Minister Boris Johnson declared a 'moment of national emergency', imposing draconian restrictions of movement to protect against the spread of the disease. Under emergency powers, police were given authority to enforce new quarantine rules, with people permitted to only leave their homes for essential supplies, or to take part in one form of daily exercise, attend medical appointments or absolutely necessary work.

As the country was gripped by fear, glued to news updates on the spread of the virus and the worsening death toll, William and Catherine gathered their team in an attempt to devise a strategy for an uncertain future. The couple had already introduced home-working for their staff in the days before the lockdown, instructing them to take care of themselves and their families before thinking about how they could help the country. One former senior courtier said:

> In the lead-up to the lockdown, everyone was ordered to pack up their things, take whatever they needed from the office and to work from home immediately. Almost straight away the thinking by the principals [William and Catherine] was, how can we as a team help, whether that was helping the NHS with the spread of information through their presence virtually or on the social media channels, local services, schools or communities. It was very much centred on using our network of contacts through government and the charity sectors to be available without becoming a distraction or hindrance to what was being advised by the government, which was changing every day.

William and Catherine, like thousands of other parents across the country, had to get to grips with homeschooling two of their children, with little clue of what to expect in a situation that deteriorated daily. The couple decamped to Anmer Hall in Norfolk and together created a timetable for George, who was six, and Charlotte, who was just four, to either do schoolwork, or arts and crafts, or take part in home-style exercise classes with personal trainer Joe Wicks, dubbed 'the nation's PE teacher' as a result of the 'PE With Joe' YouTube videos he released during the pandemic. William joked with one aide that, 'If I had any hair left, I'd have pulled it out already,' as he and Catherine felt the weight of trying to keep their children entertained while also following the lockdown rules. Afternoons were mostly spent attempting to convince the children to help with dinner preparations, creating shopping lists, baking breads and making pasta, and eating together.

Two days after the lockdown was enforced, Buckingham Palace announced that the Prince of Wales had tested positive for the virus. He was staying in Scotland on the Balmoral estate and was said to have mild symptoms, but his diagnosis sent shockwaves through the palace. A source said, 'Everyone was incredibly nervous. William spoke to his father and was given assurances that he was feeling OK, but suddenly everyone was on high alert as to what could possibly come next.'

For the first time in history the Queen took her weekly audience with the prime minister by phone. A picture released by the palace showed the monarch talking on a handset that looked as if it was from the 1970s, placed on a desk surrounded by figurines of corgis, in front of a mantlepiece with a clock flanked by statuettes of horses. It was a sign of the methods of communication that would have to be swiftly dragged into the modern world if the royal family was to carry on embodying one of the Queen's famous family mottos: 'We have to be seen to be believed.'

In a statement the Queen said:

CHAPTER TWELVE

> As Philip and I arrive at Windsor today, we know that many individuals and families across the United Kingdom, and around the world, are entering a period of great concern and uncertainty. We are all being advised to change our normal routines and regular patterns of life for the greater good of the communities we live in and, in particular, to protect the most vulnerable within them. At times such as these, I am reminded that our nation's history has been forged by people and communities coming together to work as one, concentrating our combined efforts with a focus on the common goal.

Buoyed by the Queen's words, William and Catherine got to grips with a routine that would enable them to stay connected, not only with their staff, but with the wider world. A source said, 'The prince instantly recognised that the whole operation had to shift over to video conferencing to stay connected. They were well versed in using social media as a tool, but the team put in place a schedule to connect to their charities and other organisations, where typically we would have been on the ground, and it worked really well.'

On 26 March, residents up and down the country came to their windows and doors at 8pm to join in the Clap for our Carers movement that had spread via social media. Famous landmarks and buildings were lit up blue to pay tribute to those working tirelessly in hospitals and care homes. A social media video showed William and Catherine's three children, Prince George, Princess Charlotte and Prince Louis, dressed in blue and joining the chorus of applause from their garden at Anmer Hall in Norfolk. William approved the use of a private lawn at Kensington Palace for refuelling air ambulances across London, an act praised for saving valuable time for under-siege paramedics across the capital.

He and Catherine took part in calls and video conferences, and offered condolences to the families of those who had fallen to the virus – including 55-year-old Amged el-Hawrani, who was one of the first front-line British doctors to die from Covid-19.

Over the next year, these calls and conferences would become a regular form of engagement for the couple, a way of visibly keeping up their public-facing royal duties while following distancing rules. William and Catherine could, for instance, using them to keep the spotlight on mental-health and community charities. In May 2020, Catherine launched Hold Still, a nationwide photography project launched with the National Portrait Gallery to capture life during lockdown. The project drew tens of thousands of submissions and later became an online and public exhibition and a book. A source said,

> The work going on behind the scenes was as much as the office was doing with pre-Covid engagements and tours, there was a real desire from them both [William and Catherine] to do as much as possible and that stemmed from the belief that if we could do something that went some way to either recognising or potentially alleviating the pressure on those who were working on the front line, or struggling with the isolation during such an extraordinary time, then it would be worthwhile.

Meanwhile, when coronavirus threatened to stop non-essential travel to the United States in March 2020, Harry and Meghan once again packed up their things and moved from Canada to California. No sooner had they set foot in America than the couple arranged a new date to allow them to take part in a tell-all interview with Oprah Winfrey, realising the royals' worst fears. The rest of 2020 continued to mark this distinction. On the one hand there was William and Catherine, who spent their time promoting and amplifying charities such as the National Emergencies Trust and mental health organisations such as Mind and the text service Shout. On the other were Harry and Meghan, who had chosen to step back from their royal role, signed a reported £80 million deal with the streaming giant Netflix and a further £18 million deal with music and podcast platform Spotify.

As the Sussexes settled into their new lifestyle in Santa Barbara, Meghan suffered the devastation of a miscarriage, penning an op-ed in the *New York Times* in November 2020 that described the grief felt by anyone who had experienced this trauma. By then she was already hopeful about welcoming a new addition to their family: on 14 February 2021 she announced to the world that she was expecting another child. If there had been any optimism that this new addition could bring about a renewed closeness with the royal family, it was swiftly dashed when, just 24 hours later, the US network CBS revealed that Oprah's 'intimate conversation' with the couple would finally air as a 90-minute primetime special on 7 March. In response, Buckingham Palace immediately ended negotiations about the couple's as-yet-unresolved future roles – as things stood, nothing had been agreed about what would happen after the transitional year. While graciously declaring that they would 'remain much loved members of the family', the Queen, after liaising with Charles and William, made it clear that the Sussexes' proposed 'half in, half out' model was neither feasible nor desirable. Charles and William agreed that there would be no way back for Harry and Meghan. In the same statement, the palace said, 'The Queen has written confirming that in stepping away from the work of The Royal Family it is not possible to continue with the responsibilities and duties that come with a life of public service.' Aides who remained loyal to

Harry and Meghan told how the couple were 'disappointed', while Harry was devastated at losing his patronages and military roles, which were close to his heart. One Sussex source told *The Times*, 'There is no hiding that this is a difference of opinion,' laying bare how Harry still believed he could create a new model for the family to follow. Harry and Meghan's decision to issue an immediate rebuke just minutes after the Buckingham Palace statement showed how deep the wounds remained. It read: 'We can all live a life of service. Service is universal.'

The weeks leading up to the broadcast of Harry and Meghan's interview saw the Windsors uniting as they rallied to encourage people to be selfless and have a Covid-19 vaccination for the sake of the wider community. In a video call to health leaders on 25 February, the Queen, then 94, revealed she had received one of the first coronavirus jabs in January. William would later post a photo of himself on social media with his sleeve pushed up to his shoulder while receiving the shot at a public health facility run by the National Health Service at London's Science Museum. That sense of togetherness comforted the Queen as on 1 March Prince Philip was transferred to St Bartholomew's Hospital, a specialist cardiac centre in London after spending the previous three weeks under observation for a pre-existing heart condition at the King Edward VII hospital in central London. He had been a patient at the private hospital in Marylebone since 16 February. At the time Buckingham Palace attempted to downplay the 99-year-old's admission as a precaution. William took to calling his grandmother on Wednesdays and Sundays, as well as writing letters to her detailing how the children were coping with homeschooling and how his video calls were progressing.

As the family united, so too did the palace communications operations. Senior courtiers from both Buckingham Palace and Kensington Palace had already met on several occasions to prepare several potential responses, given the global interest that would undoubtedly follow the Sussexes' interview with Oprah Winfrey. Courtiers predicted Harry and Meghan would provide further details of how they felt ostracised by the family and shut out of forging a progressive role within the institution, though no one could have guessed how weighty the couple's allegations of abandonment and racism would be. While the senior team were locked away brainstorming possible outcomes, several of Harry and Meghan's former staff, who had dubbed themselves the Sussex Survivors Club, were secretly working on a response of their own. On 3 March, just four days before the interview aired, *The Times* revealed Meghan had faced a bullying complaint made by one of her closest advisers during her time at Kensington Palace. The report by Valentine Low said the newspaper was approached by sources who wanted to give their account of the turmoil within the royal household, from Meghan's arrival as Harry's girlfriend in 2017 to the couple's decision to stand down as working royals. Low would later divulge that he had spoken to several witnesses who claimed that Meghan drove two personal assistants out of the household and undermined the confidence of a third staff member, leading to a toxic atmosphere in the workplace where staff were routinely breaking down in tears. The report also revealed the testimony given in October 2018 by Jason Knauf, the couple's communications secretary, to William's private secretary Simon Case. A spokesman for the Sussexes told the paper that Harry and Meghan were the victims of a 'calculated smear campaign based on misleading and harmful misinformation', adding that the duchess was 'saddened by this latest attack on her character, particularly as someone who has been the target of bullying herself and is deeply committed to supporting those who have experienced pain and trauma'. Buckingham Palace announced an investigation into the bullying allegations, stating that staff, both past and present, would be interviewed. The palace suggested it would seek to establish what lessons could be learned from the probe while declaring it did not tolerate bullying or harassment in the workplace.

The episode was an embarrassing one for the royal family. The sources had come forward not only due to the impending Oprah interview, but also because of concerns that nothing had been done either to investigate the claims that Jason Knauf had put forward around the alleged treatment of the Sussexes' staff, or to protect staff against the possibility of bullying by a member of the royal family. A palace insider revealed that while it was understood that William and Catherine had signalled at the time of Knauf's email that an investigation should be launched, the institution did not follow through with a formal inquiry due to fears that it could be leaked and damage the Duchess of Sussex's reputation. The source said, 'The prince was both angry and very saddened over the allegations of how the staff were treated. He knew those who had been mistreated personally and felt as though every effort that they [he and Catherine] had made to cultivate a decent working environment had been compromised.' Following the announcement of the palace's action, a spokesperson for the Sussexes said, 'It's no coincidence that distorted several-year-old accusations aimed at undermining The Duchess are being briefed to the British media shortly before she and The Duke are due to speak openly and honestly about their experience of recent years.' In a legal letter to *The Times*, lawyers for the Duchess said the media organisation was 'being used by Buckingham Palace to peddle a wholly false narrative' before the couple's television interview with Oprah Winfrey. This was, of course, strongly refuted by the palace.

Then, on 7 March, the interview aired. It is almost impossible to fathom how utterly toxic Harry and Meghan's relationship with the institution had become less than three years after a glittering wedding that was celebrated around the world. Some sources who have contributed to this biography suggest that signs that things could head in this direction were present from the start, referencing Harry's fractured relationship with William, coupled with Meghan's alleged treatment of her staff and unwillingness to observe even the most basic forms of a constitutional monarchy's protocols. As one source said, 'There is a hierarchy which dictates how things have to be arranged, from tours, engagements, what issues you choose to work on, for example. And then, when egos get involved, you're going to have a problem. The whole business of the family only works when you are playing on the same team.'

One thing for certain, however, is that when Harry and Meghan appeared on international television to accuse unnamed members of the royal family of racism, charged others with peddling lies, and blamed the institution for ignoring Meghan's cries for help as she contemplated suicide while pregnant, those at the centre of the allegations were left in utter disbelief. One of Meghan's most incendiary claims was that while she was pregnant with Archie there had been 'concerns and conversations about how dark his skin might be when he's born'. Winfrey later revealed that off camera, Harry had been at pains to stress that neither the Queen nor Prince Philip, who was still in hospital receiving treatment at the time, 'were part of that conversation'. Yet Meghan's disclosure triggered wild speculation over which royal made the comments, leading to MPs including the future prime minister Sir Keir Starmer wading into the row over the 'really, really serious issues'. At the palace, the royals were in shock.

The programme was broadcast by CBS at 8pm Eastern Time on Sunday evening in the US – 1am on Monday morning in the UK. British audiences would not be able to watch the interview until 9pm that evening, on ITV1. This meant that, as of Monday morning, none of the royal family had seen the interview, but senior staff from the three households had each gathered in their respective offices overnight to watch the programme via a mixture of internet streams and links to US television services set up by the palaces' IT departments. Those tasked with watching it live took feverish notes. By 8am, the Queen, the Prince of Wales and William and Catherine were each delivered a full report on the litany of claims. William and Catherine's team contacted them by phone once they had filed their report to give them a rundown of the comments made by the Sussexes. One former courtier said:

> It was agreed that we would contact the Cambridges first thing in the morning, which we did before arranging to meet in person at Kensington Palace.
> After the initial phone call there was a lot of backwards and forwards to William and Catherine, over email, text messages and on the phone, so they were completely across what we were dealing with. The situation was completely unprecedented and what felt like days once everyone knew the full picture was actually only a matter of hours. But it was calm and measured and they both [William and Catherine] wanted to do the right thing and support the Queen in any way they could to respond.
> Likewise between Buckingham Palace and Kensington Palace there was a lot of collaboration, everyone was feeling their way into how best to respond given what we had been faced with, but the overriding feeling was that what we had to get absolutely right was what was appropriate not only for the family who had been thrust into this situation, but also the institution.

CHAPTER TWELVE

Breakfast news bulletins led on the stories throughout Monday morning, and this continued throughout the day. News media websites, some of which had liveblogged the CBS special from their US offices, dedicated dozens of individual articles to the furore. An early draft statement was agreed and prepared by the households and presented to the Queen by 2pm that afternoon, but the monarch was in no rush to respond. Instead, given the gravity of the proclamations by the Sussexes, she decided she wanted to sleep on it. The delay, one palace insider said, allowed time for the statement to be altered to include the immortal line 'some recollections may vary'. The monarch has been credited with this phrase, which has gone down in royal history as a subtly cutting response to Harry and Meghan's devastating claims. In his book *Courtiers*, Valentine Low elaborated further, suggesting the line was presented by Jean-Christophe Grey, William's new private secretary, and it was Catherine who argued for its inclusion, even when others thought it may antagonise Harry and Meghan. The insider said:

> There is no denying the original statement that was prepared on the Monday was pored over. On the one hand, everyone agreed that it had to be carefully worded so as to not inflame the situation any further, but on the other there were certain individuals who believed it had to be stronger, to send a message that while the family was not going to get involved in a tit-for-tat row, they were not going to lie down and take everything that was going to be thrown at them. Catherine was central to that message and the most vocal in including that line.

Another source said:

The beefing-up of the original statement is a pure example of how the princess has evolved to have her eye on the future. She knew, and in fact she was very intent on making clear, that what was then being talked about all over the world after Harry and Meghan's interview was being taken as gospel and the family did in fact need to draw a line under it without opening the Pandora's Box even further. They [William and Catherine] have a deep understanding that this affected them, arguably more than any of the others in the room, because it's their future on the line, because who in their right mind is going to support them if the family is silent to claims of bullying, harassment or racism? And, more importantly, no one recognised these claims as valid. It is a good example of the princess being absolutely central to those types of conversations concerning the direction of the monarchy in such a key moment.

At 5.30pm on Tuesday 9 March, Buckingham Palace released their statement: 'The whole family is saddened to learn the full extent of how challenging the last few years have been for Harry and Meghan. The issues raised, particularly that of race, are concerning. While some recollections may vary, they are taken very seriously and will be addressed by the family privately. Harry, Meghan and Archie will always be much loved family members.'

While Catherine had demonstrated a steely resolve few had seen before, either publicly or in private, William was, according to several sources, absolutely seething. He felt betrayed by Harry to the extent that he vowed never to speak to him again. Such was his anger that he told one of his most trusted aides that he had 'absolutely no time to entertain either of them [Harry and Meghan]'.

A few days later, William's composure would be tested again when, during their first public engagement since the Oprah interview aired, a reporter shouted out: 'Is the royal family a racist family, sir?' William knew he would not let the question go unanswered. This point had, very likely, dominated his thoughts in the aftermath of the interview. 'We are very much not a racist family,' he responded. The royal family's relationship with the journalists who cover them is quite different to the relationship politicians have with political journalists. The political world is synonymous with characters who are ready to engage, even duel with one another publicly on matters of policy, coverage or even scandal when it arises. Those on the royal beat, however, maintain relationships, forced or otherwise, with a certain reverence that can sometimes seem at odds with their journalistic instincts. While the question to William had been posed by a junior news reporter at Sky News at the behest of their bosses, William and Catherine were concerned that journalists would now feel the family's private battles were fair game – that they might be subject to such taunts while on public engagements, for instance while visiting charities close to their hearts.

Exactly a month later, on 9 April 2021, the Duke of Edinburgh passed away, just two months shy of his 100th birthday. Coronavirus restrictions meant that only 30 people, all socially distanced, were allowed to attend his funeral. The image of the 95-year-old Queen sitting alone led to an outpouring of sorrow and sympathy. Harry, who flew to the UK alone after Meghan was advised not to travel due to being in the latter stages of pregnancy, followed his grandfather's modified Land Rover hearse in a line with his brother and their cousin Peter Phillips, who walked between them. As the royals mourned a figurehead of the family and the Queen bid farewell to her husband of 73 years, in an anguished encounter after the funeral the Prince of Wales begged his warring sons, 'Please, boys. Don't make my final years a misery.' The brothers now living separate lives, separated by an ocean, were as far from united as they had ever been.

13

CREATING A MODERN MONARCHY

Prince Philip had always been the head of the family. Different generations had leaned on him for personal guidance and his acceptance, or rejection, of others brought into the fold by marriage was seen as a moral compass by those navigating life within the confines of the monarchy. In the days that followed his death, William remembered his century of life as being 'defined by service – to his country and Commonwealth, to his wife and Queen, and to our family'. The prince spoke of his gratitude to a grandfather who had guided him through good times and bad, and of the kindness Philip had shown Catherine and their children throughout their time together. Philip had shown William, and in time Catherine, that while the institution was central to everything that the family did, there must be time for a life outside it. He had been a huge supporter of William's decision to delay taking on full-time royal duties, and he had also backed him in taking his time while he considered whether he had absolute confidence in his relationship with Catherine before making the biggest decision of his life. Indeed, Philip had warned his grandson against succumbing to the same curse that saw the marriages of his own children, Charles, Anne and Andrew ending in separation and divorce, which had marked both their lives and those of his grandchildren.

CHAPTER THIRTEEN

Away from the public gaze, Philip and Catherine had enjoyed a close relationship, evidenced by their years of writing letters to one another: the duke sympathised with her plight as an outsider coming into a family dynamic like no other. One former aide to the late Duke of Edinburgh noted that,

> He knew all the pitfalls of being attached to the family, the scrutiny, the focus and, at times, the general annoyance of dealing with palace life at times, which could eat you up if you weren't prepared to do things your own way. "Don't let them bully you into submission," he would say, and that went for the courtiers as well as the press. He was incredibly fond of Catherine and thought she was the best thing to happen to the royal family since he came along. [The aide delivered the last comment with a smile.]

In the aftermath of Harry and Meghan's Oprah interview, the Sussexes' version of how the family and the institution had conspired against them, and caused them to leave their royal roles, had created a siege mentality in the palace. And Harry's presence at the funeral just ensured these feelings stayed fresh in everyone's minds. William and Catherine were both wounded by the numerous accusations and the presentation of Harry and Meghan's 'truth', as Oprah put it. William was most aggrieved by Harry's assertion that he was 'trapped' in the system, while Catherine felt deeply let down over Meghan's disclosure of a private exchange, which sparked claim and counterclaim regarding the fitting of dresses before the Sussexes' 2018 wedding. That particular declaration would add further fuel to an already contentious argument over which woman made the other woman cry during a disagreement over Princess Charlotte's flower girl outfit. It compounded, in Catherine's mind, a key difference between her and Meghan, who she no longer believed she could trust. A palace source close to Catherine said, 'If you can't trust those you are supposed to be closest to, it's very difficult to have a relationship. There was definitely an issue of trust with the Sussexes coming back for the Duke of Edinburgh's funeral.'

Meghan's willingness to speak about William and Catherine also spurred a reaction, another palace insider said. 'They were both very hurt over the personal nature of some of the commentary. But there was a lot going on at that time, the conversation was dominated by the interview when their focus was on the Queen and the family coming together to celebrate a man who was dearly loved.' Another source told how Catherine was left so personally affected by the Duke of Edinburgh's death that it spurred her decision to encourage William to talk to his brother following the funeral at Windsor. Firstly, Catherine believed the family should come first. Secondly, if there was an opportunity to find out why Harry was so intent on trying to destroy the family before he did any more damage, then it should be taken. The source said:

> When you look at any decision they take, it's family-orientated. It's at the core of their existence, in terms of their own family but also the welfare of the extended family as well. The whole situation with the Sussexes was just very sad and just as Philip had a degree of empathy and understanding with Catherine for coming from outside the family at the beginning, I would say Catherine had that for Meghan as well, at least at the start and she did do a lot to help her integrate into the family in the beginning. But Meghan simply acted like she didn't need or want her help, it was very matter of fact and you could say she just dismissed her, which hurt Catherine. There was a lot of sadness there, but

CHAPTER THIRTEEN

that being said, she was very clear that any engagement with Harry or Meghan should be with the utmost of caution because it was obvious that they weren't to be trusted.

The froideur between the brothers showed no signs of thawing, despite their condemnation of the BBC following the damning report by Lord Dyson, published on 20 May 2021, into Princess Diana's interview with Martin Bashir in 1995. Still operating in silo, the princes issued individual statements from opposite sides of the Atlantic in which they both blamed the corporation for its pursuit of Diana, which they believed negatively impacted her fragile mental state at a time when she was at her most vulnerable. On the day the report was published, William damned the BBC for its 'lies' in securing Martin Bashir's interview, which he said had stoked his mother's paranoia and contributed to the breakdown of her marriage. The unprecedented rebuke followed the long-running investigation that concluded that the former *Panorama* reporter had used 'deceitful behaviour' to induce the princess to agree to the interview, resulting in a serious breach of the broadcaster's guidelines. Harry would go even further, suggesting that 'the ripple effect of a culture of exploitation and unethical practices ultimately took her life'.

A day later, Harry revealed in another documentary with Oprah Winfrey, for Apple TV, that he had used drink and drugs to mask the pain he felt over his mother's death, and accused the royal family of 'total neglect' over years of his own suffering. By this stage, William and Catherine had retreated from having any direct contact with the Sussexes, but they privately maintained that if there was a way for their children to have a relationship with their cousins in the future, they would not stand in their way. As Harry and Meghan welcomed the birth of their daughter Lilibet on 4 June 2021, William and Catherine sent a gift and a card of congratulations – although that would be the extent of their contact. One former courtier said that all talk of 'the other side' was effectively banned after the brothers honoured a previous agreement to come together at Kensington Palace to unveil a statue of their mother on 1 July, on what would have been her 60th birthday. Instead of delivering individual speeches on the day, William decided the engagement should be cut short in place of a joint statement where they said, 'Every day, we wish she were still with us, and our hope is that this statue will be seen forever as a symbol of her life and her legacy.' After the engagement was concluded, William made up his mind. He did not recognise Harry any more and his brother wasn't to be trusted.

Once it was clear that Harry and Meghan would not return to Britain or their royal roles, and as talk around the interview died down, William and Catherine were able to focus their attention on how they could support the monarchy at a key time of change. With the number of senior royals having dwindled yet further following Philip's passing, the Queen took it upon herself to lead by example, encouraging aides to fill her diary with engagements. In October the 95-year-old monarch undertook 19 official engagements in the first three weeks of the month. But the relentless pace at which she was operating took its toll. She became unwell, causing concern among her family when, on 20 October, she had to spend the night in hospital for preliminary tests for the first time since 2013, when she suffered symptoms of gastroenteritis. The Queen had been insistent on travelling to Northern Ireland for a two-day visit, until royal doctors forced her to 'reluctantly' cancel at the last minute. Since the start of the month, including her return from Balmoral, where she spent the summer, the Queen had travelled nearly 1,000 miles. As a further reminder of her advancing years, she had also begun using a walking stick in public, causing

CHAPTER THIRTEEN

Charles and William to plead with her to slow down, insisting that they would be on hand to manage the extra burden. After a period of rest, during which she also withdrew from attending the COP climate summit in Glasgow, the Queen was laid up again after spraining her back. The monarch was forced to pull out of the Remembrance Sunday service at the Cenotaph in central London in November, the first time she had missed the event through illness in 70 years.

The Prince of Wales and Prince William were by this time in daily contact, worried that the Queen was throwing herself into work at such a rate that she was in danger of becoming worn out. 'The Queen's health was a growing concern, with the overriding thought that she was burying herself in work and taking on far too many public engagements as a way of dealing with the Duke of Edinburgh's passing,' said one palace source. At the end of October, after the Queen had been ordered by doctors to cancel all public engagements and rest for at least another two weeks, William and Catherine visited her in Windsor, offering to forgo spending Christmas with the Middleton family and instead help with plans to spend the festive period at Windsor Castle. But the Queen assured them there was no need to change their plans. On 20 December, as coronavirus rates soared around the country, Buckingham Palace announced the Queen would spend her first Christmas as a widow at Windsor Castle, but would be joined by a small number of close family members including Charles, Camilla, Edward and Sophie.

In 2022, plans for the celebration of the Queen's Platinum Jubilee gathered pace. Palace aides arranged the festivities at home in the UK, while William and Catherine's senior team were busy making arrangements for a major tour of the Caribbean. The tour was billed as the perfect platform for the Duke and Duchess of Cambridge to reannounce their credentials on the international stage, where they would support the Queen while preparing for the next phase of their roles within the monarchy. A former courtier said, 'After Oprah the feeling was very much, "Right, what can we actually do to move things on and put on a united front?" That was the sole focus. Everyone knew the issues would remain with the Sussexes but it was very much about putting everything to one side and looking forward in a positive sense.'

Foreign tours are a major focus for the royal family. Often organised at the behest of the government, they provide a key route for diplomacy and the marketing of 'Brand Britain'.

This tour was incredibly important. In November 2021, Prince Charles had attended an emotionally charged ceremony in Barbados at which the Queen was formally removed as the country's head of state. Soon after, Jamaican prime minister Andrew Holness announced his country's plans to follow suit. Support for the monarchy across the Caribbean was being questioned and William and Catherine were left with a delicate diplomatic mission that they were intent on fulfilling. Their likeability around the world was seen as a huge plus both inside government and within the institution.

Like millions of others, William and Catherine had lived under lockdown restrictions for large parts of the coronavirus pandemic, and had been unable to travel since a joint three-day trip to Ireland in March 2020. But their last major international tour to Pakistan in 2019 had been a huge triumph of diplomacy that had celebrated Britain's ties with the Commonwealth. The government was hopeful of replicating this success in Belize, Jamaica and the Bahamas.

The backdrop of the tour, however, would not be a positive one for the royal family. The turn of the year into 2022 brought two other huge distractions. The Duke of York was fighting a civil lawsuit in the United States brought by Virginia Giuffre,

CHAPTER THIRTEEN

while Harry announced he was to challenge the Metropolitan Police's decision to strip him of his taxpayer-funded security when returning to the UK. Both were seen as extraordinarily risky moves, for hugely different reasons. Talks gathered at pace concerning Andrew's 'ultimate gamble' of demanding to be tried by a jury in the case. In private, William again voiced his concerns to his father that his disgraced uncle should seek to settle the case to avoid further scandal. The duke would eventually choose to settle with Giuffre for £12 million on 14 February, £2 million of which was set as a donation to her personal charity for sex-abuse victims.

Regardless of Andrew's vehement denials of the allegations that he assaulted Giuffre, William and Charles agreed that he should never be allowed to return to public duties. One palace insider told how William went even further, suggesting his uncle should not be welcomed to any event with the royal family, which was overruled by the Prince of Wales. While he was forced at the time to respect his father's will in not completely exiling his uncle, William was privately adamant that when he became king, the Duke of York would have absolutely no place within the royal fold, publicly or otherwise. Meanwhile, Harry's insistence on taking the British government to court was deemed not only unwise and no doubt personally expensive – it was also likely to create further tension between him and his father. The Duke of Sussex had already appealed to his family to intervene in a decision by the Metropolitan Police to only provide personal security to him and his family when visiting the UK on a case-by-case basis. Both the Queen and Prince of Wales told him there was no place for them to get involved on what was a matter for the government. His appeals would run until 2025, when the judgement was upheld by the Court of Appeal, leading him to claim it was a 'good old-fashioned establishment stitch-up'.

William and Catherine were set to fly to Belize for the start of the tour in March but, by then, the Queen's health was becoming even more of a concern. Having contracted Covid-19 in February, she then missed the annual Commonwealth Day service at Westminster Abbey. For the occasion, she issued a statement in which she reiterated the declaration she had made as a 21-year-old princess in 1947: 'my life will always be devoted in service.'

William and Catherine hoped their eight-day tour would provide the perfect uplift for the Queen and the Commonwealth after two years of infighting and scandal for the family. Unfortunately, it would become historic for all the wrong reasons.

Even before the engines on the Voyager ministerial plane roared into action at RAF Brize Norton on 19 March, the tour was off to a rocky start. The royals had been forced to cancel a planned visit to a cocoa farm in Belize after being denied permission to land a helicopter in an adjoining field amid a dispute between the local village of Indian Creek and Flora and Fauna International, a charity that owned an adjoining, contested property and of which William has been patron of since 2020. The indigenous Q'eqchi Maya people said they were not consulted about William and Catherine's visit, while a youth leader, Dionisio Shol, said the handling of the episode raised the issue of 'colonialism'. Rather than attempting to reschedule the visit or issuing an apology for what Kensington Palace aides told the media was a 'misunderstanding in communication', a decision was taken in haste to visit a different farm. William had been staunchly against the idea, instead offering to visit the villagers to personally apologise for the mishap, but was advised not to by courtiers on the trip. The decision proved to be a mistake after Sebastian Shol, chairman of Indian Creek village, told the *Daily Mail*: 'We don't want them to land on our land, that's the message that we want to send. They could land anywhere but

CHAPTER THIRTEEN

not on our land.' The Belize government later apologised, sparing the royal household's blushes, but it almost went unnoticed amid the images of protestors at the site holding homemade signs bearing the words 'Prince William Go Home'.

The incident would set the tone for the rest of the tour, on which William and Catherine soon found themselves at the centre of an uncomfortable storm. The surprise was not that this could happen, but rather that their team had not planned for, or understood, the potential pitfalls of visiting countries whose relationship with the royal family was a reminder of a painful past.

Central to William and Catherine's angst was the absence of their revered communications secretary Victoria O'Byrne, an experienced PR specialist known for her expertise in reputation management for high-profile individuals and governments, and for managing campaigns such as the London 2012 Olympic and Paralympic Games. Her departure from the royal household in December 2021, due to a personal family issue unrelated to her employment, in addition to the fact that a replacement had not been found in time for the tour, would leave a huge void in its execution.

William and Catherine's rescheduled visit to a chocolate farm in the coastal village of Hopkins, where they danced with locals next to the stunning coastline, appeared to be a happy one – and a good opening to the trip. But on their arrival in Jamaica on 22 October, a small protest in the capital, Kingston, threatened to destabilise the visit, with vocal demands from the crowds for William to apologise for the monarchy's role in the Transatlantic slave trade. Politicians joined the campaigners, labelling the royal visit 'ill-timed and ill-conceived' in an attempt to drum up support for a fledgling republican movement on the Caribbean island.

On the tour, the Kensington Palace communications team attempted to circumvent the issue by briefing reporters on the tour that the Cambridges were 'aware of protests', but added that any calls for a republic were a matter for the people and government of Jamaica. Nothing to see here, then. Except, the issue was growing by the hour. During the ceremony in which Barbados became a republic, Prince Charles formally acknowledged 'the appalling atrocity of slavery' in the Caribbean, saying 'it forever stains our history'. To the dismay of those gathered, and also in other Caribbean nations, the heir stopped short of issuing an apology, either on behalf of the country or the royal family. William and Catherine's tour to Jamaica coincided with the country celebrating its 60th anniversary of independence – and in preparation for their arrival a coalition of politicians, business leaders and musicians had written an open letter calling on the monarchy to pay slavery reparations. The letter stated that the Queen and her ancestors had 'perpetuated the greatest human rights tragedy in the history of humankind'. In a sign of the world the Cambridges were straddling – a future king and queen setting foot in a former colony – the writers of this open letter were gathered outside the British High Commission on William and Catherine's arrival, which delivered a damning assessment of the royal visit. Speaking to the British media, activist Nora Blake said, 'We may have been supportive of her [the Queen] before, but we are not supportive of the monarchy because we can make a direct link between the monarchy and the system of slavery, colonialism, total and absolute exploitation in the shackles of slavery.'

It was clear to those on the tour that the palace had not prepared for such a hostile atmosphere. A palace insider around at the time revealed that those on the ground were in 'a complete state of paralysis', which only exacerbated the problem. The source said, 'No one recognised what a big shift it would be for them [William and Catherine]. There were issues as clear as day

CHAPTER THIRTEEN

in front of them and they weren't acknowledged or acted upon once they became apparent, which was undoubtedly a huge failing.' One source close to William revealed how he was in touch with former courtiers back in the UK, expressing his unease at how the tour was being handled and how they were being advised. 'I think it suddenly dawned on him how inexperienced the team were to handle such a major tour and their inability to react in the right way to meet the demands of what was happening on the ground was concerning him,' said the source.

Jamaica was, and remains, at a crossroads in its history and relationship with the royals. On 23 March, in the lobby of his office in Kingston, Prime Minister Andrew Holness ambushed his royal guests as soon as they arrived, by declaring that Jamaica was 'moving on'. William and Catherine stood motionless as he delivered his prepared speech in front of more than a dozen TV cameras, photographers and reporters. The awkward encounter was not ideal, nor could it have been avoided. William and Catherine were forced to awkwardly wait for Holness to finish before engaging in the usual pleasantries, serving as further evidence that the couple had entered unfamiliar territory.

That afternoon, on a dusty pitch in walking distance from reggae star Bob Marley's childhood home, William joined local players for a game of football alongside Manchester City and England footballer Raheem Sterling, who was born on the island. The several hundred jubilant locals who filled the local streets and clambered onto neighbouring rooftops to catch a glimpse of the royals contributed towards an electric atmosphere and perhaps dulled the voices of protest. Walking off the pitch at the end of the game, the prince, flanked by his wife, momentarily stopped to greet groups of young children who were poking their outstretched hands and fingers through a metal fence on the perimeter of the playing field. As the saying goes, a picture tells a thousand words. The resulting images sparked a wave of commentary and condemnation as soon as they were uploaded to social media and news websites around the world. The couple were widely lambasted for, as the BBC's royal correspondent put it, 'what looked to many as some sort of white-saviour parody'. In PR terms, it was an absolute nightmare of a situation and totally overshadowed what had been a remarkable reception from locals.

In the evening, at a dinner hosted by the governor-general, Sir Patrick Linton Allen, William made a considered speech that denounced slavery as 'abhorrent', saying that 'it should never have happened'. The speech was immediately seized upon by the Advocates Network, a human rights coalition of 100 Jamaican individuals and groups, that criticised William's lack of a direct apology on behalf of the royal family as 'tone deaf'. Yet worse was to come.

The next day, on their final engagement in Jamaica, William and Catherine attended the inaugural commissioning parade for service personnel who had completed the Caribbean Military Academy's officer training programme. With William dressed, for the first time, in the No.1 Tropical dress of the Blues and Royals – a white high-collared tunic, instead of dark blue, accompanied by matching trousers in a suitably lighter, warm-weather material – and Catherine choosing a white crocheted Alexander McQueen dress, the future of the monarchy resembled the main characters of a period drama rather than the relatable faces of a new generation. The Jamaican government had requested the couple ride in the same open-top Land Rover that had been used by the Queen on visits to the island in 1962. On examining the schedule, William had voiced his concern at the optics of such an exercise and instructed his staff to suggest that he would instead inspect a guard of honour and engage in conversation with the troops.

'We were overruled,' said a former courtier. 'We attempted to negotiate a viewing of the vehicle instead, as it had been specially reconditioned for the tour, but the host government insisted they be driven around in it, the local defence team thought it was appropriate. As always with these types of tours, it's a balancing act.' The decision to concede on such an important part of a programme that had already presented several flash points would be a monumental error. Another former courtier said, 'There were discussions, but we didn't have total control. The bosses [William and Catherine] certainly did suggest if they could meet the protestors and engage with them, just as they suggested doing things such as the Land Rover tour in a more modern way. But we were told the host country wanted it to happen so it went ahead. Obviously after the event there were huge takeaways.'

Professor Rosalea Hamilton, a civil rights campaigner and founding director of the Institute of Law and Economics in Jamaica, delivered an eviscerating verdict on William and Catherine's decision to pose in the Land Rover, saying the images 'signify this young generation is continuing the monarchical traditions of holding one race superior and another inferior'.

William's landmark address, where he had hoped to present the monarchy as partners in a new future, was buried as soon as it was delivered. Catherine and William had become the story. The palace team's inexperience had been utterly exposed. Press officers had just moments before been excitedly briefing journalists about the prince's uniform and Catherine's choice of outfit, seemingly blind to the queries from the less obsequious members of the press corps about the wisdom of the Land Rover stunt. The reaction of the media at home was no better. In his withering assessment of the tour, the BBC's Jonny Dymond uttered a line that will go down in tour history: 'Quite how defeat was plucked from the jaws of victory in Trench Town, Kingston, may one day become the stuff of public relations legend.' He was right. This tour had already become notable for all the wrong reasons.

As soon as they were back on the plane on the way to their next and final stop, in the Bahamas, the tense atmosphere was palpable and William let his feelings be known. Deep down he had known the optics of riding in the Land Rover was a bad idea and still had let himself be persuaded otherwise. A palace source said:

> The prince was as upset as he was furious. All their good intentions before and during the tour, the work they put in, didn't matter. It was evidence of a changing world and there was a great deal of reflection after the tour. William and Catherine suffered from having an inexperienced team around at that particular time, and in trying very hard to foster a welcoming atmosphere at work. A lot of the people on the tour were good at planning, telling the media when to be on a bus or where to stand, but pretty woeful in any type of execution and it came to bite them.

William had been humbled. He had attempted the difficult balancing act of representing the monarchy, paying homage to the traditions of the past and leaving a good impression on the host country, but it hadn't worked. Another former palace staffer said, 'He didn't blame anyone, but he was angered at how the situation had gone from bad to worse. It was a watershed moment in terms of him knowing, there and then, that he wouldn't be put in that sort of situation again.'

As the wheels went up for the last stage of the tour, there was more bad news on the horizon. William and Catherine were made aware that a government committee in the Bahamas were urging the royals to issue 'a full and formal apology for their crimes against humanity'. William could no longer ignore the elephant in the room. He phoned the Queen and the Prince of Wales as soon as he arrived and explained that he planned to deliver an honest assessment of the tour in an attempt to regain the narrative of the previous week.

In what was deemed a significant break with royal protocol, something that left his communications team extremely anxious, William addressed the issue head on at a reception hosted by the Bahamian governor-general on 26 March: 'This tour has brought into even sharper focus questions about the past and future. In Belize, Jamaica and The Bahamas, that future is for the people to decide upon,' he said.

'Foreign tours are an opportunity to reflect. You learn so much. You learn so much. What is on the minds of prime ministers. The hopes and ambitions of schoolchildren. The day-to-day challenges faced by families and communities. We have thoroughly enjoyed spending time with communities in all three countries, understanding more about the issues that matter most to them.'

He then went further than any other member of the royal family had acknowledged before, adding: 'Catherine and I are committed to service. For us that's not "telling people what to do". It is about serving and supporting them in whatever way they think best, by using the platform we are lucky to have. It is why tours such as this reaffirm our desire to serve the people of the Commonwealth and to listen to communities around the world.'

It was clear that William and Catherine would be approaching things very differently. Senior aides said that in the future he wanted to 'listen and learn and not lecture'. Kensington Palace would also undergo a radical shift in its communications strategy, with William and Catherine both agreeing they would not shy away from tackling the big issues that would directly affect them in the years to come. It would be the start of a significant change, heralding a new beginning and renewed vision of their roles as a future king and queen.

14

THE CAMBRIDGE WAY

Years of infighting and scandal at the heart of the royal family had damaged its reputation; in 2022, following the bruising Caribbean tour, there were fears that the monarchy was no longer fit to face the future. Aides conceded that accusations that the tour was both 'tone deaf' and smacked of 'colonialism' had deeply affected William and Catherine. 'They were upset by the criticism', one former aide remarked. 'But they weren't about to sit around and complain, they wanted to act and look at things with a different lens to see if they could have a different effect in the future.'

William understood that a new way forward was desperately needed to guarantee the monarchy's survival. He was acutely aware that either his father's reign or his own could be marked by the desertion of a significant number of countries from the Crown; the world was changing and the monarchy needed to be agile enough to deal with those changes. 'It was a case of wanting evolution, more than revolution,' a former senior courtier said. 'Things had to change and the best way to do that would be to be very aligned on a new message moving forwards. A "Cambridge way" of doing things, where [the Prince and Princess of Wales] could say, this is the model and these are the principles we want to follow.'[2] Another aide said, 'While William and Catherine had the utmost respect for the Queen and the Prince of Wales, they understood they couldn't rely on those foundations as a measure

CHAPTER FOURTEEN

of success for the future. If they wanted to be considered relevant in the future, they had to move with the times and be alive to the issues that people were experiencing right now.'

As they settled down to evaluate the tour, William and Catherine identified two key issues/errors that had had a catastrophic effect on the outward presentation of the tour. Firstly, cancelling the engagement at the first cocoa farm in Belize had been a mistake. The family whose sustainable cocoa farm they had been due to visit were devastated at losing the opportunity to highlight their work that a visit from the royals would have provided. The owners had arranged national broadcasters and reporters to cover the Duke and Duchess's visit, which they believed would result in a much-needed boost to their business in a competitive international market.

The second, of course, was deciding to board a Land Rover that the Queen had used in the 1960s – which could have been seen as archaic, as well as imperialistic – at the behest of the Jamaican government. A palace source said, 'That was the moment that hurt the most and the one that could have been avoided. It was one thing to be criticised for shaking the hands of young children through a fence, which was unfortunate but widely seen as not a true representation of the warm welcome they had received in Trench Town, but the Land Rover incident was totally avoidable.' Conversations between William and Catherine's senior team had taken place right up until the day of the event, and aides admitted, in hindsight, that they had made an error of judgement: 'Royal tours are about striking a balance and incidents like this can quickly cause offence to the host nation, but on reflection there were reservations that should have been acted upon.'

For generations, the royal family had been judged on its ability to remain apolitical and tread carefully when it came to complex diplomatic issues. William believed that if he was going to be taken seriously and be seen as genuine when he came to reign, he had to stand up for what he believed in and be seen to live by the principles that mattered most to him: respect, empathy and fairness. One of his most senior advisers disclosed that when they conducted their evaluation of the tour William let it be known that he wanted to be able to speak if he felt that the monarchy had something to say. The trusted motto of 'never complain, never explain' was outdated, and the royal family needed to evolve. Why couldn't William meet with the protestors? Why couldn't he be the one to forge new relationships with nations that sought to forge their own destiny away from the Crown? These burgeoning issues were ingrained in William's mind. If change was to come, which it undoubtedly was, then why fight it? Similarly, Charles had been vocal in private that the royal family would not stand in the way of realms that wanted to explore a republican future, but the institution was slow to recognise the ways in which the world was changing.

William wanted change to be a factor, but change that he could support. Change for good. Some may have been concerned that he was suddenly going to launch the Crown into a campaign of political and moral judgement – that was not his intention at all. Neither was this move from him a criticism of the Queen or his father, far from it. It was just that, with the world changing, William knew the tried and tested routes had to be updated: he needed to carve his own path.

William and Catherine wanted to place a focus on building bridges between communities and generations 'with humility and a willingness to be educated and learn from different experiences'. The trouble with having humility as a focus when you are a prince who lives in a palace and enjoys an incredible amount of privilege, is pretty obvious. Yet William knew that a shift to an approach built on empathy and understanding needed to be

CHAPTER FOURTEEN

central to the monarchy if it were to move forward. He wanted all of his visits, whether at home or abroad, to be driven by causes that mattered, and for the family to be able to be more open and honest when on these tours whenever it felt appropriate. One palace source said:

> The prince had always seen his role as helping people, whether that is directly or being someone who can use his position to bring people together to create change for good. When that mission is clouded by noise from outside factors, you have to look at the things you can control. Questions were rightfully asked, such as should they have gone to meet the protestors, could they have sat down with them and listened? They might not have been able to solve anything, but they would have had genuine interest in what they had to say while showing genuine humility. The questions need to be asked, what feels instinctively right in any situation? There was definitely a shift in mindset [towards] learning, understanding and education.

William and Catherine even started to question whether their future international visits should even be called 'royal tours'. A former senior aide said:

> There were discussions that perhaps the term was old-fashioned. Did the phrase conjure up feelings of imperialism, was that one of the sensitivities that needed to be top of the agenda moving forwards? We certainly reflected a lot on how things had shifted ... The bosses came away feeling that they genuinely want to learn and understand, and the comms that should be done before a visit were really important. If you take the protests that

happened at the start of the tour, it wasn't the number, but the message, and one of the main takeaways was certainly that there needs to be more of a learning agenda that should be more explicitly talked about in an authentic, genuine way.

William and Catherine's first tour of the post-Covid-19 era was a harsh wake-up call: the world was evolving. The accusations of being out of touch and, worse still, conducting a tour that smacked of colonialism, were deeply wounding to the couple. The murder of George Floyd by a police officer in the United States and the rise of the Black Lives Matter movement had made all institutions ask questions of themselves. The post-tour assessment provided pause for thought over how much planning had gone into travelling to a region where anti-monarchy sentiment was growing, and the failure to identify the obvious pitfalls when operating in an environment that required added sensitivity. William and Catherine both knew their strengths lay in their warmth, their affection for meeting different people from all walks of life, and a genuine willingness to help others. They may not have been able, from a political standpoint, to directly address the country's, or even the royal family's, connections to slavery and the evils of the past, but both William and Catherine knew that the survival of the institution would one day be solely in their hands and they could never allow themselves to be so exposed in the future.

In the wake of the tour, William and Catherine were also eager to examine their purpose, and their capacity to use their incredible profile to have a positive impact across local, national and international communities. They decided that they wanted the central pillars of their work – from campaigning on the environment and homelessness, to the early-years development of children, and highlighting British crafts and industries – to take on an even bigger significance to their working lives. Senior members of the family had previously stacked up engagements, some even competing with one another over how many they could complete before the end of the year, when the 'hardest-working royal' totals were compiled by the press. William and Catherine's new strategy would be to abandon the impulse to engage in the biggest number of engagements and instead focus wholly on those that would create 'maximum local and global impact'.

Redefining the pillars of their public role and the results they wanted to achieve with their platform would represent a significant shift in how the royal family had operated for generations. Queen Elizabeth II was the patron of more than 600 organisations during her reign, while Prince Philip was associated with nearly 1,000 throughout his life – as a patron, president or honorary member. William and Catherine recognised that they would not be able to make the impact they wanted by spreading themselves so thinly. They wanted to slim down the number of patronages they were associated with, focusing far more of their energy into the causes to which they believed they could make the biggest difference. William and Catherine now each maintain between 20 and 30 combined royal and military patronages. In 2023 they took part in 185 and 132 public engagements respectively. Compared to Queen Elizabeth II or Charles, when he was Prince of Wales, who on average performed between 400 and 500 public engagements a year, it is a paltry figure. However, courtiers will go to lengths to explain how the number of behind-the-scenes weekly meetings they both attend to plan and execute their engagements has 'redefined the role for the global impact they are having'.

One former courtier said,

> They have subtly redefined what it means to be a senior member of the royal family. And when you look at what their public role is, the idea of creating long-lasting projects

that had the capacity to create generational change was very much accelerated after the pandemic. Together, they were the driving force behind that change to take on less patronages but focus on larger issues at the heart of everyday life. That would be their legacy.

William and Catherine wouldn't be starting from the ground up – they had already been launching causes close to their hearts for some years. This book has already shown how one of William's passions from an early age, heavily influenced by his father and grandfather, was the environment. He had studied geography at university and in the past has frequently spoken of his ambition to work in conservation around the world as part of his royal duties. In October 2020, William launched the Earthshot Prize, an ambitious environmental project designed to provide recognition and support to those inspiring innovators and entrepreneurs who are searching for solutions to the planet's most pressing environmental challenges. Taking its inspiration from John F. Kennedy's Moonshot speech – the American president's challenge to his nation to place a man on the moon and return him to earth by the end of the 1960s – Earthshot is designed to run for ten years, awarding five winners £1 million in prize money each year.

A project like this was unprecedented for a member of the royal family and almost did not come to fruition. William was anxious on several levels. He did not believe he would achieve the funding needed to stage the awards over a decade, let alone the vast sums for the prizes. Furthermore, he was concerned that innovators wouldn't engage with the idea in sufficient numbers if it was not executed properly. In one moment of malaise, in the spring of 2020, it was Catherine who convinced her husband to continue with the idea. 'Catherine was the one who convinced him to pursue it,' said a former senior aide.

CHAPTER FOURTEEN

The world was locked down with no real end in sight over when it would reopen, big businesses and benefactors were looking at ways their operations were going to change, international travel was all but over, or at least there was no way of knowing when it would reopen again and the world was rapidly changing almost on a daily basis. There was a period when William was going to call it a day, believing that the task was insurmountable, maybe to park it and revisit it but a lot was up in the air. But Catherine persuaded him not to give up, to keep on going, because when the world did open up and look very different then the whole project and the awards were exactly what was going to be needed, because at its core it was all about optimism and hope and she could see that it would be a success as much as William did. It tells you a lot about their relationship and support for one another.

The Earthshot Prize has gone on to receive nearly 6,000 entries in five years, shortlisting 75 finalists and awarding £25 million to its 25 winners. The conservationist Robert Irwin, son of the late Steve Irwin, one of the most influential environmentalists in history, said William's idea was 'leading the way' and would 'inspire' the next generation. Robert became a global ambassador for the prize in 2024, shortly before meeting William in Cape Town, South Africa, for the fourth annual event. After walking in the shadow of the iconic Table Mountain, Robert said William was 'leading with a sense of positivity'.

The Earthshot Prize really stands out as a global mission that leads with a sense of hope, and let's be real, we need hope more than ever before. We also need solutions to the big issues that face our precious planet. The Earthshot Prize exemplifies a sense of urgent optimism. I have the privilege of carrying on a conservation legacy that my dad and my family created, and that is something very important to me. It makes me feel incredibly excited and hopeful when I get to join forces with like-minded causes dedicated to making the world a better place.

Turning his attention to William, Irwin said,

He knows that he can put a spotlight on people making a real difference. He takes this responsibility very seriously, and he has a great ability to direct attention to where it needs to be ... I am always impressed by his knowledge and dedication, and in the conversations I have had with him, I often learn something new. Most importantly, though, he truly cares about a healthy planet for our future generations.

A former senior adviser said,

There was definitely a shift in attitude following the Caribbean tour. A lot of the work had already been operating in the background, if you look at Earthshot, for example, that started in 2018 and launched in 2020, but these were projects that would go beyond turning up for the odd engagement, they would become the fabric of their work over decades. Whether that was creating partnerships, involving different sectors, commissioning research, it was a clear evolution. Then you add to that their own personal profile, of being willing and able to carry that messaging through on a huge scale, it is a very exciting proposition.

Earthshot would therefore just be the beginning. Thirty years after being taken to visit a homeless shelter as a child by his

CHAPTER FOURTEEN

mother, William launched his Homewards project in June 2023 with one goal: to demonstrate that it is possible to end homelessness, 'making it rare, brief and unrepeated'. On 18 June 2023, William announced he would use land he inherited through the Duchy of Cornwall on his father's ascension to the throne, for social housing. In an interview with the *Sunday Times* he said he felt that too often 'people don't even look at' the homeless.

> How many people stop and talk to somebody who is homeless? Very few of us. In my job I get to meet these people. I get to hear the stories; I get to feel it; I get to see it. That for me, and I've heard this from them themselves, matters an awful lot. They've become invisible. It's really important that society acknowledges that there is somebody there and they're having a tough time. It shouldn't happen, but it's right there, you can't ignore it.

As part of a five-year project, William set up a transformative programme operating across six locations in the UK that would each benefit from £500,000 funding. It would bring together dozens of partner organisations, from front-line homelessness charities to big businesses, setting them on a path towards ending homelessness for good. In an ITV documentary released in October 2024, he spoke about his mother's influence and his inspiration for taking on a subject that he realises could leave him open to criticism considering his incredible privilege. 'I feel with my position and my platform, I should be delivering change. I have taken some inspiration and guidance from what my mother did,' he said. 'It's a five-year project, it's ambitious, it's big. I make no bones about that. It's going to be a lot of hard work. The ultimate ambition is to prove that we can prevent homelessness in these regions so then others will come along and go well, if they can do it, why can't we?'

This coalition, like William's others, would involve experts, political leaders and specialists aimed at shaping programmes for purpose with clear ambitious goals. Gordon Brown, who served as Britain's prime minister from 2007 to 2010, became a partner in William's Homewards project in 2025. Brown believes that William's late mother had a profound effect on his commitment.

> The way in which he was influenced by his mother from a very early age has shaped his passion, his dedication and his commitment to these causes ... William really believes that we have to do something about the problems that people, who for whatever reason are left behind and lose out, are going through. His focus on the causes of homelessness and then on how to prevent it and on building the necessary partnerships, that is really the way forward. I see this charity and this movement that he has created going from strength to strength. He is only at the beginning of what will be a very big success story because he has this huge convening power to bring together charities, companies, local authorities, foundations and governments, so we are going to witness something very big which will change lives. He is changing people's view of what homelessness is and what can be done about it. His mother changed people's views on AIDS, she changed views on landmines and he is doing the same with those who find themselves homeless. By having empathy and respect at the heart of everything he does, looking at the causes and effects of homelessness and working out ways to bring partnerships together, that is changing the way we look at the issue. The whole country should be very proud of what he is doing.

Catherine would take a few more years to set up her first project. While she received some criticism for the time it took her to

CHAPTER FOURTEEN

become a leading member of the royal family, that wasn't through a lack of passion. Those who have been alongside her since those early days speak of her sincere desire to use her profile for the benefit of others. Family has always been the cornerstone of her life: from growing up with two loving parents, and siblings who to this day have remained two of her closest confidants and supporters, to having a clear view of how she wanted to bring her own family up, it is the bedrock of her existence. Following her marriage to William, Catherine identified that her increasing profile would provide opportunities to work with experts from almost any field of her choosing. In the background, she quietly set about reaching out to academics, teachers, educators and charities, to determine where she could be of use. In her conversations with experts on issues such as mental health and addiction, Catherine learned that very often the suffering of the most vulnerable people she met could be traced back to the earliest years of their lives. Aides who worked with her at the time said she quickly embarked on a 'fact-finding mission' to learn more about how the early years, and especially the first five years, of children's lives really shape their physical and mental health, and well-being later on as adults. Catherine decided that in order to be taken seriously, while she was still accumulating the necessary background experience, she could achieve her ambitious plans by forming collaborative partnerships between experts and organisations to raise the salience of early years as an issue.

Her first major step was in 2018, when she established a steering group to explore how best to support academics, practitioners and charities in their work to provide all children with the best possible start in life. In 2020, Catherine launched a nationwide public survey called '5 Big Questions' to gather views from parents and carers about early childhood, looking at the opportunities children from different backgrounds have, what they need, and how the country can help the youngest generation. The project was praised by the Queen, government ministers and charities such as the Anna Freud Centre, which specialises in child mental health research. It was with family in mind that she set up the Royal Foundation Centre for Early Childhood in 2021, with the aim of improving the lives of generations of young people. Using her experience from a decade of working behind the scenes meeting academics, business leaders, charity bosses and families, Catherine announced that the centre would focus on researching people's experiences in early childhood and examining the cause of today's hardest social challenges, such as addiction, family breakdown, poor mental health, suicide and homelessness.

Jamie Lowther-Pinkerton, William and Catherine's former private secretary, said:

> Catherine laid the groundwork over many years but it would be fair to say she hasn't broken cover until recently. But it's never been about putting herself at the centre of what she is doing, she has always sought to bring people and organisations together to make a difference, which is the real difference in how she and William operate. For Catherine, I would say this shows she has made considered choices, done due diligence and chosen causes that are incredibly important to her. In order to bring the spotlight to bear, you have to know what you are talking about and whenever she talks about the early years especially, she has now become a true force to make a real difference in people's lives. From the start of her involvement with the family, there was a real emphasis that it is a long race and you are far better off at getting it right if you take your time, but from the very start she was incredibly interested in taking

CHAPTER FOURTEEN

early years on and what she has achieved in the field already is a great testament to that work over many years.

Courtiers suggest Catherine has applied herself in the background to educate herself on the central issues of her projects so that she can offer something that goes beyond her profile. Giovanna Fletcher, host of the hugely successful parenting podcast *Happy Mum, Happy Baby*, said how she was taken aback not only by Catherine's knowledge of the early years, but also her humility in discussing her insecurities as a parent when she made a surprise appearance on the podcast in February 2020.

> Having met her previously, I knew she was a great listener, I knew that everyone she met, she was fully invested in what they were saying and had a real quality on how to build conversations with people that she was intent on learning from. But the knowledge that she has built up in the early-years sector, the dedication she has given to it and the different people she had brought together means that she can speak as an authority on the subject, which is incredibly impressive. Her dedication to the early years is beyond just caring, it's an investment in the future of the next generation, and her willingness to share her own personal experiences of motherhood, parenting and her influences is incredibly inspiring. When someone is in her role, you would assume they would have all the confidence in the world, but her humility is what sets her apart.

In 2023, Catherine launched the next stage of the Centre for Early Childhood's work with the Shaping Us campaign. Billed as a landmark project, the Duchess believed that more needed to be done to build on the success of 5 Big Questions survey and build a public awareness campaign around the importance of early childhood in shaping adults and society. Catherine believed that while the Centre for Early Childhood was building a strong body of academic research, the general public would struggle to identify what its objectives and results were if they could not see their impact on the real world. The result was to collaborate on a special 90-second animation film, showing how a little girl named Layla is shaped by her interactions with the people and environment around her, from pregnancy to the age of five. At the launch, Catherine said, 'The way we develop, through our experiences, relationships, and surroundings during our early childhood, fundamentally shapes our whole lives. It affects everything from our ability to form relationships and thrive at work, to our mental and physical well-being as adults and the way we parent our own children.'

Mental health campaigner Fearne Cotton, who worked with Catherine on a number of events and helped launch the project, said:

> What I think is so remarkable about Shaping Us is how the Princess of Wales has gathered just the most brilliant minds to really create something that is game-changing. I work in the mental health space and one of the bits that we are still missing culturally is the awareness of the profound effects our childhoods have on us, and her focus on this issue has changed the whole narrative of how people are thinking. She is not only coming at this from her position as a mother, but also knowing that she's got such great potential to influence, and I couldn't think of a better way to use a platform like this. As a society, as parents, we are facing such a strange landscape of great change and the awareness and protection of our children's mental health and the way we

CHAPTER FOURTEEN

can react to this as parents, care-givers and families, should be top of the agenda.

This sense of family would lead William and Catherine to make one of the biggest decisions of their lives, when, in summer 2022, they decided to move from Kensington Palace to Windsor. This decision was set against a backdrop of the Queen's failing health and the couple's desire for their children to spend more time with their great-grandmother, who had moved to Windsor permanently at the start of the pandemic, as she entered her final years. This brought most of the family physically closer together as they prepared to celebrate the Queen's Platinum Jubilee – with the exception of the Sussexes, of course, which remained a thorny issue. On 1 June the couple flew in for the Jubilee celebrations from their home in California, after behind-the-scenes negotiations that had guaranteed them a full security detail when attending events across the bank holiday weekend. Harry and Meghan arrived by private jet, with their two children Archie and Lilibet, and were greeted by three of the Queen's protection officers, who whisked them to Frogmore Cottage in Windsor.

On the public stage, the tensions within the family were evident across the weekend of celebrations. At Trooping the Colour on 2 June, the official celebration of the sovereign's birthday, Harry and Meghan were relegated to watching from a window in the Paymaster General's Office with a view over Horse Guards Parade. At a service of thanksgiving at St Paul's Cathedral on 3 June, they arrived to a mixture of cheers and some boos from the crowd outside, and were deliberately seated on the opposite side of the aisle to the Duke and Duchess of Cambridge, to avoid any awkward visuals. When they arrived, William and Catherine did not glance in the Sussexes' direction before taking their positions. A former courtier said, 'It all had to be carefully choreographed, mainly to limit what the press could make over Harry and Meghan's attendances at the events. Everything was done to make sure the focus was on celebrating the Queen.' After the service, Harry and Meghan chose not to attend a reception at Buckingham Palace with other royals, instead returning to Windsor early.

On 4 June Harry and Meghan threw a small birthday party for their daughter's first birthday, creating an opportunity for the Queen to meet her great-granddaughter for the first time. Despite the warmth extended to the monarch, the Sussexes did not meet William and Catherine – relations between the couples remained incredibly fractured. Harry and Meghan also decided to skip the music concert outside Buckingham Palace later that day, where Prince Charles and William made speeches in honour of the Queen's incredible milestone anniversary.

Despite the evident difficulties after so many years of instability, portraying the cohesiveness of the royal family on the weekend of the Platinum Jubilee celebrations was very important to Queen Elizabeth II. That meant that, although her health was failing, the Queen was determined to not only attend the celebrations, but also to appear on the iconic Buckingham Palace balcony with her three heirs, Princes Charles, William and George, for the finale.

On 5 June 2022, Elizabeth II stepped out onto the balcony to huge cheers from the thousands gathered below. Palace sources at the time said the 96-year-old monarch wanted 'the world to see the heartbeat of her family and the future of the monarchy'. It was indeed a powerful message. In what she may have known would be her final balcony appearance, she possibly felt that with Charles and William emulating her sense of duty and dedication, the country and the Commonwealth were in safe hands. Less than three months later, the landscape of the British royal family would change for ever.

15

THE WORLD MOURNS

At 6.30pm on Thursday, 8 September 2022, Buckingham Palace announced the death of Queen Elizabeth II. After a record-breaking 70 years on the throne, the monarch had passed away peacefully at the Balmoral home that she loved so much.

Just two days before, on Tuesday, 6 September, the Queen had appeared frail, but in good spirits, when she welcomed incoming Prime Minister Liz Truss at Balmoral, having accepted the resignation of Boris Johnson after the Conservative party had been plunged into turmoil. But then, at 6pm on Wednesday, the first signs of serious concerns about the Queen's health emerged, when Buckingham Palace announced that following doctors' advice to rest, the monarch would not be able to attend a virtual meeting of the privy council that evening.

More rumours about the Queen's condition began spreading from 10am on Thursday, resulting in a cascade of calls from royal correspondents to the palaces and their sources in an attempt to shed light on the fast-moving situation. When, at 12.32pm, Buckingham Palace said the Queen was under 'constant medical supervision' but remained comfortable at her home in Aberdeenshire, it provoked a frantic chain of events. Prince Charles, the Duchess of Cornwall and Princess Anne, who were already in Scotland, quickly made their way to Balmoral – signalling the gravity of the situation. Prince William had been notified just before midday of his grandmother's deteriorating

THE WORLD MOURNS

condition, by an aide of his father's, although he was urged not to travel to Scotland right away to avoid causing alarm among the general public. An hour later, at 1pm, William was contacted for a second time and a private jet was organised to get him to Scotland as quickly as possible. Aides arranged for Prince Andrew and the Earl and Countess of Wessex – Edward and Sophie – to accompany him on the flight. Prince Harry and Meghan, who by chance were in the UK, having attended a number of engagements in the preceding days, including an appearance at the One Young World Summit in Manchester, announced that that they would both travel to Scotland. It quickly emerged, however, that they would not be part of the royals' travelling party. Such was the state of the relationship with the Sussexes, William had not reached out to his brother, leaving him to make his own way. William, Andrew, Edward and Sophie scrambled to RAF Northolt in South Ruislip, west London, boarding RAF flight KRF23R at 2.39pm, touching down at Aberdeen Airport around 3.50pm. By the time they landed, the Queen had already died.

While it was assumed that she would also travel with her husband, Catherine made the decision to stay behind. That morning, before news of the Queen's worsening condition started to be relayed, William and Catherine had taken their three young children to their first day at Lambrook School in Berkshire, where they were starting following their move to Windsor. 'As ever, the decision made was the right one for their family,' a courtier said. Catherine called her mother, Carole, and asked her to come over to their Adelaide Cottage home to provide extra support for the children when they returned home from school. After picking them up herself and excitedly finding out about their first day, Catherine delivered the sad news that their beloved 'Gan-Gan' had passed away peacefully.

CHAPTER FIFTEEN

While Catherine would have been welcomed at Balmoral, her absence provided an opportunity for Charles to appeal to Harry to join his family alone. In his memoir, *Spare*, Harry recalled a phone call his father made to him, writing: 'He said I was welcome at Balmoral, but he didn't want ... her. He started to lay out his reason, which was nonsensical, and disrespectful, and I wasn't having it.' A source close to the King has since refuted Harry's version of events, saying the King never expressed such a view. 'Any suggestion that the King [Charles] said he "didn't want" Meghan there is simply untrue. It was explained to Harry that as the Princess of Wales [Catherine] was not going, perhaps it would be best for Harry to attend on his own, alongside his family, who at the time were dealing with an incredibly stressful situation. How the Duke of Sussex took offence to that is a matter for him.' At 1.52pm Harry, who was due to attend a charity event in London that evening, announced that he was cancelling his plans and would travel to Scotland separately, but 'in co-ordination with other family members' plans'.

Just after 5pm, the royal party, driven by William in a dark green Range Rover, and followed closely by royal protection officers, arrived at a rain-drenched Balmoral, a little while before dusk descended. Inside the Queen's favourite home, where he had spent many wonderfully happy summers as a child with his father, grandparents and the wider family, and in later years with his own wife and children, William was greeted by his aunt Princess Anne and his father. The group were taken separately to the Queen's room to say their final goodbyes. At 6.30pm the flag at Buckingham Palace was lowered, and the Palace announced in a statement: 'The Queen died peacefully at Balmoral this afternoon. The King and The Queen Consort will remain at Balmoral this evening and will return to London tomorrow.' Harry would not arrive at the castle until shortly after 8pm. Harry only discovered his grandmother had passed when he opened the BBC news app on his phone after the plane had landed. Changing into a black tie, he stepped off the plane into a thick mist and made his way to a waiting car. Anne was on hand to meet him at the castle door and took him to the Queen's room to bid a final farewell. William had already left, choosing to stay with Charles and Camilla at their Birkhall home, close by on the estate, and so conveniently avoiding Harry who was left to have dinner with Anne, Andrew, Edward and Sophie. Harry left at dawn the following morning as Operation Unicorn, the codename for the contingency plan that had been put in place were Her Majesty to pass in Scotland, was executed. Charles III was King, and the Carolean era had begun.

It is perhaps the most peculiar conundrum about being heir to the throne: the job you have been prepared to do since birth is wholly contingent on the death of a beloved parent. In the BBC interview to celebrate Queen Elizabeth II's 90th birthday, William echoed the sentiments his father had expressed many times before him: 'I certainly don't lie awake at night waiting or hoping for it,' he said. 'Because it sadly means my family has moved on, and I don't want that.' And yet both men are expected to be completely ready when the time comes. A source said: 'William wasn't being cute with that response. You can be perfectly mindful of how you envisage your future playing out and what you can do to effect that without wishing it to become a reality sooner than it has to be.' Another source said that William's focus had 'stepped up a gear' in recent years, mainly owing to his increased maturity, the death of his grandmother and absence of his brother. 'A slimmed-down monarchy will obviously present those options which have to be considered regardless of what anyone else thinks,' the source added.

The next day, 9 September, after returning to London, the King delivered his first address to the nation. From the

CHAPTER FIFTEEN

Blue Drawing Room at Buckingham Palace, where the Queen recorded so many of her Christmas messages, Charles described the 'loss beyond measure', of his 'darling Mama', a pain that was softened only by the memory of the inspiration she gave and of a life led by example. Charles, who had waited more than 50 years to take the throne, promised to honour the vow his mother had made on her 21st birthday in 1947, in Cape Town, South Africa, dedicating herself to a life of service to her country, its people and the Commonwealth. Courtiers were pleasantly surprised at the reaction to the King as he toured the United Kingdom following his accession. For years, palace officials had gamed scenarios where the country would not welcome Charles as monarch, such was the nervousness about his divorce from Princess Diana, his infidelity and his eventual marriage to Camilla Parker Bowles, who was for many years seen as public enemy number one by the British tabloid press. Charles's relationship with Camilla, who would now be Queen, had survived years of intense scrutiny, and their public image had undergone a huge transformation in the two decades since their marriage. It is both a testament to all of this and the way in which Charles has largely been accepted into the hearts of the nation that his emotional address was universally praised.

It was in this deeply moving message that the King announced that William and Catherine, from that moment, would be known as the Prince and Princess of Wales. 'With Catherine beside him, our new Prince and Princess of Wales will, I know, continue to inspire and lead our national conversations, helping to bring the marginal to the centre ground where vital help can be given,' Charles said. Charles had of course discussed his plans with his son and daughter-in-law in the years leading up to his accession. Queen Elizabeth II was also in favour of the titles being bestowed upon William and Catherine on the event of her death. But it was not all plain sailing. The last Princess of Wales had been William's mother, Diana, and courtiers said that while Catherine had a full appreciation of the history associated with the role, she was determined to find her own path. But Catherine had also privately expressed to William and to Charles her reservations about taking over the title, conscious of the British public's exceptional feeling for, and connection to, Princess Diana even 25 years after her death. 'This tells you how considered she is,' said a former senior aide to both William and Catherine.

> She is benevolent with her intentions, but also wishes to carve out her own role for both herself and her family, which in many ways looks very different to how generations of royals have acted in the past. She is very aware the pace that she wants to progress and the way in which she sees her future role within the institution, and I think when she was convinced to take the title on, and there was a bit of convincing, she felt that while there would be inevitable comparisons with Diana, she could manage it in her own way while having full respect for the way Diana carved out a very different role for herself within the royal family.

William returned to the family home on 9 September, he and Catherine focused their attention on how best they could pay their respects to the Queen over the coming days. The future that they had discussed in private so many times over the years was now a reality.

In an emotional tribute to the life and legacy of his grandmother, released on the morning of Saturday 10 September, William thanked the Queen for being present in every significant moment of his life:

CHAPTER FIFTEEN

I have had the benefit of The Queen's wisdom and reassurance into my fifth decade. My wife has had twenty years of her guidance and support. My three children have got to spend holidays with her and create memories that will last their whole lives.

She was by my side at my happiest moments. And she was by my side during the saddest days of my life. I knew this day would come, but it will be some time before the reality of life without Grannie will truly feel real.

I thank her for the kindness she showed my family and me. And I thank her on behalf of my generation for providing an example of service and dignity in public life that was from a different age, but always relevant to us all. My grandmother famously said that grief was the price we pay for love. All of the sadness we will feel in the coming weeks will be testament to the love we felt for our extraordinary Queen. I will honour her memory by supporting my father, The King, in every way I can.

The Queen had doted on him from a young age and been there to offer protection following the breakdown of his parents' relationship and the tragic death of his mother. With her passing, William was at once confronted with the next stage of his life beginning. His father was the new monarch, and he was now next in line to the throne. It was time to draw on the preparations William and Catherine had made in the years before now, the laying of the foundations, everything they had done to get their own family ready for what lay ahead.

That day, they decided they would travel the short distance to Windsor Castle to spend some time viewing the floral tributes and take the opportunity to thank some of the hundreds of well-wishers who had gathered to pay their respects. There was one small issue, however. Less than half a mile away, Harry and Meghan were at their Frogmore Cottage home, having decided to stay in the UK until the Queen's funeral nine days later. There was only one thing to do. In honour of the promise he had made to his grandmother, that he would not shut his brother out for ever, William picked up his phone and tentatively texted Harry. They had not spoken since Prince Philip's funeral in April a year earlier, nor had they exchanged messages apart from the gift and card that William and Catherine had sent to Harry and Meghan on the birth of their daughter Lilibet that June. 'He thought it was an important show of unity at an incredibly difficult time for the family', a source close to William said. William's short invitation for Harry and Meghan to join him and Catherine for a public walkabout was equally brief, but quickly set in motion the opportunity for the two couples to at least put on a show of unity at such a testing time.

The media had been briefed that William and Catherine planned to view the flowers and meet the public at around 4.30pm, but it was not until 5.15pm that they pulled up to the gates at the end of the Long Walk in a black Audi driven by William, with Catherine in the passenger seat and Harry and Meghan riding in the back. The two couples, who had once been dubbed 'The Fab Four' were back together, if only for a fleeting moment. Despite the rows and the heartache caused by the bitter split, Catherine was quoted by the *Daily Telegraph* as saying to one well-wisher that 'at times like this you've got to come together'. After spending 40 minutes viewing the displays and taking even more flowers from members of the public who had stood there for more than 12 hours, William again offered his brother and sister-in-law a lift, driving off to their nearby homes on the Windsor estate. Perhaps William had Charles's words from his first public address ringing in his ears: the Queen had always demonstrated the capacity to

CHAPTER FIFTEEN

see the best in everyone. For now, while the country mourned, their frigid relationship had momentarily thawed.

Four days later, on 14 September, the coffin of Queen Elizabeth II was transported from Buckingham Palace to Westminster, where it would lie in state until her funeral on 19 September. King Charles III, Princess Anne and Princes Andrew and Edward followed their mother's coffin, while William and Harry walked side by side behind them. Both were determined that their relationship should not overshadow events, aware the eyes of the world were also on them. The sight of William and Harry united again, and walking behind the Queen's coffin, evoked memories of the day in 1997 when, aged 15 and 12, they had walked behind their mother's. The mourning wives of Windsor were waiting for them to arrive at Westminster Hall. Queen Camilla, the new Princess of Wales, the Countess of Wessex and the Duchess of Sussex stood side by side in a line before the committal service began. A day later, William admitted to well-wishers at Sandringham, the Queen's Norfolk home, that his solemn walk behind the coffin had brought back painful memories: 'Doing the walk yesterday was challenging. It brought back a few memories. It's one of these moments where you kind of think to yourself, "I've prepared myself for this, but I'm not that prepared."'

A close friend of William's said of the time: 'What was important to both William and Catherine was to get among the people and thank them. They had lost someone very special to them, William of course losing his grandmother, the person who had provided so much guidance to him throughout his entire life, but he realised the country was hurting too.'

The Queen's grandchildren took part in a public vigil on Saturday 17 September, with William and Harry leading their cousins: Prince Andrew's daughters Eugenie and Beatrice, Prince

Edward and Sophie's daughter Lady Louise Windsor and son, James, James (formerly Viscount Severn, now Earl of Wessex), alongside Princess Anne's son Peter Phillips and daughter Zara Tindall. On the eve of the funeral, the King hosted 500 world leaders and dignitaries at Buckingham Palace while the Princess of Wales hosted Ukraine's first lady Olena Zelenska at a private meeting at the palace, reinforcing Britain's commitment to the country that had been at war with Russia since February of that year. Catherine had met President Volodymyr Zelensky and his wife in 2020, but her high-profile meeting was clear evidence of the bigger role she would now play in royal duties and unofficial diplomacy.

On 19 September, the Queen was laid to rest. Kings, queens, presidents and world leaders flocked to Westminster Abbey for the grand state funeral, and thousands packed the streets from Westminster to Windsor to pay their respects as she made her final journey. The Queen's coffin was taken to Windsor Castle and, in a private family ceremony, lowered into the vault of St George's Chapel, reuniting her with her cherished husband, Prince Philip.

Even though William and Harry had stood shoulder to shoulder to honour their grandmother, soon after the funeral they would go their separate ways again. In the hours following the Queen's death, Charles and William discussed Harry and Meghan's attendance at the events that would follow. One source close to William said that both father and son agreed they would 'exude extreme caution around them', fearing that anything they did say could be used as material in Harry's upcoming memoir, which had been announced in June 2021 and was initially scheduled for publication in late 2022 – but would be delayed to early 2023 following the Queen's death.

Sources close to William suggest a turning point in his relationship with Charles came when the Prince of Wales began

CHAPTER FIFTEEN

to grow his own family. While William's bond with his father throughout his childhood and adolescence may be described as complex, those close to him will relay that as both men have matured it has evolved into one founded on mutual respect and understanding. William has developed a sincere appreciation and understanding of the demands that Charles felt as a parent in a troubled marriage, and as a single parent under intense circumstances. William also recognises how his father allowed him, with the late Queen's blessing, to seek a life outside of the institution for longer than he had been permitted himself.

William, in turn, has a growing appreciation of the issues his father has had to deal with in his life, while also valuing Charles's love and guidance throughout his darkest times. In a 2018 BBC documentary celebrating Charles's 70th birthday, William praised his father's commitment to the causes he had championed throughout his life, and his dedication to duty, as well as the fact that he is a 'brilliant' grandfather. Reminiscing about finding his father in his study asleep on his desk, with piles of letters and papers surrounding him, William reflected on whether reaching his eighth decade would present an opportunity for Charles to slow down.

> I think now he's reached his 70th year, it's a perfect time to consolidate a little bit because as most families would do, you are worried about having them around and making sure their health's OK. And he's the fittest man I know but equally I want him to be fit until he's 95. So, having more time with him at home would be lovely, and being able to, you know, play with the grandchildren. Because when he's there, he's brilliant. But we need him there as much as possible.

It is true that there have been competitive tensions along the way – the overlapping of tours, the way in which William has become a leading light in the conversation on environmentalism and against climate change, an issue that Charles had led on for more than 50 years – but insiders suggest that much division presented in the media between the two men has been 'largely manufactured' and a 'deep and profound respect for one another' exists. Of course, they are incredibly different individuals. They have their own, divergent, attitudes concerning tradition, the way in which family life competes with the expectation of duty, and their eagerness for change in a rapidly evolving world. And while they have many interests that are aligned, and which seem to have grown ever stronger in recent times – the environment, conservation, the military, a life of service – they are two men who embody very different historical eras. While the King indulges in a passion for literature, classical music and the arts, William has no problem in letting it be known he would rather blast out Australian rock anthems by AC/DC, and has a particular reverence for noughties dance music. The King's passion for Shakespeare has not been passed down, with William being renowned for being more of a 'box-set guy', according to one aide quoted in Robert Hardman's *Charles III*.

Another major difference lies in William's attitude to the Prince of Wales title. As Robert Hardman identified in his book *Charles III*, William made three early decisions that each represented a break from his father's approach. William would not spend months at university learning Welsh. It is an issue he has drawn much criticism for and one, it is fair to say, he cannot really hide from. Secondly, he would not buy a home in Wales, although he does technically have the use of a farm in Llwynywermod that is owned by the Duchy of Cornwall estate he inherited on Charles's accession. Thirdly, and most staunchly,

CHAPTER FIFTEEN

he showed no desire to take part in a grand formal investiture like his father's, which was televised in 1969. While these departures from tradition might appear to signify a distinct lack of interest in the office, or indeed the country, courtiers say that couldn't be further from the truth. Indeed, both William and Catherine have huge affection for Wales, having spent some of their happiest moments together in Anglesey, and have visited the nation five times in three years. 'Both William and Catherine don't do things for show, or for the sake of it,' one palace aide said. 'They love Wales, they love the people and the country, and that commitment will only grow stronger. But for the prince, many of these traditions of the past are rather performative. They would rather demonstrate their commitment through their work.'

Charles and William had been united throughout the Sussexes' departure and the scandal involving Prince Andrew and his relationship with Jeffrey Epstein, which has brought them ever closer together in recent years. 'While [the King] loves both his sons equally, his relationship with the Prince of Wales is something that has strengthened over the period of difficulty experienced by the family as external battles have occurred,' said one source. Sources close to the King suggest that one of his main objectives since ascending the throne at the age of 73 has been to prepare William for his time as monarch as best he can – recognising that it's perhaps the most important thing for him to do considering the age at which he took the Crown.

One of the King and William's first joint ventures in their new roles was, on 14 November 2022, to effectively strip Andrew and Harry of their roles as Counsellors of State. Up to that point, under the Regency Acts of 1937 and 1953, those tasked with handling affairs of state in the monarch's absence had been the sovereign's consort plus the first four adults in the line of succession. If the King were to be incapacitated and the Prince of Wales, for example, overseas, then the duty would have fallen to the Duke of Sussex, the Duke of York or Princess Beatrice. Conveniently bypassing a major overhaul of the Act, the King declared that he would be 'most content' for Parliament to amend the rules by adding the names of the Princess Royal and Prince Edward to the list, while stating that only working royals would be able to stand in for him.

While the Duke and Duchess of Sussex had stood dutifully in memory of the late Queen, the bitter split from the royal family endured. That December, they were due to appear in an intimate documentary series that would lift the lid on their time in the royal family, part of their $100 million deal with the streaming service Netflix. And that wasn't the end of the difficulties at Buckingham Palace. In November, Prince William's godmother and one of the late Queen's closest confidantes, Lady Susan Hussey, stood accused of racially abusing a black guest at a Buckingham Palace reception. British-born domestic abuse campaigner Ngozi Fulani claimed that Lady Susan Hussey, who remained in an honorary role as chief-lady-in-waiting at the grace of the King, repeatedly questioned her on her heritage, asking 'What part of Africa are you from?' When informed by the guest that she was British, 83-year-old Lady Susan remarked, 'No, but where do you really come from, where do your people come from?' When Ms Fulani first raised the issue some days later on 30 November, the palace launched an investigation into the 'unacceptable and deeply regrettable comments' and promptly dismissed the veteran royal aide from her role. The row erupted as William and Catherine prepared for the start of a three-day visit to Boston in the United States, as part of the prince's second annual Earthshot Prize awards. In the wake of the Duchess of Sussex's claims that unnamed members of the family had discussed her unborn child's skin tone, William moved quickly to condemn Lady Susan's

CHAPTER FIFTEEN

remarks, saying through an aide that 'racism has no place in our society'. Lady Susan later met with Ms Fulani at Buckingham Palace and offered her sincere apologies for the comments that were made and the distress they caused to Ms Fulani.

William and Catherine hoped to move on swiftly – he wanted to celebrate one of his flagship projects and they were on their first foreign tour together as Prince and Princess of Wales – but just 24 hours later another bombshell would present itself in the form of a trailer for Harry and Meghan's Netflix show.

In royal circles, this trailer was considered a blatant attempt to hijack the Waleses' visit; it included a dramatic voiceover from Harry saying 'no one sees what's happening behind closed doors' as Meghan appears in the background, stretched over an armchair, apparently crying. The next day the *Daily Mail*, quoting royal sources, called it a 'declaration of war', while *The Times* presented the Sussexes as 'Self-styled victims' who were 'pulling no punches'. The Sussexes may or may not have had anything to do with the timing of the release, but they must have understood the consternation it would cause. And yet, though it was certainly unwelcome at a time when the royal family was still reeling from the death of Queen Elizabeth and dealing with the racism accusations, it served to bring William even closer to his father. 'They were in constant contact over that period,' one courtier revealed. 'They were completely aligned that if there were any further accusations they believed to be untrue then they would be ready to respond.' In the end while the documentary did garner hyperbolic headlines claiming the Sussexes were intent on bringing down the monarchy, palace officials described the six-part series documentary as a 'drawn-out whingefest'.

Soon after the senior royals spent Christmas together at Sandringham that year, there was Harry's memoir to deal with. In the days leading up to publication on 10 January 2023, Harry took part in several high-profile interviews where he said he wanted to make peace with his father and brother. These assertions seemed astonishing when, on 5 January, leaked copies of the hugely anticipated book emerged across Europe, with stories that were as wounding as expected. Across more than 500 pages, Harry vented at the lack of compassion from his family for his mental health issues, accused his brother of assaulting him, and suggested Catherine made life difficult for his wife as she entered the royal fold. Further insult to Charles included Harry labelling him an 'old man' and claiming that Camilla leaked stories about Harry through the palace – which added to the overall feeling that Harry's relationship with the rest of his family was terminal. A source close to William said:

> At first he [William] was incredibly angry. The situation had spiralled out of control but the book reinforced his view that he [Harry] was not to be trusted. [William] was incredibly let down and immensely sad, but in a way it made him more determined to rally around his own family and his father and I think what you've seen since then is a complete dedication to concentrate on the things you can have an effect on, or what you view as important, and engaging [with Harry] did not come under that.

Another source gave a fascinating insight into how Catherine dealt with the criticism: 'Her attitude was consistently "this will pass". Whenever William would get riled up about it, she would calm the situation down and bring him back to what matters most to them. That is their family and what they are doing.'

Eight months would pass before the nation geared up for the King's Coronation. Although in that time Charles's estranged son, an unsavoury allegation of racism at the heart of the insti-

CHAPTER FIFTEEN

tution, and the threat of protests overshadowing his big day, had threatened to blow his reign off course, by and large, the nation had taken to the new-look royal family. The tide of public opinion was turning against the Duke and Duchess of Sussex, largely due to them earning tens of millions of pounds in the corporate world while still engaging in a one-sided war of words from the other side of the world. Charles was being widely welcomed by crowds up and down the country as he sought to hit the ground running during his first year at the helm. For many, it would be the first Coronation they had witnessed, and the rolling news coverage, countless camera angles and days of build-up swept much of the country into a state of excitement. William sealed his father's crowning with a kiss on his father's cheek, pledging his loyalty to him. Their double act was evident for the world to see, signalling not only a new era but William's emergence as a king in waiting.

16

IN SICKNESS AND IN STRENGTH

The first anniversary of the Queen's death was a reminder, not only the passing of time, but also the fractiousness within the royal family that she had left behind. William and Harry had not spoken since the late monarch's funeral and a gulf remained between them. In September 2023, when the Duke of Sussex visited his home country to complete a handful of public engagements, no time was set aside to meet with Charles or William. It's easy to guess what Her Majesty would have made of the continuing rift between the Sussexes and the rest of her family, but it was clear that despite an unofficial truce that had held until her funeral, her passing had done little to bring the two warring sides together. The end of Elizabeth's reign had been far from harmonious. One of her sons was embroiled in a tawdry sex scandal and a beloved grandson was continually lashing out at the institution she had led so gracefully for so long. Yet despite the family troubles that had dogged the last years of her life, the Queen had been at peace and with no regrets when she passed. According to the Right Reverend Dr Iain Greenshields, then Moderator of the General Assembly of the Church of Scotland, Elizabeth had been in a reflective mood at the time, reminiscing on her Platinum Jubilee and the influence of her father on her strong faith. In the summer of 2022, just

CHAPTER SIXTEEN

weeks before the monarch's death, Dr Greenshields had spent a few days at Balmoral. He was part of an exclusive guest list who dined with the Queen, including Sophie Wessex, the Princess Royal and her husband, Vice Admiral Sir Timothy Laurence, and John Warren, the Queen's racing manager. Dr Greenshields – who stepped down from his post in May 2023, delivered the homily at the Service of Thanksgiving for the life of the Queen at St Giles's Cathedral, Edinburgh, on 11 September 2022, and attended her funeral at Westminster Abbey – revealed in an interview in the *Daily Mail*: 'At one point in our conversations she went to the window and said, "who would not want to be here". She was in a very peaceful, private place. She was at peace.'

At 9.50am on 8 September 2023, as the nation remembered the life and legacy of Elizabeth II, and the more than 70 years she spent on the throne, Harry made a solo pilgrimage to his grandmother's final resting place at St George's Chapel, in the grounds of Windsor Castle. As if further evidence of Harry's estrangement from the rest of his family were needed, the King was 500 miles away in Balmoral, where he spoke to staff and a small group of well-wishers after a church service at Crathie Kirk, the Queen's favourite place of worship. In a recorded message, the King paid tribute to his mother, saying he recalled with 'great affection her long life, devoted service and all she meant to so many of us'. Charles also took the opportunity to make special mention of Camilla, as the world was still getting used to the notion of referring to her as the Queen. 'I am deeply grateful, too, for the love and support that has been shown to my wife and myself during this year as we do our utmost to be of service.'

After Harry visited the chapel in Windsor, which had been unlocked especially for his private vigil, he headed to Germany for a launch event ahead of the 2024 Invictus Games in

Dusseldorf. He had been less than half a mile away from William and Catherine's Adelaide Cottage home; neither party sought to arrange a meeting. Not long after, the Waleses took a helicopter to Pembrokeshire.

The Prince and Princess of Wales were attending a private service of remembrance at St Davids Cathedral, which Elizabeth II had visited on numerous occasions throughout her reign. William clasped his hands and bowed in silence as Catherine laid a bouquet of ivy, eucalyptus and white roses by a portrait of the late Queen. The princess later told well-wishers how she continued to remember Elizabeth with great affection, telling them: 'We all have wonderful memories of her. We have to hold on to them, cherish them.'

The late Queen's unifying force, which had for so long bound the family together, had seemingly been extinguished with her passing. On the King's 75th birthday, on 14 November, Harry did reach out to his father, but it would not be enough to secure an invitation to the extended royal family's annual Christmas gathering at Sandringham. While friends of the Sussexes who were quoted in a *Sunday Times* article suggested that the couple wanted to 'change the state of play', and would 'readily accept' an invitation to the festive gathering, the King was in no mood to indulge them. 'Trust and goodwill were not available at that particular juncture,' said a senior royal source. Perhaps the King knew what was coming: less than two weeks later, on 26 November, after months of dealing with the allegations from Harry and Meghan of bias, mistreatment and racism at the heart of the institution, the monarchy was faced with more claims of jealousy and infighting from the Sussex camp, including Charles being disappointed by William's failure to involve him in his big environmental initiative, the Earthshot Prize, and Catherine ignoring Meghan's 'cries for help'.

CHAPTER SIXTEEN

Omid Scobie, the co-author, with Carolyn Durand, of *Finding Freedom*, which had charted Harry and Meghan's escape from The Firm, released a damning new book, the sensationally titled *Endgame*, which promised to examine the royal family 'in crisis'. Scobie – dubbed 'Meghan's mouthpiece' by the *Daily Mail* and the 'Sussexes' journalist supporter-in-chief' by the *Guardian* – had stressed in pre-publication interviews that he had not interviewed Harry and Meghan as part of his research. But he also admitted that sharing mutual friends with the Duchess of Sussex gave him the advantage 'with getting information and breaking details'. Whatever his previous protestations, the actual scale of the advantage he had enjoyed when producing his previous tome was revealed when, in November 2021, Meghan was forced to apologise to the Court of Appeal for making a misleading statement in her privacy case against the *Mail on Sunday*'s publishers in regards to the publication of a private letter to her father. She admitted that, far from having exerted no influence over the international bestseller *Finding Freedom*, she had in fact authorised her former communications secretary Jason Knauf to provide information to the authors.

Scobie's new book was, unsurprisingly, dismissed by both Buckingham Palace and Kensington Palace, with one source quoted in the *Daily Mail* labelling it 'vicious … plain nasty' and 'depressingly poisonous'. But other insiders pointed to what they saw as the worrying trend of the Sussexes' use of favourable media. In an interview with the *Sunday Times*, Scobie portrayed William as 'hot-headed' and power-hungry, and suggested he was actively allowing aides to engage in an ugly briefing war against his brother. Scobie went further, describing Catherine as an underachiever who was so afraid of public criticism that she was reluctant to step out of line or engage in anything riskier than the most basic of duties. Palace sources naturally leapt to the defence of the Waleses: figures quoted in an article in the *Daily Mail* blasted the claims as 'outrageous', and accused Scobie of 'peddling' what they described as conspiracy theories 'dressed up as fact'. Reflecting on the period, one senior palace source offered another view.

> What everyone fails to remember every time there is a raft of these types of headlines painting a war between two houses, is that there is a family at the centre of all of this ... one that has been torn apart in quite distressing circumstances and not for the first time. However, what was concerning was Harry and Meghan's free use of the media when it suited them, either with Netflix or Harry's books, or perhaps leaking details to a friend, to portray the family as constantly out to get them, when they knew full well they [the royal family] were extremely unlikely to respond. There is and will always be a dignified silence but those comments and continued criticism were absolutely extremely hurtful.

Yet away from the imputations of spite and bigotry, far worse was to come. While Harry had attempted to walk back some of Meghan's claims about his family's racism, Scobie found himself at the centre of a media storm when it emerged that a Dutch translation of the book that had gone on sale in the Netherlands contained the names of the two royals who had, Meghan claimed in their interview with Oprah Winfrey, raised 'concerns' over Prince Archie's skin colour. Neither Harry nor Meghan had been willing to name those at the centre of the allegations, although Harry had told Winfrey off camera that it had not been the Queen or Prince Philip. Much to the fury of both the family and the palace, this had led to a public game of 'Guess Who?' On 29 November 2023, on his *TalkTV* show, the journalist Piers

CHAPTER SIXTEEN

Morgan was the first to name the King and Catherine as the two senior royals. They had been identified by the Duchess of Sussex in letters she wrote to Charles on the issue in 2022, and also named in the translation of Scobie's book. The *Guardian*, the *New York Times* and the *Daily Mirror* followed suit. Then, Saskia Peeters, one of the Dutch translators, challenged Scobie's claim that he had not mentioned the names in his book, insisting that they were included in the manuscript she was given to work on by the publisher Xander Uitgevers. Palace sources described the entries as a 'mendacious smear' and royal lawyers were called in to consider legal action as the publisher was forced to withdraw from sale, then pulp, copies across the Netherlands.

Whereas the furore filled the news agenda for days, a palace source tells of an 'almost serene calmness' from both Catherine and William:

> There's no getting away from it, it wasn't pleasant. But no one was in a state of panic, there wasn't any crisis to fight back. They knew it would be handled appropriately in-house and the whole scenario was so preposterous that it was more hurtful than anything. Here are two people who spend their time doing all they can for the benefit of others and their characters were being smeared in the most appalling manner. The message was to keep calm, stay together and carry on, and that was from the very top.

Another well-placed source suggests William was vexed at the audacity of dragging his father and wife into the racism row without any foundation. 'He was pissed off,' said the source. 'He thought it was callous and purposeful. To be accused of something so abhorrent was completely beyond the pale and couldn't be further from the truth of how they are as people and as a family.'

In the lead-up to Christmas, the family put on several displays of unity. On 5 December they welcomed more than 500 dignitaries to Buckingham Palace for a glittering diplomatic reception. Then, on 8 December, William and Catherine took their three children to Westminster Abbey for the princess's annual Together at Christmas carol concert, accompanied by other members of the royal family. In his Christmas message, the King spoke of peace and compassion amid wars in the Middle East and Ukraine, and quoted the Bible in a call for 'peace on Earth and goodwill to all'. In a clear sign of his wish for further harmony in his family, Charles invited his former sister-in-law, Sarah, Duchess of York, to join the royal family and walk alongside her ex-husband Prince Andrew to church at Sandringham. It would be the first time she had participated in this tradition in 32 years. The King's decision to bring his brother back into the family fold was an issue William fundamentally disagreed with, to such a degree that he challenged Charles directly. A source with knowledge of the conversation said that William was 'very much put in his place', and that while he did not agree with the view that Andrew's exile should be limited, he did not provoke his father further. William's negative view of his uncle Andrew had predated the Duke of York's fall from grace. For years the Prince of Wales had questioned what benefit his uncle was to the wider operation. 'Long before he was embroiled in the scandal [involving Virginia Giuffre], he'd always thought his uncle was a bit of an ignoramus,' a palace source revealed.

> He would question 'what does he actually do?', but it was more than that. He'd seen how Andrew behaved in front of staff, ordering people about, the aggressive or dismissive manner, they'd never seen eye to eye. William has a relationship with his cousins [Princesses Beatrice and

CHAPTER SIXTEEN

Eugenie] ... so he takes no umbrage with them, but there's no love lost for Andrew or Sarah.

In an alternate dimension Andrew probably thought there would be a way back into public life if the scandal or the headlines died down, but it would have always had to be while his brother was King. William didn't think either of them [Andrew or Sarah] should be anywhere near the family, publicly or otherwise, but he was overruled by his father.' William and Catherine joined the family at Sandringham alongside the King and Queen. Here, for the first time, in an arrangement familiar to many blended families across the country, Camilla's children and grandchildren were present for the extended festivities.

The harmonious scenes were to last only slightly longer than the Christmas leftovers. As soon as the new year had begun, Andrew was once again in the spotlight, facing a raft of lurid allegations. His fate was sealed following the release of court documents related to a New York defamation case brought in 2015 by Andrew's accuser Virginia Giuffre, against Ghislaine Maxwell, the duke's former friend who procured underage girls for Jeffrey Epstein to abuse. Details in the legal papers suggested the Duke of York had indulged in 'daily massages' during frequent visits to the late paedophile's Florida mansion, had committed 'acts of sexual abuse' and took part in an 'underage orgy'.

William again implored the King to act: to strip Andrew of his titles and banish him from the family for good in order to protect the reputation of the institution. While Andrew had always vehemently denied the allegations, both publicly and privately to his family, one palace source close to William said:

The Prince of Wales was adamant the whole episode would never go away and, despite how others may have felt, there was absolutely no upside in Andrew being protected. His view was crystal clear, Andrew shouldn't be anywhere near the family under any circumstances, not by association, not at family functions, anywhere. Every single time there was a new revelation, which no one knew when it was coming or what the next one would be, it was a stain on all of the family.

The King had begun attempts to coax his brother out of his 30-room Royal Lodge mansion on the Windsor estate, but Andrew – and 'Fergie', who still lived with him rent free – was in no mood to move. The duke told his brother he was 'going nowhere', antagonisingly pointing to the 'cast-iron lease' that he had signed on the property with the Crown Estate in 2002. The *Times* newspaper would quite aptly later dub the row 'The Siege of Royal Lodge'.

There was more drama to come. While the start of the year usually represents a gentle beginning to the royal calendar, 2024 was about to change all that. On 17 January, shortly after 2pm, Kensington Palace announced that the Princess of Wales had undergone planned abdominal surgery the previous day. Catherine had not appeared unwell during the Christmas celebrations at Sandringham, but the news was followed by a statement explaining that she would remain at the London Clinic in Marylebone for up to two weeks, and most likely be off royal duties until Easter.

The announcement caught everyone, including the typically well-informed royal corps, completely off guard. At just 42, Catherine was usually the picture of health. An incredibly active young mother, always enthusiastic about taking part in physical or sporting challenges when they presented themselves on royal engagements, the princess had not had any major health issues since her pregnancies. But a potential two-week stay in hospital

CHAPTER SIXTEEN

set alarm bells ringing. As is standard practice for senior royals, the palace disclosed few details about the princess's condition and instead wheeled out a familiar phrase to journalists: there would be 'no running commentary'. No further updates would be given unless there was 'significant new information' to impart, the palace said. Given the magnitude of the issue – that a senior member of the royal family was in hospital receiving medical treatment and would be off royal duties for the foreseeable future – and of course noting that there would be much unhelpful speculation, courtiers did let it be known that Catherine's condition was 'non-cancerous'. In the announcement, Kensington Palace said the princess wished to apologise for postponing planned engagements, and that the Prince of Wales would also take a leave of absence to support his wife and care for their three children. The statement noted that the princess 'appreciates the interest this statement will generate' and stressed that Catherine wanted her personal medical information to remain private. It continued: 'She hopes that the public will understand her desire to maintain as much normality for her children as possible.' But then, as newsrooms around the world scrambled to deliver the information to their readers and viewers, and health experts were lined up to somewhat unethically speculate on what condition the princess might have, there was an extraordinary and unprecedented development.

A little over 90 minutes later, Buckingham Palace announced that the King required hospital treatment for an enlarged prostate. In a rather more matter-of-fact tone, the palace's statement said that his condition was benign and he would be admitted for a 'corrective procedure'. 'In common with thousands of men each year,' it continued, 'the King has sought treatment for an enlarged prostate. The King's public engagements will be postponed for a short period of recuperation.' Nothing like this had occurred before, at least in living memory, and it set royal journalists into a spin. Were the King and Catherine's conditions more serious than the palace was letting on? What would happen to their engagements? Who would run the monarchy if Charles and William were stepping back for any amount of time? The timing of the announcement about the King also seemed particularly odd, given the palace would have been aware of the princess's condition, and only added to the overall concern. It would later emerge that the timing of the statements was not deliberate. The King had been due to meet Cabinet ministers and foreign dignitaries on both 17 and 18 January, at Dumfries House in Scotland, until he was advised by doctors to cancel all appointments. Fearing the news could leak and send journalists already processing the princess's condition into a tailspin, the King and his senior team decided to get ahead of the media storm.

What was plainly evident, however, was the different ways in which the two palaces had chosen to address each event. The princess had very much wanted details of her condition to remain private, something that nobody could begrudge. On the contrary, the King was convinced that by discussing such an issue openly and in a positive manner, he could encourage others, specifically men of a certain age suffering from similar symptoms, to seek treatment. 'That was in no doubt from the King himself,' said an aide. 'Thousands of men will go through this at some point in their lives, most at His Majesty's age or even younger, so he was very much of the opinion of, "Let's get it out there and do some good."' Indeed, the King's inspirational decision had an immediate effect, with the National Health Service reporting an upturn of more than 1,000 per cent in visits to its web pages on prostate issues and symptoms.

While much of the focus was on Catherine and the King, William was left in an extraordinary position. Suddenly, with

CHAPTER SIXTEEN

three children to care for at home and no live-in staff at their Adelaide Cottage home, and with his wife and father in hospital, his future was looking decidedly different. 'When Catherine went in, he was fairly resolute,' said a close aide.

> They both very calmly told the children what was going on and how long Catherine would need to be away for, but explained other than that everything would continue as normal and when she came home, she would need to rest up for a bit. At that time it seemed to all be perfectly in hand, they were the calmness in the storm certainly. But away from the children he was of course incredibly pensive. His father's illness brought into focus just how quickly his life, and that of his family as well as the whole landscape of the institution, could change very quickly.

As questions began to be posed by the press about who was actually running the institution, it emerged the next day in *The Times* that Buckingham Palace had quietly made provision to prevent both the Dukes of York and Sussex from acting as substitutes for the King. While both remained 'Counsellors of State', meaning they were part of the cohort of understudies to the monarch in the line of succession who could, in theory, officially carry out duties if the sovereign were unwell or abroad, the King had discreetly moved to sideline them in an act instigated shortly after he ascended the throne. In a previously unnoticed statement to the House of Lords on 21 November 2022, the royal household had confirmed that only 'working members of the royal family will be called on to act as counsellors of state'.

Nine days after Catherine was admitted to hospital, the King arrived at the front of the London Clinic where he would be having his treatment, waving to well-wishers as he entered in a purposely choreographed move. During his stay, Charles was even seen 'tottling' along the corridor on his way to Catherine's private room, the two of them placed on the same floor of the hospital. William and Catherine had decided early on that they would not take their three children to the hospital, due to the dozens of journalists who spent days camped outside, despite pleas from the palace. Instead, Catherine was able to keep in touch with her family through video calls from her bedside, catching up on what George, Charlotte and Louis had been doing at school and asking if 'Papa' had been able to cook for them while she had been away. Carole and Michael Middleton were regular visitors to the Waleses' home during Catherine's stay, with William also having assistance from the children's nanny, Maria Turrion Borrallo.

On 29 January, a little less than the two weeks it had initially been suggested her stay might last, Kensington Palace announced that Catherine had been discharged. She managed to leave the hospital via a back door so as to not be seen by the photographers camped outside the entrance. Their attention was, anyway, drawn by the King, who, acting as a decoy, strode out through the front accompanied by Camilla, waving to well-wishers and journalists alike.

Palace aides said that the princess was 'doing well' and 'making good progress' and had returned home to convalesce. It was the longest Catherine had been away from her children and they from her, even more so than William and Catherine's eight-day trip to the Caribbean two years prior.

While the King and Catherine concentrated on their recovery and William cleared his diary to help support his wife, the Queen became the de facto central figure of the monarchy, taking on almost daily public engagements. On 4 February Camilla and Charles appeared together in public for the first time since he was discharged from hospital, attending their first Sunday church service in three weeks, in Sandringham, where he was resting up. Waving to onlookers outside St Mary Magdalene Church, as he and the Queen were greeted by the rector of Sandringham, he appeared to be in great spirits. But earlier that week, the monarch had been told by royal doctors that he had cancer. He was placed on an immediate course of treatment and ordered to put his public engagements on hold for the foreseeable future. A statement on 5 February was distributed by Buckingham Palace, revealing that during the King's treatment for benign prostate enlargement, a 'separate issue of concern was noted'. This revealed a form of cancer. Again, the King insisted he share the diagnosis, in the spirit of helping others, and was positive about the outcome.

Prior to the announcement, Charles called all members of his family, including his sons William and Harry. The Duke of Sussex immediately made plans to jump on a plane to see his father in London, arriving at lunchtime the following day. The meeting at Clarence House was brief, lasting less than 40 minutes, before Charles left to return to Sandringham. Harry was in the UK for a mere 26 hours and, notably, while he had been granted an audience with his father at short notice, he did not see William or Catherine.

Despite the King's insistence that he was feeling well and determined to face the diagnosis head on, William was concerned for his father's welfare and implored him to take the necessary time to recuperate. William told Charles he was ready to return to his duties now that Catherine was at home and he would be on hand if his father needed him to take on any extra responsibility. True to form, as good wishes poured in from all over the world including from presidents and prime ministers from the United States to Ukraine, Charles insisted he would carry on with his weekly audiences with the prime minister and daily state boxes from home, although he would shelve larger public engagements for the time being.

In recent years, a vast gap has emerged in the reporting of the royal family between traditional British media and the subsequent commentary on social media. This has never been more evident than in the early months of 2024.

When the Princess of Wales entered hospital on 16 January, and was then ghosted out two weeks later to disappear completely from public view for potentially months on end, it created an incredible vacuum of information. This was quickly filled by hurtful and often dangerous speculation and commentary by thousands if not millions of people who consumed and shared untruths and fake news. Despite Kensington Palace publicly stating the Princess's condition was non-cancerous, the conjecture around her hospital stay ranged from her suffering a terminal illness to a diagnosis of drastic cosmetic surgery gone wrong. The social media landscape filled with conspiracy theories, which seemed to grow more out of control with every day that went by. At first the palace did not publicly respond to hearsay, with sources dismissing the 'outrageous speculation'. But privately, as calls came in constantly from international outlets requesting updates, frustrations were mounting. On 27 February the rumours were stoked further after, at the last minute, William pulled out of a memorial service for his late godfather, the former King of Greece, Constantine II, citing a 'personal matter'. Outside of the UK, wild claims made by journalist Concha Calleja on Spanish TV – that Catherine was in an induced coma following 'serious complications' from her abdominal surgery – started to be widely covered. Kensington Palace strongly denied the claims, calling them 'total nonsense' and 'fundamentally totally made up', but it did little to stem the tide. By the beginning of March,

CHAPTER SIXTEEN

lurid conspiracy theories about Catherine's condition were being discussed by national newspaper columnists and on daytime television; they also became trending topics on X (formerly Twitter). A senior palace aide said at the time: 'There are a lot of people who need to take a long hard look at themselves and what they are stirring up. At the heart of all of this is a young mother, who has every right to recuperate in private. Neither she nor her family are immune to what is being speculated upon, which is both hurtful and outrageous.'

On 2 March, in a rare update, Kensington Palace, as well as saying that the princess was 'doing well', took the extra step of speaking out on the 'madness of social media', in an attempt to address the deranged rumours. After weeks of hysteria and wild speculation, on 10 March the palace released a photograph taken by William of Catherine and their three children. The beautiful family portrait, which showed the princess smiling in the garden of their home, surrounded by George, Charlotte and Louis, who were dressed in autumnal outfits, was not meant to be distributed as a 'proof of life' response, but rather to celebrate Mother's Day, which fell that Sunday. Within hours, though, the palace and the world's media had both been sent into a frenzy. Eagle-eyed self-appointed social media sleuths pointed out several issues with the image. From Louis' unusually positioned finger, to Charlotte's mismatched cuff and Catherine's misaligned jacket zip, all was not as it seemed. Suggestions that the image had been doctored, or, worse still, was a complete fake led several of the world's largest and most respected picture agencies, including the Associated Press, Reuters, Agence France-Presse, Getty Images and the Press Association, to one by one issue kill notices, which saw the photograph removed from their libraries. The result was chaos inside the palace, as dozens of calls and emails were coming in from all over the world, as well as questions over who had signed off on the photograph. Catherine, who was supposed to be recovering from major surgery, instead found herself at the centre of an even bigger international situation.

The next morning, at 10.28am on Monday 11 March, the princess issued a personal statement in which she admitted to editing the image. Publicly taking the blame for the furore, the princess wrote on X: 'Like many amateur photographers, I do occasionally experiment with editing. I wanted to express my apologies for any confusion the family photograph we shared yesterday caused. I hope everyone celebrating had a very happy Mother's Day. C.'

Despite Catherine's *mea culpa*, the frenzy would not die down. PR experts waded in, questioning how the palace had allowed a situation like this to happen, and suggesting the palace was in a full-blown crisis. In reality, it was not. 'The princess just wanted to put out a nice picture and on any other day, or moment in time, there would not have been such hysteria,' a senior courtier said. The following week, grainy footage taken by a member of the public sitting in a car, which showed William and Catherine leaving a farm shop on the Windsor estate, appeared online. In perhaps the most emblematic moment of the irrationality of the time, on 20 March the *Daily Mirror* revealed how a criminal investigation had been launched at the hospital where Catherine had been treated, over claims that three staff had allegedly tried to access the princess's private medical records. The security breach, confirmed by the Information Commissioner's Office, which was leading the criminal probe, made headlines around the world for days. Yet on the day of the *Mirror*'s world exclusive the princess was not concerning herself with the probe or the people at the centre of it. She was steadying herself for something much more life-changing.

Two weeks before that moment on a warm spring afternoon in March when she had sat down to pose for a photograph with

CHAPTER SIXTEEN

her family, Catherine had been contacted by her medical team at the London Clinic. With William by her side, the Princess of Wales, who had previously been in for a major, yet routine abdominal operation, was told that secondary tests had shown cancer was present in her body. The advice was an immediate course of preventative chemotherapy in order to give her the best chance of a full recovery.

Friends of Catherine say that although she was caught completely in shock, she remained composed. Her first thoughts were of her children and her husband. William, according to friends, later told how he was in 'a state of disbelief'. First his father had been diagnosed with cancer, and a month later his wife was now facing a similar challenge. Both he and Catherine knew there would have to be a public statement, but for the moment this was not their immediate concern. Catherine called her parents and her siblings to tell them, then she and William resolved to gather the children and impart what they knew in the best and most positive way possible. By the time she'd informed their most senior aides, Catherine had already decided to make a personal statement. She had seen the positivity and warmth that had greeted the King when he had been so open about his own diagnosis – there had been an outpouring of public emotion and the Buckingham Palace post room had filled with thousands of cards. More than that, though, the princess believed that her experience could benefit others in similar distressing circumstances. Catherine's family rallied round, with her sister Pippa helping to write the script for the short video statement. Dressed in a simple striped jumper and jeans, sitting on a wooden bench and surrounded by a serene spring backdrop of daffodils – a world away from the disgraceful chaos peddled by faceless social media trolls – Catherine calmly described how the diagnosis had come as a 'huge shock' on top of an 'incredibly tough couple of months for our entire family', but that together they were concentrating on 'doing everything we can to process and manage this privately for the sake of our young family.'

The princess added:

> As you can imagine, this has taken time. It has taken me time to recover from major surgery in order to start my treatment. But, most importantly, it has taken us time to explain everything to George, Charlotte and Louis in a way that is appropriate for them, and to reassure them that I am going to be OK. As I have said to them: I am well and getting stronger every day by focusing on the things that will help me heal; in my mind, body and spirits.

She said the family now needed 'some time, space and privacy', but in typical fashion ended on a positive note with a message for others. 'At this time, I am also thinking of all of those lives who have been affected by cancer. For everyone facing this disease, in whatever form, please do not lose faith or hope. You are not alone.'

The message, recorded in complete secrecy by a BBC special events team, was broadcast on the 6pm national news and online. Much like the announcement of the death of Elizabeth II, it felt like an earthquake whose reverberations were felt around the world. 'The days beforehand were filled with shock, but at that moment, it was genuinely as if the world stood still,' said a senior courtier.

> Everyone knew it was a huge moment. The princess delivered her message with such grace, perfection and empathy, it was incredibly emotional. But to know both she and William had had to prepare themselves to tell their

CHAPTER SIXTEEN

three young children that Mummy was ill and would have to go back to hospital, but that she would be OK, was just extraordinary. Everything they live for is for those children, they are their absolute world. There were a lot of tears from everyone.

William had been floored by the news, yet what shone through to those who know him best was his immense pride in his wife. A close friend spoke of the prince's reaction:

It was like being hit by a bus, sudden, brutal, and completely disorienting. One moment life was normal, and the next, everything changed. He worships her, truly. She's his world, and when the diagnosis came, it was as if the ground beneath him vanished. He talked about the rug being pulled, but it was more than that, it was heartbreak, fear and helplessness all at once. Watching him go through it was deeply emotional. You could see it in his eyes; in the way he held himself. But through it all, his devotion to her never wavered. He's been by her side every step, and the depth of his devotion is something that stays with you. It's love in its rawest, most powerful form.

17

HEALING

Away from the public gaze, William and Catherine did what they could to ensure that life carried on as normal for their three young children. The Prince of Wales took charge of the school drop-offs, while Catherine's parents and siblings were regular visitors to the family home in Windsor. Quiet evening dinners were enjoyed at home, playdates were organised to keep the children entertained and there were weekends away at the Middletons' family home in Berkshire – all part of enveloping George, Charlotte and Louis with as much love and support as possible. While the children benefited from having their mum at home all the time, the road of treatment and recovery was not simple.

Once the initial shock of her diagnosis had passed, the schedule of regular hospital appointments and the time needed to recuperate and regain enough strength to start each week, both physically and mentally, took its toll. 'Throughout everything thrown at her, she was incredibly upbeat,' a friend said. 'Even in her darkest moments, and there definitely were some around the treatment, both dealing with the physical and mental side effects, it was a pretty gruelling time. But her focus was always on her children. Doing everything she could to do the right things around her treatment, her recovery, and being as positive and optimistic as possible was all for them.' Another friend told how William and Catherine's relationship entered its strongest phase, through 'mutual love and support'.

CHAPTER SEVENTEEN

They are both incredibly proud of each other. In the moment, it was obviously very stressful for them both. William had both his father and his wife diagnosed with cancer within days of each other, then through Catherine's treatment, as well as having to split his focus to deal with all that and making sure the children weren't affected, it was a lot. They were both very conscious of protecting them as much as possible. Catherine's admiration for the way in which William took on all of that, keeping the children entertained and occupied, being constantly sanguine even when he had the weight of the world on his shoulders, allowing her to concentrate on her treatment and recovery, is something she will be eternally grateful for.

From the start of her programme of treatment, Catherine immersed herself in what she described to friends as 'natural healing'. Leaning on her love of the outdoors, alongside her weekly treatments at the Royal Marsden hospital in Chelsea, west London, when she was able, Catherine embraced the art of '*shinrin-yoku*'. A national pastime in Japan, also known in the West as 'forest bathing', it has been credited with reducing stress and promoting well-being. Studies over the past 20 years suggest that the practice of bathing in natural light and absorbing the quiet atmosphere of beautiful scenery and clean fresh air, in a forest or similar environment, can reduce stress, fatigue and balance the nervous system. 'She is a big believer in the natural world and its ability to help us heal,' said a friend. 'Having that mantra definitely helped the family connect during her treatment because they were able to spend so much time together, and getting outside in nature was a huge factor in her recovery.'

Daily meditation also formed an important part of Catherine's routine, helped by the renowned contemporary artist Chris Levine. Levine, famous for his work using light and holograms, is celebrated for creating one of the most iconic photographs of Queen Elizabeth II, *Lightness of Being*, in which he produced a series of stunning images of the late Queen in a tranquil pose amalgamated from more than 8,000 images taken across two sittings in 2004. Catherine's patronage of the National Portrait Gallery, which in 2012 exhibited Levine's *Equanimity*, the first-ever holographic portrait of Queen Elizabeth II, established the connection and the two have remained in contact ever since. A friend said:

> Every cancer journey is different, but all are complex and unpredictable. Yes, she was scared of what the future may hold, as was William, but they spoke a lot about what they were feeling, they shared what information they deemed appropriate at the right times with the children, and it worked for them as a family. They were able to turn that fear into love and that helped them all incredibly.
>
> What Catherine was able to do was really centre in on what was important to her, which was being around her family, and her loved ones, and concentrating on the little moments, whether that was being outside, meditation, the stillness of being, which all contributed to the bigger picture around getting better as quickly as possible.

As Catherine grew in strength and confidence, William was able to return to royal duties and, when asked by well-wishers on engagements, provided basic updates on how his wife was progressing with her recovery. So, for instance, on 5 June, William and the King, who had attended his first public engagement since his own diagnosis just a month before, attended the commemorations in Portsmouth for the 80th anniversary of

CHAPTER SEVENTEEN

D-Day. During a conversation with 100-year-old D-Day veteran Geoffrey Weaving, the Prince of Wales revealed Catherine was 'getting better'.

Ten days later, on 15 June, Catherine gave the country a huge boost when she was well enough to attend Trooping the Colour, the King's official birthday celebrations in central London. In her first public appearance since Christmas Day, the Princess of Wales emerged from Buckingham Palace in the Glass Coach to loud cheers from the crowds, looking radiant and laughing with her three children all the way up the Mall to Horse Guards Parade. Kensington Palace was keen to stress that the princess's appearance did not represent a full return to public life as she continued her treatment, and she did not attend the annual Garter Day at Windsor or Royal Ascot the following week. Catherine's next public outing would not be until a month later, on 14 July, to attend the men's singles final at Wimbledon, receiving a standing ovation as she arrived on Centre Court wearing a striking purple Safiyaa dress, alongside sister Pippa and nine-year-old Princess Charlotte.

On 11 August Catherine and William teamed up in a video montage of famous faces congratulating the Great Britain team who were competing in the Paris Olympics. While Catherine looked happy and well, the brief clip garnered far more worldwide attention for the fact that William was sporting a 'holiday beard'. The topic of royal beards had been a dramatic source of contention between William and his brother, according to Prince Harry's memoir. Harry's desire to keep his beard for his wedding to Meghan had apparently angered William – it was said that the Queen had disapproved of William having one for his own nuptials – to the point that William attempted to force him to shave it off. Intriguingly, though, Harry revealed how his beard took on a symbolic importance for him, helping him with his crippling anxiety and calming his nerves. Was this new beard William's own security blanket? Was he presenting a new image in public after all the stress and strain he had been under? 'Not really,' says an aide. 'At first he blamed it on laziness, and then he actually quite liked it so thought, why not keep it for a bit.' While William, and presumably Catherine, were fans, it appears there was one person in particular who was not. 'Charlotte didn't like it the first time. I got floods of tears; the first one, I got tears, so I had to shave it off,' William said in a newspaper interview later in the year. 'And then I grew it back. I thought, hang on a second, and I convinced her it was going to be okay.'

Aside from the trials and tribulations of managing Catherine's cancer diagnosis and treatment, the family were enjoying life together in their bubble. Weekends were spent in Norfolk, walking and sailing across the Norfolk broads, or with the Middletons in Berkshire. Catherine's appeal for 'time, space and privacy' during her cancer announcement had been heard and respected by the media, allowing her to fully engage with both her clinical and therapeutic treatment plan. Although she had begun a gradual return to public life, the palace continued to urge caution over her eventual resumption of full-time duties. In particular, the King was happy to allow his daughter-in-law to take all the time she needed. In late August, Charles was delighted when William and Catherine confirmed at the last moment that they would come up to stay with him and Camilla at Balmoral for the end of the children's summer break. On 25 August, Catherine and the family attended a church service at Crathie Kirk. During the break, Catherine was able to relax and celebrate for the first time in months, having finished her course of chemotherapy. While she was not in remission, plans were being made for her to return to a 'light programme of engagements over the coming months as she continued to chart her recovery'.

CHAPTER SEVENTEEN

While William had taken a leave of absence from front-line royal duties, two awkward yet pressing issues still confronted the institution. Prince Andrew and Prince Harry, or the 'Dukes of Hazard' as courtiers had dubbed them, and the unresolved, though very different, problems they presented were still on the agenda. The King had ordered the removal of Andrew's personal security detail, in the hope that his brother's ailing finances would force him to decide, of his own volition, to leave Royal Lodge. William, who had long urged his father to take a stronger line with his uncle, saw it as a step in the right direction but was still incredibly nervous about the US authorities' continued appetite for speaking to Andrew over his links to Jeffrey Epstein. On 29 August, not having spoken directly for months, William came face to face with Harry, who had flown in from California for the funeral of their uncle, Lord Robert Fellowes, who had married their mother's sister, Lady Jane Fellowes. The warring brothers sat apart at the back of the church and did not speak to one another, despite, as the *Sun* reported, finding themselves only 'five yards from each other' after the service finished. At the wake, William and Harry mingled with family and friends, including Diana's younger brother Earl Spencer, and at one stage were practically standing 'back to back'. And yet, according to fellow mourners, again they did not share a conversation. While William may have been forgiven for having other things on his mind, the froideur was a clear demonstration that he was in no mood to entertain his brother despite previous attempts at an intervention from the Spencer family.

As the summer holidays drew to a close, Catherine was ready to start the next part of her healing journey. With the children settled back at school, she announced via an incredibly slick video by the talented London-based filmmaker Will Warr that she had completed her chemotherapy. In the deeply personal video, the princess said her nine-month battle with illness had been a 'scary and unpredictable' time for the family, but the experience had reminded her and William to 'reflect and be grateful for the simple yet important things in life, which so many of us often take for granted. Of simply loving and being loved.' A soothing voiceover accompanied segments showing the couple together and with their children in Norfolk, walking through woods and playing on the windswept beaches at Holkham.

Throughout her journey, Catherine had absorbed nature's powerful healing properties and had come out the other side with an intense desire to share her experience with others. Although she still wished the exact nature of her abdominal surgery and subsequent cancer diagnosis to remain private, during their summer break to Balmoral Catherine had spoken with the King at length about his willingness to be so open with his health issues. 'Once she was clear from her treatment, there was a real determination to move the dial and turn her experience into something positive,' said an aide.

> The video announcing her cancer diagnosis had been watched millions of times around the world, and it was evident from the amount of supportive letters and cards received, and by talking to the charities and NHS staff, just how much it had resonated with people, urging so many to be aware of the signs and symptoms of cancer wherever possible. The princess recognised there was an amazing opportunity to do more to help others and share some of her experiences, because it is so often a complex and scary situation for so many.

The location of the video, taken near the family's sanctuary of Anmer Hall, away from the royal bubbles of London or

CHAPTER SEVENTEEN

Windsor, was chosen deliberately to show how beneficial her surroundings had been. And the relaxed scenes in which William and Catherine played cricket with their children, lay on a blanket together, embracing and even kissing at one stage, showed more than ever how William and Catherine were changing the narrative around them and shaping how they wanted to be perceived in the modern world. The couple were displaying togetherness and a vulnerability, like no member of the royal family had done before. In a world where displays of affection are rarely seen publicly, and historically not even handed down to children, the presentation of this rock-solid family unit was incredibly unique. Six months after she calmly stared into the camera to deliver the news of her unexpected diagnosis, Catherine explained how she felt when her world was turned upside down. 'As the summer comes to an end, I cannot tell you what a relief it is to have finally completed my chemotherapy treatment,' Catherine said.

> The last nine months have been incredibly tough for us as a family. Life, as you know, it can change in an instant and we have had to find a way to navigate the stormy waters and road unknown. The cancer journey is complex, scary and unpredictable for everyone, especially those closest to you.
> With humility, it also brings you face to face with your own vulnerabilities in a way you have never considered before, and with that, a new perspective on everything.

As Catherine said, her focus would now turn to doing whatever she could to 'stay cancer free'. She was able to plan a select few engagements and take meetings at home or at Windsor Castle with those working on her main projects, such as the Centre for Early Childhood or Shaping Us. Those close to the princess suggest that over the course of her treatment and recovery, she experienced a profound change in the way she saw her future role. Firstly, she had been humbled and overwhelmed by the level of support from the public. But it was her new sense of hope and appreciation for life, and the strength that she had drawn from her loved ones, that would govern her way forward. It had been an incredibly tough time but she was ready to put herself out there again.

Senior aides supported the princess's desire to begin with a handful of public engagements and advocated for a greater degree of flexibility than usual, to allow her the space to return at her own pace. Few had expected to see Catherine until the Remembrance Sunday service at the Cenotaph in London in November, but a surprise engagement on 2 October at Windsor Castle marked her return to public duties. William had been moved by the story of a teenage photographer called Liz Hatton, which he had learned about through his patronage of London's Air Ambulance Charity.

Brave Liz, from Harrogate in North Yorkshire, who was just 16 at the time, had given up on her studies as she battled a rare and aggressive form of cancer. The desmoplastic small round cell tumour is so rare that just 12 cases are diagnosed in England each year and there is no standard care treatment. Liz was undergoing chemotherapy but her prognosis was desperate; in January 2024 she had been given between six months and three years to live.

And yet she was determined to make the most of the time she had left and had created a photography 'bucket list'. To help her, William had invited Liz to Windsor to capture a royal investiture, and she believed that her role would be limited to briefly capturing William handing out honours to sports stars including cyclist Mark Cavendish, rugby referee Wayne Barnes and footballer Alistair McCoist. But, following the engagement, William took her to a private room to meet Catherine, who told the teenager how her creativity and strength had inspired both her and William. The two were pictured sharing a warm embrace on the front pages of the next day's newspapers. Invitations flooded in after the meeting, with Liz eventually managing to photograph comedian Michael McIntyre, circus performers, dancers from the Royal Ballet, and stars on the red carpet at the MTV Europe Music Awards. She also worked with one of her photography heroes, Rankin, on a fashion shoot. Eight weeks after her visit to Windsor, on 27 November, she passed away surrounded by her family. Reflecting on Liz's invitation to the Castle, her mother Vicky Robayna said:

> All any parent wants is for their child's dreams to come true, and the Prince and Princess of Wales were a big part in making that happen. [Her] final two months were the happiest we had ever seen her, and a lot of that was down to their kindness, we truly can't thank them enough. Before that day at Windsor Castle, Liz had had some opportunities, but the meeting really brought her into the public eye and allowed her dreams to become a reality.

Since Liz's death, her family have fundraised for research into desmoplastic small round cell tumours, and were invited by William and Catherine to attend a Buckingham Palace garden party in 2025.

Soon after, the warmth and empathy Catherine had displayed with Liz and so many others would be called on again. The role of being a senior royal involves striving to be in tune with the people they serve. At times of national celebration, the monarch and his family should be there to congratulate, and in times of distress become a source of comfort. On a warm summer's day in July that year, the community of Southport in north-west

England had been rocked by a senseless attack at a children's Taylor Swift-themed dance and yoga event. In an episode of absolute horror, 17-year-old Axel Rudakubana walked into the Hart Space dance studio, armed with two knives. Six-year-old Bebe King and seven-year-old Elsie Dot Stancombe died at the scene, while nine-year-old Alice da Silva Aguiar died in hospital the following day and ten other children were injured. In the hours and days that followed, riots started across the country, fuelled by misinformation on social media that the suspect was an illegal migrant. Hours after the attack an account on X called 'Europe Invasion' posted that the suspect was 'a Muslim immigrant', a claim that was entirely false. The post was seen by close to 4 million users. Despite an official police statement that the suspect had been born in Cardiff, people continued to share this information online. Some of the claims were amplified or repeated by well-known influencers such as the controversial personality Andrew Tate, who had millions of views repeating false narratives. The false details shared online led to much higher engagement on posts that linked Southport with terms such as 'muslim', 'islam' and 'asylum', ensuring a far-right edge to the widespread disorder.

Like many other parents across the country, William and Catherine had been left deeply shocked by the details of the case. In the aftermath both the prince and princess spoke to their team about what assistance they could offer through their network of charity contacts, either to the victims' families, the survivors, or the emergency responders. At first it was suggested that William should plan a visit to Southport alone, in a show of support for the town. But this plan was soon expanded. 'When it came to planning the visit, Catherine felt compelled to go,' said an aide.

CHAPTER SEVENTEEN

As parents they felt utterly powerless after the tragedy, but in their public role, they wanted to show support to the town and the families of those so deeply affected. A lot of their work, or certainly how they see their roles, is about helping people and building a human connection. That is what they can offer, by being there and saying, 'we stand by you', it is incredibly important as ambassadors of the monarchy to have that meaningful connection with the country, especially at times of such sadness.

On 10 October, William and Catherine made an emotional visit – the princess's first public engagement since completing chemotherapy treatment – to the town, in private comforting the families of the three girls who lost their lives in the attack, and taking part in an event with some of the emergency responders who helped on the day. The couple also spoke to mental health practitioners who had been working in the local community to deliver long-term support to those affected by the tragedy. Following the visit, Phil Garrigan, chief fire officer for Merseyside Fire & Rescue Service, praised the couple, saying: 'The Princess of Wales broke off and came back into the building to give a hug to the people who responded because she could see the emotion in them and could see it was difficult for them to relay their feelings and to say how impactful events have been. I think that just shows a really caring side and is very, very touching.' William and Catherine later posted on social media that the visit had been a 'powerful' reminder of the need to support one another 'in the wake of unimaginable tragedy'.

On 23 January 2025, Rudakubana was sentenced to life imprisonment, with a minimum term of 52 years. No motive for the stabbings was identified at his trial. The couple returned to Southport nearly a year later, on 23 September 2025, speaking to teachers and pupils at Farnborough Road Infant and Junior Schools and Churchtown Primary School, the schools attended by Elsie, Alice and Bebe.

William and Catherine have both always seen communities and what they can offer as the foundations of their public roles. From Catherine's early-years work, to William's efforts with the environment, people and places are at the heart of what they do. The Prince of Wales's connection to homelessness has spanned more than 30 years, beginning in 1993, when he was 11, with his first visit to The Passage homeless shelter in London. Diana's charity work had influenced him, leading him to take on patronages with the national charity Centrepoint in 2005 and The Passage in 2019. Helping the homeless and trying to alleviate the causes of homelessness has gone on to form one of the pillars of his work, namely in the form of Homewards, his five-year programme to show it is possible to end homelessness, and taking part in a landmark documentary for ITV to coincide with the charity's launch in the UK in October 2024.

Being a member of the royal family has its obvious perks and privileges, and its fair share of criticisms too. One particular piece of opprobrium that has been directed at William in recent years has been his suitability to campaign on an issue such as homelessness, no matter how incredibly close to his heart it is. William decided to tackle this head on in the powerful two-part documentary. 'Why else would I be here if I'm not using this role properly to help people who are in need,' he said. 'I don't believe we should be living with homelessness in the 21st century. At some point you've got to say, "Right, come on, we're actually going to do something that's really going to make a difference to people's lives."' William also used the film to demonstrate the reasons why he is so invested in the issue. Reflecting on his 1993 visit to The Passage with his mother and brother Harry,

CHAPTER SEVENTEEN

William talked about how his life had been shaped by his experiences, and how Princess Diana had helped him formulate a different view of the world from an early age. Speaking to Mick Clarke, chief executive of The Passage, he said: 'She made sure that when we grew up that the life outside palace walls thing was real, you know, not just a statement. It was an actual fact.'

On his motivation for using his profile to shine a light on the issue, he added: 'I've slowly tried to work out what can I bring to the role and the platform that I have. What do I feel works? What do I feel people want to see from me? And I have taken some inspiration and guidance from what my mother did, particularly with homelessness. And that's grown more over the last few years.'

Mick Clarke said:

What is plainly evident in all the times I have met Prince William is his genuine authenticity, whether it is carrying out public engagements or private visits to the charity. He never leaves without speaking to everyone, he is interested in their individual stories. Many people who use our services, from the very nature of their lifestyles, have a sixth sense with people. But they take to William immediately. They can sense he cares, why else would he be there? He certainly doesn't need to be.

He's got a brilliant sense of humour, he's quick-witted, and in a world which is rushing at a million miles an hour, he is a very good listener. All of this puts people at ease and that is a huge advantage when trying to find out how you can help someone.

There are far easier issues to get involved with and he knows by being involved he will come in for, in my view, unfair criticism, but it's never fazed him. We are so grateful he is our patron and, through his work, we are slowly making homelessness be seen as a societal issue, and something which isn't just on the fringes of every community.

As William returned to full-time royal duties, one of his other landmark projects, the Earthshot Prize, travelled to Cape Town. Taking the awards to the African continent early on in their history had been a huge goal of the prince, who wanted to spread to the four corners of the globe the ten-year project's message of optimism about the search for planet-saving solutions. After travelling to the iconic Table Mountain and celebrating the winning innovators at a star-studded awards ceremony, William sat down with British journalists on the tour to speak about the 'hardest year in my life' – a reference to his wife's and father's cancer diagnoses. The fact he uttered those words after losing his mother at 15, and walking behind her coffin just six days after her death, goes some way to revealing the enormity of what he had faced. During the week I covered the tour in South Africa, William appeared relaxed and composed, as he felt his way back into royal life after having taken so long away from regular front-line duties.

But while he had appeared in good spirits, playing rugby with local schoolchildren, walking across the beautiful coastline as he spoke to park rangers about the challenges of their roles protecting endangered wildlife, the impact of the past year was also clear. In a subtle sign of pressures the last 12 months had exerted on William, throughout the week he had sported a homemade bracelet given to him by his daughter Charlotte, with the word 'Papa' spelled out in white beads, a 'relic' he said, from the Taylor Swift concert they'd attended during the summer. Addressing his relaxed demeanour he clarified, 'It's interesting you say that, because I couldn't be less relaxed this year, so it's very interesting you're all seeing that.' When asked how the preceding months had been for him and his family, William presented himself at his rawest, sighing and lowering his voice. 'Honestly? It's been dreadful. It's probably been the hardest year in my life. So, trying to get through everything else and keep everything on track has been really difficult. But I'm so proud of my wife, I'm proud of my father, for handling the things that they have done. But from a personal family point of view, it's been, yeah, it's been brutal.' When asked how the princess was getting on, William smiled and said, 'She's doing well.'

In another huge boost for the monarchy, on 9 November Catherine appeared at the Royal British Legion's Festival of Remembrance at the Albert Hall. The following day she joined William and the King on the Foreign Office balcony for the Remembrance Sunday service at the Cenotaph in London. Both events signify the importance that the royal family attach to commemorating the fallen. Catherine also took centre stage at the glittering banquet at Buckingham Palace on 3 December held during the state visit of the Emir of Qatar, then again three days later at her Together at Christmas carol concert at Westminster Abbey. At Sandringham, William, Catherine and their children joined the King, Queen and their extended family (though not Prince Andrew: following allegations he was linked to Chinese spy Yang Tengbo, he was forced to pull out of the annual family gathering), for a 'decidedly more relaxed affair' than previous years' celebrations, according to one insider. 'After all they had been through, it was a time for looking forward to new beginnings and embracing the power of togetherness they had as a family.'

The new year brought good news and with it the chance to celebrate what a difference 12 months can make. On Catherine's 43rd birthday, on 9 January, William posted an incredibly heartfelt message on social media, saying: 'To the most incredible wife and mother. The strength you've shown over the last year has been remarkable. George, Charlotte, Louis and I are so proud of you. Happy Birthday, Catherine. We love you.' Just days later, on 14 January, the Princess of Wales confirmed she was in remission from cancer and visited the Royal Marsden in London, where she had been for many private appointments throughout her chemotherapy treatment. Her decision to revisit the scene of her darkest hours was a reminder of the promise she had made to help those facing challenges similar to what she had coped with. While she had remained discreet about both her abdominal surgery and cancer, the princess was happy to share candid details of her hospital experience with fellow sufferers. After joking about the novelty of entering the hospital through the front door, having made 'so many quiet visits in secrecy', Catherine gestured to her arm and chest to discuss the semi-permanent 'port' mechanism used to deliver the vital medicine during treatment. 'I got so attached to it,' she said, then joked that she had hesitated when finally told, 'you can have it taken out'.

In a statement following the visit she thanked staff at the hospital for looking after her so well. 'My heartfelt thanks goes to all those who have quietly walked alongside William and me as we have navigated everything. We couldn't have asked for more,' she said. The language used in that statement, while no doubt written with joy, also gave a telling insight into what the future holds for Catherine and her family. While she spoke of her 'relief' and how she remained 'focused on recovery', she also said: 'As anyone who has experienced a cancer diagnosis will know, it takes time to adjust to a new normal. I am however looking forward to a fulfilling year ahead.'

What would the new normal look like, many wondered? Would the monarchy be forever changed by its collective experience of the unprecedented events of the previous 12 months?

CHAPTER SEVENTEEN

While the King had at the first opportunity thrown himself into more work and public engagements, with those close to him remarking that he knew no other way, William and Catherine had responded to their ordeal in a different way. It had not only centered them further as a couple and as a family, but made the foundations of what they had built over 20 years together appear more important. Sources close to them said the experience had also had a profound effect on how they viewed their future as individuals and also regarding the future of the monarchy that they would one day helm. Catherine and William's experiences of their own vulnerability as a family, as well as some of the tragedies they have witnessed, helped cement their conviction that empathy and kindness should be at the heart of their vision for the future of the monarchy.

18

A NEW ERA

In an interview for the late Queen's 90th birthday in 2016, Prince William spoke of being consumed by the challenge of how to 'modernise and develop' the royal family and make it 'relevant in the next 20 years' time'. Nearly a decade on from those comments, which were seen as him boldly stepping out of the shadows cast by his grandmother and father, William gave an indication of how the passage of time has shaped his view of how the monarchy should operate and present itself in the modern age. Being at the centre of a thousand-year-old institution can weigh heavily on an individual. The traditions of the past are so deeply woven into the fabric of your existence, and synonymous with how much of the world views you. But is it realistic, or indeed correct, to blindly follow everything that has been laid out before you since your birth? Prince William does not think so. 'Change is on my agenda – change for the good,' he said in October 2025. In one of his most personal interviews ever, the Prince of Wales set out his vision for a modern monarchy; one that is fit to lead in an ever-changing world. He talked about how he seeks to question the purpose of his role and the institution at large, and how he wants his son and heir, George, to view his place within it. Although what the monarchy will look like when George takes the throne is, at this stage, anyone's guess.

These past few years have seen incredible change, filled with levels of scandal and infighting not seen in a generation, with

CHAPTER EIGHTEEN

questions raised in Parliament over the privileges afforded to the royal family, and a growing anti-monarchist movement that asks whether we should even have a monarchy at all. 'I want to question things more,' William said. 'I want to create a world in which my son is proud of what we do, a world and a job that actually does impact people's lives for the better.' The somewhat unlikely prompt for such a candid reflection was Canadian actor and comedian Eugene Levy. As part of the third series of his award-winning Apple TV+ series, *The Reluctant Traveler*, Levy did what perhaps no interviewer has ever properly done when presented with the chance to sit down and speak to a senior member of the royal family: he listened. In doing so, he garnered a telling insight into how William and Catherine see their future. They do not see their path as predetermined, but one that they have the capacity to change through their own actions, and in doing so remind the world of the power and influence the institution can still exert.

There can be no doubt that the monarchy is in a state of flux. The death of Queen Elizabeth II, after more than 70 years on the throne, would always present challenges for the new monarch. Charles was 73 when he became king; revolution was far from his mind. And a cancer diagnosis 18 months into his reign has naturally added to the uncertainty about how long Charles III will stay on the throne, making it harder to project the sort of steady reassurance that the country and the Commonwealth perhaps needed. The Duke and Duchess of Sussex's departures from royal life, as well as the manner in which their relations with the rest of the family have fractured, possibly beyond repair, have added to the weight of responsibility those left must feel. A vulgar scandal involving the man regarded as the late Queen's 'favourite son' not only rocked the institution to its foundations, but has served to make further examination of William and Catherine's public roles more more likely. All of this, coupled with Charles's long-held desire for a slimmed-down monarchy that is more accountable and financially more palatable to the public on whose support it ultimately relies, has created a pervasive sense of uncertainty.

But this is precisely why the Prince and Princess of Wales's vision is what is needed. It's a vision that instinctively upholds the values and traditions of the past yet isn't afraid to make changes and lead in a bold new direction. William is certainly up for the challenge. 'I enjoy that change, I don't fear it. That's the bit that excites me, the idea of being able to bring some change. Not overly radical change, but changes that I think that need to happen.' While old heads within the institution may worry, William's reassurances are worth noting. 'I think it's very important that tradition stays, and tradition has a huge part in all of this. But there's also points where you look at tradition and go: "Is that still fit for purpose today? Is that still the right thing to do? Are we still doing and having the most impact we could be having?"'

As many of those who have so graciously given their time and considerable insight when contributing to this biography have noted, William and Catherine's leadership will be shaped by the pressures and expectations they will always face, but the opportunities they feel lie in front of them also give them the chance to craft something closer to their own image and values. We are living in a time where our planet's climate and environment are in great peril, millions of children do not get the start in life they deserve, and homelessness in all forms is on the rise due to a range of social and economic factors. If not them, then who? William and Catherine want their roles to be a blend of tradition with modern sensibilities, continuity with reform, and duty informed by deep personal conviction. In his conversation with the travelling British media in South Africa in 2024,

CHAPTER EIGHTEEN

William spoke about the way in which he sees his role evolving, firstly as Prince of Wales, and then when he becomes king.

> I'm also going to throw empathy in there as well, because I really care about what I do. It helps impact people's lives, and I think we could do with some more empathetic leadership around the world. So that's what I'm trying to bring, that's what Catherine is trying to bring as well. I sit here right now doing Earthshot and projects like Homewards as well, and who knows what's going to come next, but it all centres around those values of trying to help deliver change and make those lives better.

With William, almost everything seems to come back to the need to effect the real change that he sees as part of his destiny. Many of those I have spoken to during my extensive research for this book have spoken of William's appetite for recalibrating things both inside the institution and, after so much turmoil in recent years, for reshaping the public's view of what the monarchy stands for. William characterised his 'different' approach as being 'royal with a smaller "r"'.

> I can only describe what I'm trying to do, and that's I'm trying to do it differently and I'm trying to do it for my generation. And to give you more of an understanding around it, I'm doing it with maybe a smaller 'r' in the royal, if you like, that's maybe a better way of saying it. So, it's more about impact, philanthropy, collaboration, convening and helping people.

But what does this all look like in practice? Well, subtle signs have already emerged and they suggest that what's coming will be more substantial than just William's choice of sustainable trainers, or Catherine's slickly produced Instagram videos espousing the impact nature can have on our mental health, laudable as those things are. The objective is to make the monarchy inclusive, to weave it into the cultural landscape of this country and beyond. Talking about mental health, the value of family, sharing parental responsibilities, being open about your mistakes. All of this contributes.

In the course of these discussions, it's important to remember that King Charles has been a pioneer. In the 1970s he was a man so ahead of his time that his comments on the scourge of plastics and the perils of climate change were dismissed as lunacy. In the same decade, Charles established the Prince's Trust (now the King's Trust), which since 1976 has directly helped more than 1.1 million young people from disadvantaged communities to develop the confidence and skills they need to realise their ambitions. Yet many parts of the operation remain unchanged. Both Buckingham Palace and Kensington Palace have in the past suffered with an image problem. The lack of women in senior roles as well as the ethnic mix of employees is being addressed with each year that passes, and William has already begun plans for how the Duchy of Cornwall can better serve the public at large. William and Catherine represent rebirth and reinvention at a time when it is needed most. The days when William was dubbed 'Workshy Wills' or a 'reluctant royal', or Catherine dismissed as 'Waity Katie', have been consigned to the distant past. Our future king and queen now rank as the most popular royals in almost every national or international poll of note, regularly recording favourability ratings well above 60 per cent. The quiet revolution is upon us.

The coronation of King William V will also be distinctly different from his father's and every other monarch's before him.

CHAPTER EIGHTEEN

While Charles's lasted three hours, down from four for Elizabeth II, William's will be concise, at a maximum of 90 minutes, says one source. Those who know him best say they do not expect the vast number of costume changes of previous crownings, nor, as reported in the *Sunday Times*, will the service invite the congregation to swear their allegiance to the King, his 'heirs and successors'. 'If you want to know what it will look like, you only need to look at William and Catherine as a couple,' one former senior aide to the couple says. 'They have a modern outlook, they are relatable and the people they surround themselves with share those values. Everything they set out to do is with other people in mind. That certainly doesn't include the entire nation swearing allegiance, it's about collaboration at work to get the best result for the most amount of people. That is the ultimate goal.'

If harmony is indeed William and Catherine's focus, then there are further examples in front of us. The result of Harry and Meghan's exit has been a family split in two. Even Harry, after spending the best part of the last six years raining down on his relatives, has said in a BBC interview that he 'would love a reconciliation'. At such a time, consonance can perhaps only be delivered through distance, and distance is what has been delivered. A key decision for William and Catherine has been shutting Harry and Meghan out, for their own well-being as well as for the protection and prosperity of the institution. While 'recollections may vary' on the most fiercely contested matters, especially the hurtful accusations by the Sussexes of racism and abandonment, the future king and queen have steadfastly taken decisions to protect their own future, such as ensuring their children grow up in the most balanced and well-rounded environment possible to prepare them for the future, whatever that may be.

While, of course, the issue of Prince Andrew's association with a convicted sex offender is entirely different from the situation with the Sussexes, William and Catherine's personal view has again been that their best option is to keep their distance from the source of the problem. They knew that the disturbing claims of sexual abuse that have pursued Andrew for more than a decade, allegations he has always vehemently denied, had permanently damaged him in the public's eyes. And his now famous BBC *Newsnight* interview, where he failed to apologise for his connection to Epstein, or acknowledge the victims of sexual abuse, was, for William and Catherine, terminal for their relationship with him. The late Queen sought to protect her son from complete banishment, clinging to the hope that he would one day be exonerated. Similarly, while acknowledging that his brother could never return to public duties, Charles attempted to honour his mother's wishes and for a long time stopped short of pushing for Andrew's complete banishment. By contrast, William made it clear that once he became king there would be no such mercy.

Since 2019 the ever more depressing drip of information relating to Andrew and Epstein has presented a serious challenge to the institution. Buckingham Palace has not acted for the prince since he stepped down from public duties, suggesting he was a private individual, and in doing so sought to further distance itself from him. But with every Balmoral meet-up or Christmas walkabout that came around, questions were raised as to how close to the King, or William, Andrew actually was. Did the royal family think this would all blow over if they kept quiet, or kept him close? William and Catherine have never seen it that way.

On 31 January 2025, email correspondence from Andrew to Epstein – which emerged from legal filings in London involving the case of former boss of Barclays Bank, Jes Staley, who had been dismissed from the bank due to his relationship with Epstein (in June 2025 Jes Stanley lost a legal challenge against a decision to

CHAPTER EIGHTEEN

ban him from top financial jobs in the UK) – appeared to fully contradict the prince's claims that he had stopped seeing the billionaire after early December 2010, when they were pictured together in New York's Central Park. Andrew suggested he had flown to the city 'with the sole purpose' of ending his relationship with Epstein, and that during their walk they had agreed to part company, with the Duke of York stating: 'And to this day I never had any contact with him from that day forward.'

But the emails showed that Andrew contacted Epstein on 28 February 2011 to discuss a *Mail on Sunday* article that included a picture taken in 2001 of the prince with his hand around the waist of a 17-year-old Virginia Giuffre, in Ghislaine Maxwell's mews house in Mayfair. A day after the article ran, the prince wrote: 'Keep in close touch and we'll play some more soon!!!!' The shock inside the palace was matched only by the level of revulsion from the public. Just weeks after the emails were published, on 25 April 2025, mother of three Virginia Giuffre tragically took her own life. Her death would leave many unanswered questions, but in October 2025, ahead of the publication of her posthumous memoir, the King and William signalled the end had finally come for Andrew. More emails, this time released to the US Congress, exposed Sarah Ferguson's correspondence with Epstein, which continued even after his sex-abuse conviction. Charities she had been associated with for decades publicly denounced her and cut all ties, condemning her to a similar fate to her ex-husband. On 18 October, Buckingham Palace announced that Andrew would relinquish all of his titles, though he would remain a prince by nature of his birth. However, as the pressure ramped up further, MPs publicly threatened to delve into Andrew's opaque finances, which he had used to maintain his lifestyle and make the £12 million out-of-court settlement to Giuffre in 2022. The scandal overshadowed the

King's historic visit to the Vatican, where he became the first monarch in 500 years to pray with the Pope, leading him on 30 October to declare he had stripped his brother of all his titles, honours and styles. Andrew and Sarah would also be bound to finally leave their Royal Lodge home. While Andrew would be provided a smaller home on the Sandringham estate and a livable allowance by the King, Sarah would leave with nothing. Henceforth, Charles's brother would merely be known as Andrew Mountbatten-Windsor. While some press reports suggested William and Catherine had 'pushed for Andrew to be ousted', those closest to them disagree. 'Both the Prince and Princess of Wales supported the King's actions, and His Majesty was aware of their feelings. But it was entirely the King's decision. Unlike some members of the family, William is fully aware of his constitutional role and while it is true he was consulted, he would not seek to demand anything of the monarch as he trusts his final judgement,' said a senior palace insider.

William is interested in the decisions his father is responsible for, but he appreciates the need to keep his distance. If the King had not taken such drastic action with Andrew amid growing public anger, as the late Queen failed to do, then William would have surely acted when he takes on the top job. What is abundantly clear, now more than ever, is that William remains utterly focused on his own future.

Whereas the King has a decent roster at his disposal, with the Princess Royal – often dubbed the 'hardest working royal' for the amount of public engagements she completes – still maintaining public duties at an extraordinary pace, William will have to do more with fewer players at his disposal. Gone are Harry and Meghan, and now the former Duke of York is in disgrace. The statistics are clear, the Prince and Princess of Wales take on fewer public engagements than previous

CHAPTER EIGHTEEN

generations of royals (notwithstanding Catherine's illnesses throughout 2024 and continued recovery), and the supporting cast is looking thin. But they have found peace carving out their own future on their own terms. With many of the senior royals growing towards a natural retirement age, the Duke and Duchess of Edinburgh (Prince Edward and his wife Sophie) will find their roles naturally elevated. Some sources also believe William and Catherine will call on the part-time royals, such as Princesses Beatrice and Eugenie and even Zara Tindall to help with engagements on an ad-hoc basis, such as they have done with garden parties in the summer months, but this too poses its own problems about whether a 'half in, half out' model, such as the one proposed by the Sussexes, is actually workable and even acceptable with the public.

Their eldest son, Prince George, who will one day succeed William as king, will celebrate his 13th birthday in July 2026. By then Princess Charlotte will be 11 and Prince Louis 8. William and Catherine will also have celebrated their 15th wedding anniversary. Suddenly, in an institution where the wheels of time can move slowly, life appears to be flashing by at an extraordinary pace. There will be a time, perhaps in the not-too-distant future, when the foundations they have built, as a couple and as a family, will form the bedrock of the institution.

It is clear both William and Catherine want their children to be aware of what their future holds and yet be not overawed by the responsibility of duty in whatever form that may take. In recent years they have introduced their children to more of public life, especially in events or issues close to their hearts. In December 2025, William brought George to one place that has held special significance in his life, the homelessness charity where he was first introduced to the issue 32 years ago by his mother in 1993. During a visit to The Passage in Westminster,

London, the Prince of Wales and his son helped prepare lunch for 150 people supported by the charity at their annual Christmas lunch. George signed the visitor's book on the same page as his grandmother and dad on 14 December 1993, taking genuine interest in the history before his eyes.

Mick Clarke, chief executive of the Passage, said the young prince 'Very much like his dad, just wanted to get stuck in and help. A lovely kid is how I would describe him,' the charity boss said. 'And he just really seemed very interested in the work that we do and particularly in talking to people who have used our services.' Describing the signing of the book with Princess Diana's name as a 'lovely, beautiful moment' he said 'it kind of felt full circle, really - 1993 through to 2025, with William bringing George'. There can be no doubt that this introduction for George, and most likely William's other children when the time is right, demonstrates to the next generation the importance of using their position and profile to help the most vulnerable in society.

As king and queen, William and Catherine will have the ultimate power to shape the monarchy in their own image. Simon Case, who served as William's Private Secretary from 2018 to 2020, has explained how the prince and princess's emphasis on family and people will be their greatest strength.

> If you look at the foundations of their work, most notably environmental protection, mental health, focus on the early years, addictions, homelessness, these are all issues that are entirely focused on the basic needs of society in order to flourish. Coupled with their attention to their own family, and how that will in turn affect the wider institution, these are the fundamental principles of who they are as people.

CHAPTER EIGHTEEN

You have fundamentally misunderstood them as people if you don't acknowledge that while family may be important to them, it's not something you can take for granted, close family is something you actually have to work at. That same level of dedication is evident in their work. The times have changed, the reach of the royal family and [their] individual profiles is absolutely extraordinary in the digital age. But by centering on specific issues, you know they mean business, that if they are going to take on an issue it's because they care and they want to make a difference. Queen Elizabeth II is the very best example to date of a monarchy in dialogue between sovereign and people, and each sovereign will bring their own approach, but William and Catherine are best prepared to respond to what the people ask of them in any given situation.

Concentrating on a smaller number of projects in order to make a greater impact comes with its own risks. Programmes such as Earthshot, Homewards and the Centre for Early Development all have political implications and consequences. Campaign too much and you've crossed the line into meddling with or criticising government policy. Do too little and, well, you're back to the accusations of being work-shy. But those who know them well suggest that the Prince and Princess of Wales are driven by the opportunity to affect generational change. Jason Knauf, former senior adviser to William and Catherine as Duke and Duchess of Cambridge, and now CEO of the Earthshot Prize, said:

> They have shown that there will always be things that are unique to each generation, that reflect changes to the media, changes to society.
> You'll still see total respect for the family, for the institution and for the traditional moments that people the

world over really love and appreciate and care about too, but there will be subtle updates that, like any monarch, they feel they need to make.

When they became Prince and Princess of Wales, as difficult as that moment was with the death of Her Majesty, it felt natural. While there have been huge changes for them and the family in recent years, they were very determined before a change of reign that they would be operating in such a way, whether that be domestically or internationally and their charitable initiatives, that they felt that they had the credibility to be public servants at that level.

Now we are seeing a natural and smooth evolution as they continue to grow, but it hasn't seemed unnatural that they are the main support to the King. That is exactly what they will want to make sure happens for the next change of reign, whenever that may be, that of course there will be a moment of grief for them and the country, but they are responsible for being as prepared as they possibly can be and that the people have the confidence that they can represent the country and the realms in the right way, that not only is a success both nationally and internationally, but also seems authentic and natural to them.

Through almost one hundred interviews and speaking at length to dozens of sources, many who have worked side by side or been close to the Prince and Princess of Wales for many years, it appears that William and Catherine have reached a stage where they are comfortable making plans at their own pace. The events of the last two years, since the King and princess's cancer diagnoses, have allowed them to slow down and appreciate the here and now. 'Family is everything,' said a close friend.

They are committed, kind and empathetic. And when they needed people to be with them, ultimately, on the whole, people were. That's the type of world they want to live in. They are still growing as people, working things out. They aren't the finished article, and they don't pretend to be. If William is unsure of something, whether it's a direction or a project, Catherine has been there to offer support or reassurance, and the same in return. That's the aura they have, why people are loyal to them, because it's reciprocated. Everything is done with kindness and dignity, and that's all we should all strive for.

When considering all these factors, and questioning what the future will hold for William and Catherine and indeed the monarchy, it is worth reflecting on the Prince of Wales's own words in Cape Town. 'I sit here right now doing Earthshot and doing all the projects I'm doing, like Homewards as well. And who knows what's going to come next, but it all centres around those values of trying to help deliver change and make those lives better.'

ACKNOWLEDGEMENTS

The role of a royal correspondent with an affiliated media organisation inevitably provides a privileged position at the heart of an institution intrinsically tied to history. I have been privileged to be at the centre of so many landmark moments of recent years and for that alone I am hugely grateful to the editors who have entrusted me to document such momentous occasions.

To my colleagues at the *Daily Mirror* for their patience and encouragement, Tom Carlin, Dominic Herbert, Dean Rousewell, Nick Dorman and Louise Sassoon. To my peerless former editors Alison Phillips, Paul Henderson and Lloyd Embley, thank you. I am particularly indebted to the late, great, Peter Willis, former *Mirror* editor and founder of inspirational Pride of Britain Awards. His trust in me, through complete blind faith, to hire me for my first job in national newspapers is a kindness I will never forget. His counsel and friendship is dearly missed by all who knew him.

I am particularly indebted to my editors at Ebury, Lorna Russell, Josh Ireland, Michelle Warner, and the extended Penguin Random House family, including Lucy Brown and Ellenor Jermyn, for their guidance and professionalism throughout the whole process of creating this book.

A special thanks to Abigail Le-Marquand Brown for granting me the opportunity to make it possible, and for the trust placed in me to deliver this definitive account of the Prince and Princess of Wales's life together. I will forever be grateful.

Many of the sources I have had the pleasure of dealing with throughout my 20-year career as a journalist, and during my

ACKNOWLEDGEMENTS

eight years as a royal correspondent, have done so under the condition of absolute anonymity. I thank them for their professionalism and often friendship when they have gone above and beyond to assist me. I am hugely indebted to them.

I am also immensely grateful to those who have kindly lent their support and considerable time to this book and who were able to speak on the record to assist my research into key moments of the Prince and Princess of Wales's lives. Particularly Jamie Lowther-Pinkerton, Simon Case, Jason Knauf, Nick Loughran, Ed Perkins, Patrick Jephson, Gordon Brown, Sarah Brown, Kent Gavin, Nicholas Witchell, Jennie Bond, Giovanna Fletcher, and Fearne Cotton.

I would like to make special mention of Louise Flood of the *Daily Mirror*. There are few people in any career whose kindness and professionalism can be matched. I am not alone when I say it has been the utmost pleasure to have your friendship and guidance throughout my career and listen to the stories of former legendary Mirrormen and women, such as the doyen of royal reporters James Whittaker, and others through your magnificent 40-plus-year career with the *Mirror*.

Thank you also to my travelling companion for more than a decade, *Mirror* chief photographer Ian Vogler, a tremendous professional and life-long friend.

I have also been fortunate to work with many who I consider to be masters of their craft in what is often a tumultuous industry. Ian Gallagher and Shekhar Bhatia are two such individuals whose kindness and guidance has been a permanent fixture.

To many colleagues on the royal rota who I have accompanied on royal visits and overseas tours. Thank you for your companionship and good humour.

I am eternally grateful to the inimitable Lorraine Kelly, and the *Lorraine* show's incomparable editor Victoria Kennedy, as well as all the team at ITV, with notable mention to producers

ACKNOWLEDGEMENTS

Jo Williams, Fiona Strang and Camille Solomon. Their support and encouragement to me and to my extended broadcasting career when in 2018 I walked into their studio as a complete novice, has been a true gift. You are the best in the business.

There have been many biographies of members of the royal family whose insight has been of particular interest in my research and who have also helped me in shaping my royal coverage for the *Mirror* and beyond. Special mention to Robert Hardman, Andrew Morton, Valentine Low, Robert Jobson, Ingrid Seward, Katie Nicholl and Norman Baker.

I also want to thank the teams at Channel 9 *Today Show* including Karl Stefanovic, Sarah Abo, producers Josh Kuskoph, Madison Williams, Brayden Dykes and Matthew Russell; and Channel 7 Sunrise presenters Natalie Barr, Matt Shirvington, producers Matthew Simmonds, Holly Fallon, Paul Burns, David Walters, Glen Caro and Zac Donovan. I have been privileged to have your support over the years.

Huge thanks also to the teams at True Royalty and Love Monday, especially executive producer Kerene Barefield and presenter Kate Thornton.

The undertaking of a considerable project such as this usually involves considerable sacrifices along the way. Creating this book of which I am immensely proud, has meant I have been less than available over many months of research and writing. To my amazing wife, Katie, for her unwavering support, love, patience and encouragement during this process and throughout our marriage. This book is dedicated to you and our three beautiful children.

To my mum and dad, Linda and Tony. I am forever thankful for your unending love and constant support to me and my siblings Charles, Lillee and Alice. To my extended family, Paige and Nick, Sarah and Matthew, whose love and guidance I am privileged to have. I love you all.

IMAGE CREDITS

Plate section 1
P. 1 top © Anwar Hussein, bottom left © Tim Graham, bottom right © PA Images
P. 2 top ©WPA Pool, middle © PA Images bottom © Ted Blackbrow/Daily Mail/Shutterstock
P. 3 top © Anwar Hussein, bottom left © Shutterstock, bottom right © UK Press
P. 4 top left and top right © PA Images, middle © Shutterstock, bottom © Max Mumby/Indigo
P. 5 top left © Associated Press, top right © Antony Jones, middle left © Shutterstock, bottom © Chris Jackson
P. 6 top © Associated Press, middle and bottom © PA Images
P. 7 top and middle © George Pimentel, bottom © Shutterstock
P. 8 top left © Pascal Le Segretain, top right © Samir Hussein, bottom left © Chris Jackson, bottom right © PA Images

Plate section 2
P. 1 top © Mark Nolan, middle © Alan Davidson/Shutterstock, bottom © Pool
P. 2 top © WENN Right Ltd, middle © Nicky J Sims, bottom © Max Mumby/Indigo
P. 3 top © Abir Sultan, middle © Pool, bottom © Daniel Leal
P. 4 top © Pool, bottom © WPA Pool
P. 5 top © Comic Relief, middle © Chris Jackson, bottom © Stephen Lock/Pool/Shutterstock
P. 6 top and middle © Pool, bottom © PA Images
P. 7 top left © Chris Jackson, top right © Samir Hussein, bottom © WPA Pool
P. 8 top © Kensington Palace / BBC Studios, middle © Samir Hussein, bottom © Anadolu